What the reviewers said...

"At the turn of the century, the story of a girl raised on an isolated farm in the province of Manitoba who became one of the first women members of a provincial parliament, managed to run a household of a husband and five children, and pursue a career as a novelist was something of a phenomenon."

—*Radio-Canada International*

"She is as vivid as a tiger lily at a funeral."

—*Alberta's Western Living*

"Nellie McClung is one of Canada's most colourful, outspoken, and important historical figures."

—*Canadian Materials*

"I do not want to pull through life like a thread that has no knot. I want to leave something behind me when I go; some small legacy of truth, some word that will shine in a dark place."

—*Nellie McClung*

Presenting Goodread Biographies

The Goodread Biographies imprint was established in 1983 to reprint the best of Canadian biography, autobiography, diaries, memoirs and letters in paperback format.

Books in the series are chosen from the hardcover lists of all of Canada's many publishing houses. By selecting a wide range of interesting books that have been well received in the bookstores and well reviewed in the press, we aim to give readers inexpensive and easy access to titles they missed in hardcover. A new selection of books is added to our series twice yearly, every spring and fall.

You'll probably find other books in the Goodread Biographies series that you'll enjoy. Check the back pages of this book for details on all titles in the series. You'll find our books on the paperback shelves of your local bookstore. If you have difficulty obtaining any of our titles, get in touch with us and we'll give you the name of a bookstore near you which stocks our complete list.

OUR NELL

OUR NELL

A SCRAPBOOK BIOGRAPHY
OF NELLIE L. McCLUNG

CANDACE SAVAGE

Goodread Biographies

Published in hardcover in 1979 by Western Producer Prairie Books
Published in paperback in 1985 by Goodread Biographies
Canadian Lives series publisher: James Lorimer

Canadian Cataloguing in Publication Data

Savage, Candace, 1949 -
    Our Nell

(Canadian lives)
Reprint. Originally published: Saskatoon:
Western Producer Prairie Books, 1979.
Bibliography: p.
Includes index.
ISBN 0-88780-134-X

1. McClung, Nellie L., 1873-1951. 2. Feminists — Canada — Biography. 3. Women's rights — Canada — History. I. Title. II. Series..

HQ1455.M22S38 1985   305.4'2'0924   C85-098269-3

Goodread Biographies is the paperback imprint of
Formac Publishing Company Limited
5359 Inglis Street
Halifax, N.S.
B3H 1J4

Printed and bound in Canada

I have seen my country emerge from obscurity into one of the truly great nations of the world. I have seen strange things come to pass in the short span of one lifetime, and I hasten to set it down while the light holds. People must know the past to understand the present and to face the future . . . .

In Canada we are developing a pattern of life and I know something about one block of that pattern. I know it for I helped to make it, and I can say that now without any pretense of modesty, or danger of arrogance, for I know that we who make the patterns are not important, but the pattern is.

Nellie L. McClung, 1945

CONTENTS

PREFACE

This is the story of Nellie Letitia Mooney McClung, perhaps the most celebrated and controversial woman ever to figure in Canadian public life. Most of us are familiar with some aspect of her reputation, whether as a politician, an author, or a feminist reformer. But because there has never before been a full-scale study of her life, few of us appreciate the scope of her achievements, and fewer still have a sense of her as a person who, not so long ago, thought and laughed and cared deeply about the world in which she lived.

It is true that Nellie herself has left us with two volumes about her life, *Clearing in the West* and *The Stream Runs Fast*. Of her sixteen books, they are among the most satisfying. What set them apart are the same characteristics which distinguished Nellie — her openness and spontaneity. She never tried to hide behind a contrived or pretentious style. When reading her words, one often has the impression of a speaking voice, a human presence. And that is one reason I have quoted freely from Nellie's writings in this book — because she offers herself to her readers with such generosity.

Still, effective as they are, Nellie's autobiographical works do have their shortcomings. Like most of us, she is not always to be trusted as a witness to her experiences. Sometimes she is modest, sometimes arrogant, sometimes forgetful, sometimes selective in what she chooses to tell. Occasionally, one suspects, she gives way to her storyteller's taste for drama and rearranges events a little to heighten the effect. She writes with the passion — and lack of perspective — of a participant.

What this book sets out to do is combine the immediacy of Nellie's own writings with the detachment of more distant observers. To this end, I have selected passages from Nellie's works — her autobiography, novels, stories, articles, notebooks, and miscellaneous jottings — and woven them together in such a way that they tell her story from beginning to end. Then, I have added the comments of her contemporaries — journalists, friends, and family — people who watched her close at hand. Finally, I have provided my own analysis and insights, both to offer a point of view from the present and to keep the story on course.

When I started work on this project, I felt rather diffident. Nellie McClung was a Great Woman in my mind, a source of inspiration, unimpeachable and remote. But the more I learned about her, the more "real" she became. I began to see her as a living, breathing human being, with talents, follies, and limitations, who had lived her life with sincerity and verve. Instead of a sterile admiration, I could respond to her with affection and respect. I hope that you will feel the same.

A great many people have contributed to the preparation of this book. My first thanks must go to Lorna Rasmussen and Anne Wheeler (Mugdha) for getting me started on the research and to Gwen Thorrsen, Jeanne Walters, Maxine Wray, Frances Wright, the executive of the Calgary Local Council of Women, and the Saskatchewan Arts Board for their financial assistance.

Those who contributed information include the late H. B. Beynon, Mollie A. Burry, Ada Cameron, Nena M. Eastes, Gladys Erhardt, Mrs. E. Friesen, Alice L. Glendenning, Susan Gunn, Rosa Gurney, the late Edna Jaques, Lillian Kidder, Ruby M. Lewin, Mrs. G. A. McDonald, Ella B. Madsen, Joyce O'Bryne, Charles S. Oke, Miss H. M. Purdy, Mrs. A. Richardson, Earle F. Riley, Mr. and Mrs. M. A. Robertson, Ascheneth Sharp, Mrs. W. C. Taylor, P. Tivy, Mrs. Clarence Truman, Retta K. Turple, J. Wallcraft, Irene F. Woodyard, and Mr. and Mrs. A. H. Woolsey.

The Mooney-McClung family have been generous with their time and knowledge. Florence (McClung) Atkinson, Nellie McClung (junior), and Ruth Scott helped me as they were able. Special thanks must go to Margaret McClung, Mark McClung, and Weston Sweet. The excerpts from Nellie McClung's writing appear in this book by arrangement with the McClung estate.

Archivists across western Canada have been consistently helpful, as has the reference staff of the Saskatoon Public Library. I also appreciate the expert assistance of Gwen Rigby who typed (and retyped) the manuscript.

The manuscript was read by three of my friends, Katherine Arbuthnott, Rob Sanders, and Vera-Marie Wolfe. I have benefited greatly from their perceptive comments and their encouragement.

My deepest debt is to Arthur Savage, who accompanied me on research trips, read untidy manuscripts, helped me make difficult decisions, praised me outrageously, and generally saw me through. To him, my gratitude and my love.

CHAPTER ONE

PRAIRIE CHILD

I believe a happy childhood is the best fortification
against life's sorrows!

Nellie McClung is the kind of personality you can't miss. Drop her into a Canadian Club, a Press Club, a political meeting or her own Methodist Church, and things begin to fizz. Most people like her. Some don't. But everybody has to have an opinion of some sort, for she's as vivid as a tiger lily at a funeral.

Out in the West where Nellie . . . comes from, they don't believe in hiding your light under a bushel nor caching it behind the conventions. They don't approve of blondined minds, marcelled convictions, and Missus-grundified accents of expressing them. If the Lord made you out-and-out, you'll get on in the West; if not, you'll get out.

—Natalie Symmes, 1916[1]

She is a bit of a paradox, this breezy western writer, speaker and reformer. A stiff backbone, a virile manner and argumentative tones contradict the peace and quiet in her eyes. Even in repose you know instinctively that she is a fighter. But such a square fighter. And the thread of charity runs throughout mingled with the tenderness of a big-hearted woman.

—newspaper article, 1918[2]

She was a lovely woman — the greatest Christian I ever knew.

—Edna Jaques, 1977[3]

When Nellie McClung's public career was at its height, in the years during and after the First World War, she left her mark on almost everyone she met.* There was something about her manner on a lecture platform — her spontaneity, her high spirits, her sly wit — which made her hard to resist. Prairie women, in particular, were open to her charm: she could make them laugh; she could make them cry. She could fire them with a vision of the shining new world which would be theirs when they won the right to vote.

Not everyone shared in this exultation, of course. People who disagreed with her views on women's suffrage and prohibition thought she was a nasty busybody who ought to be at home darning her husband's socks. But these detractors were in the minority, at least during the years when her influence reached its peak. Then, when Nellie McClung pushed, the world moved, or so it seemed.

One of the most attractive things about Nellie at this stage in her life was her matter-of-factness (a characteristic which endeared her to those who knew her well). She refused to let the sudden surge of fame sweep her off her feet. However much she enjoyed the thrill of apparent power, she never let herself forget that she was one of the "common folk." Ever since her youth, she had felt a special allegiance to "the people who do the work of the world."[4]

Her own family, the Mooneys, had been backcountry farmers. On 20 October 1873, the day Nellie was born, they lived on a hundred rock-strewn acres in Grey County, Ontario, just outside Chatsworth and near Owen Sound. Nellie's father, John Mooney, had moved there in 1841, at the age of 29. Irish-born, he'd been driven from his homeland by the famines and had toiled for ten years to clear away the dense forest of hardwoods which covered his land. His wife, the former Letitia McCurdy, had emigrated from Scotland in 1857, faced with the necessity of making her own way in life, and had married the following year. One of Nellie's earliest and clearest memories of her mother was that she seldom stopped for rest.

There were six children in the Mooney household. Will, the eldest, was fifteen when Nellie came along. After him the family records listed George, Elizabeth (or Lizzie), Jack, and Hannah. Nellie Letitia was the baby of the family, and that privileged position may help to explain the confidence and high optimism with which she later faced the world.

---

*Two typefaces are used throughout this book. Italic type identifies explanatory or transitional passages. Roman type is used for sequences made up exclusively of excerpts from the writings of Nellie L. McClung and others. See, for example, page 4. For the sake of consistency, a few minor changes (to spelling and capitalization, for example) have been made in the excerpts.

But if being the youngest had its advantages, it certainly didn't protect Nellie from her share of the family chores. Hard-working woman that she was, Letitia Mooney was a past master at finding things for other people to do. She had the qualities of a good general, Nellie affectionately recalled, and her husband liked to tease that she could keep forty people busy. To be sure, there was never any lack of work on that Ontario farm, not even for the littlest child. As far back as Nellie could remember, she had lived with responsibility. If nothing else, she could be sent to water the barrel of ashes from which her mother made soap. The Mooneys always had homemade soap, home-cured hams, homespun clothes: everything possible was produced at home, for the family was chronically short of cash.

The fact was that the Mooney land, in spite of all it had cost the father in labor, was stubborn and niggardly. The family could never expect more from it than subsistence. Even by rushing from dawn to dusk they could not get ahead. And now, in the 1870s, reports were coming in from western Canada which made their struggle especially hard to bear. The Riel Rebellion had brought the "great lone land" to the attention of easterners, and a few young adventurers had set out to see it for themselves. In the late seventies, one of them returned to visit his family in Grey County, bringing eye-witness information about the Northwest and its unimaginable expanse of rich, deep, prairie sod.

No one listened more attentively than Nellie's big brother, Will, and her mother. Will wanted a better future for himself, and Letitia was willing to consider any hardship for the sake of those to whom she was bound by duty and love. Besides, if her eldest son was interested, that was reason enough for her to take the matter seriously, for as Nellie once grumbled, "Mother had the Old-world reverence for men, and attributed to her sons qualities of wisdom and foresight which, no doubt, surprised them."[5]

In the spring of 1879, Will headed west, and a year later, in May 1880, when Nellie was not quite seven, the rest of the family left Ontario to join him on the five quarters of land he had picked out, eighty miles southwest of Portage la Prairie, near present-day Wawanesa. The buffalo had disappeared from the area just one year before. This was virgin country and the Mooneys would inhabit it alone for a while. (The first neighbors — three miles distant — would not arrive until 1881; that year all of Manitoba held fewer than 66,000 souls.) There were no doctors nearby, no churches, no schools for Nellie and the other children to attend. In fact, there was not even a practical all-Canadian route from Manitoba to Ontario, so the family traveled by steamship to Duluth *and then north by train to Saint Boniface. From there it was 180 miles of mudholes and gumbo to their new home, a plodding three-week journey by ox-drawn wagon, Red River cart, and foot.   As Nellie remembered the journey, her mother had walked every step of the way.*

Nellie L. McClung, 1935

It was a warm clear day with blue shadows toward the end of September when we left the main road, and turned southeast on the Yellowquill trail toward the Assiniboine River. The muddy roads with their terrors were past for we were now traversing a high sandy country with light vegetation, and raspberry brakes. The blue sky had a few white clouds that held the colors of the sunset. The hills around were pricked with little evergreen trees. The oxen sensing the nearness of home, stepped livelier and everyone's spirits rose. . . .

In the early dawn [of the next morning] we forded the river. The big oxen drawing the covered wagon, and driven by Will, went first and when we saw them safely climbing up the opposite bank it was easy to get the little oxen to take the water. The pony cart came next and the cow followed. She had all the intelligence of a good dog and needed no guidance.

We crossed just above the junction of the two rivers, the Souris and Assiniboine. . . . And so the last barrier was passed. . . .

No one could fail to be thrilled with the pleasant spot that Will had found for us. A running stream [Spring Brook] circled the high ground on which the log house stood. Away to the south, hazy in the distance, stood the Tiger Hills; to the northwest the high shoulder of the Brandon Hills, dark blue and mysterious, enticed the eye. Near the house there were clumps of willows on the bank of the creek and poplar bluffs dotted the prairie north of us.

Before we were unloaded from the wagons, mother was deciding the place she would plant the maple seeds she had brought with her from Winnipeg, the hardy Manitoba maple. . . .

[When the time came, I] . . . walked proudly behind my father, in the clean new furrows in my bare feet, as he broke the new sod on our farm, and as the coulter cut the sod, and the share turned it over, I knew he was doing something more than just plowing a field. I knew there was a significance in what he was doing, though I had no words to express it.[6]

Nellie L. McClung, 1920

I have always regarded the fact that I was born and brought up in the country as one of the happiest circumstances of my life, for there life is simple and sane, and normal, with a clear line drawn between right and wrong. The currents of thought run deep in the country, and not only deep but unimpeded. Country people have time to tidy up their minds, classify their emotions, and, generally speaking, get their souls into shape. Personality develops more readily in the country too, with its silences and its clear spaces which bring meditation to the heart![7]

Nellie L. McClung, 1930s

Two hundred miles from a railway helps a child to keep free from the entanglements of civilization! I had plenty of time to think my own thoughts. . . .[8]

Nellie L. McClung, 1947

A person can face life better, can accomplish more, on the basis of a secure and happy childhood. I was a big girl before I knew that homes could ever break up. To me, home was the Rock of Gibraltar. That's a wonderful bulwark with which to face the world.

My people were working people. We had little money. We children were taught to appreciate little pleasures. A pair of new shoes was a thrill. I've always kept that feeling. It has kept me young. Always I have some small thing to be happy about.[9]

Nellie L. McClung, 1946

I distinctly remember that I had a very happy time working outside; that is, bringing up the cows, doing my share of the milking and particularly in harvest time I had the great joy of bringing out the lunch to the men. Occasionally I drove the horse rake to gather up the strands of grain that the binder had missed. I never associated these things with the idea of work. In fact, I think if the bitter truth were told, I was not very fond of work, and I remember that when the dishes were coming up to be washed, my sister Hannah often remarked that I had a way of disappearing or becoming involved in something outside which claimed my close attention.[10]

Nellie L. McClung, 1913

There now! I forgot to tell you of my proudest achievements. I trapped thirteen mink one fall when I was twelve years old. Yes, sir! I have the skin of one, tanned it myself. Thirteen is an unlucky number — for mink.[11]

LESSONS

As far as little Nellie was concerned, the move to Manitoba had been the lark of a lifetime; every day was a new adventure. And that feeling didn't leave her until long after the Mooneys were settled in their new log home. For the next three years, she enjoyed the freedom of the prairie.

But every now and then, something happened which broke her carefree mood. Her sister Lizzie fell ill with pneumonia in the stormy, snowbound winter of 1881, and her mother, finally, despairingly, gave her up for dead. There was no help for miles around, not even anyone to whom Letitia could go for comfort. If it hadn't been for the providential arrival of a young Methodist missionary, bearing medicine, the family knew that Lizzie would have been lost.

It takes only one experience like that to teach you the true value of neighbors. Even young Nellie took the lesson to heart. Each new outfit which pulled into the community was cause for celebration. The newcomers brought with them the promise of companionship, help in times of crisis, and perhaps (as Nellie was quick to realize) even fun.

Nellie L. McClung, 1935

Settlement went on apace . . . [in our area], and soon we had, much to our delight a real neighborhood. . . . Frank Burnett, who was a natural leader, began to talk of a picnic early in the summer of '82. . . . A committee was formed and a program of sports arranged. There was to be a baseball game, married men versus single men; a pony race, an ox race, a slow ox race, and foot races. I was hoping there would be a race for girls under ten, or that girls might enter with the boys. But the whole question of girls competing in races was frowned on. Skirts would fly upward and legs would show! And it was not nice for little girls, or big ones either, to show their legs. I wanted to know why, but I was hushed up. Still, I kept on practising and tried hard to keep my skirts down as I ran. I could see it was a hard thing to do. In fact, I could see my dress which was well below my knees, was an impediment, and when I took it off I could run more easily. I suggested that I would wear only my drawers (we did not know the word bloomers). I had two new pairs, held firmly on my "waist," with four reliable buttons. My suggestion was not well received. Then I wanted a pair of drawers made like my dress; for that would look better than white ones with lace. Lizzie thought this a good idea, but mother could not be moved. There was a stone wall here that baffled me. Why shouldn't I run with the boys? Why was it wrong for girls' legs to be seen? I was given to understand that this was a subject which must not be spoken of. . . .

The next year, 1883, we had a picnic in the same place, and we had a horse race that year, for the settlers had added horses to their equipment. . . .

[It] . . . was not nice to watch for one horse was ridden by a real jockey in a red cap, and he beat his horse from one end of the half mile to the other, with a short black-snake whip, and I was glad he did not win. . . .

In the slow ox race, our black and white Jake was entered, and I was glad no one would beat him; for one rule of that race was there would be no whips or switches. Each man would ride his neighbor's ox, and endeavor by words of entreaty or hand slaps to get the ox to move as fast as possible. Someone could run behind the ox and push him or slap him, and someone could go ahead with a pan of oats to coax him. The slowest ox would win the race. . . . Jimmy Sloan, who worked for one of the neighbors would ride Jake.

Just then the women came up the hill, Mrs. Dale wheeling her baby in the carriage. We had been watching the baseball game, but I ran over to Mrs. Dale's carriage to see if I could wheel the baby. Being the youngest of my family I had never had the care of a baby, so it was a treat to me to wheel a carriage. Mrs. Dale gladly relinquished the baby, and I kept the carriage moving as I watched the slow ox race forming at the far end of the field. Little Jake took his place with the other four oxen. And the word was given!

The race began, and the fun was on. In spite of entreaties Jake kept his pace. He merely shook his ears, but refused to quicken his steps. The people cheered and shouted, and three of the oxen began to trot, Jimmy Sloan waved his straw hat, from side to side, ki-yi-ing like a coyote to frighten his mount.

Suddenly, I saw Jake dart forward with a bellow of pain — he began to gallop like a wild thing, and threw his rider in his frantic lurchings. He was coming straight for the end of the field, still bellowing — a horrified silence fell on the people. What did it mean?

Had he gone crazy? He was making straight for the shelter of the trees, where I stood with the baby carriage. . . . My heart turned cold with terror! Someone was screaming! He changed his course a few feet from me, and crashed into the brush! As he passed I saw that his white side ran with blood!

The picnic broke into an uproar. Jimmy Sloan had used spurs! The race was spoiled — all the fun had gone out of it. Then the truth came out. Jimmy Sloan had been drinking. He would never have done this if he had been himself; there wasn't a better boy in the country than Jimmy Sloan.

I couldn't walk; my knees had gone weak, and my memory of the picnic is confused from that point. I know Mrs. Dale came running and her face was white and sick looking. There was great indignation, high voices and excitement. Who had brought liquor to our picnic? . . .

That was my first direct contact with the liquor business and coming so early in life, it left a mark. The maddened ox, blind with pain, coming bellowing toward me and the baby asleep in her carriage — that was my nightmare for many years and still holds an allegory which has not lost its meaning as the years go by. I know there is a pleasant aspect of this matter of drinking, and when many people think of it they see the sunkissed vineyards, where the grapes hang purple and luscious, and the happy people sing glorious songs of praise, for the wine that cheers their labors, and warms their veins. Some think of how it loosens the tongue and drives out self-consciousness, and makes for good fellowship when people meet. I think of none of these things. I remember a good day spoiled; peaceful neighbors suddenly growing quarrelsome, and feel again a helpless blinding fear, and see blood dyeing the side of a dumb beast. . . .

It is strange to look [back] on these days when men were divided into two classes; they either drank, or they didn't drink. No woman drank, needless to say.

No doubt our severe climate and the pioneer conditions helped to draw this clear line. Man was pitted against the forces of nature every day, and could not afford to be off his guard for one moment. We had no bridges to give safe passage over streams; no road signs, no protecting railings. In summer the work had to be done, and done on time; every day was precious; there was no place for loiterers! And in winter with storms and low temperatures, long journeys and dark nights every faculty was needed; clear eye, strong arm, good judgment, courage, which is quite different from foolhardiness. . . .

As cold and hard a country as ours has one unalterable law — the survival of the fittest. The incompetent were like little candles in the wind.

When we knew that a man drank to excess, we regarded him with a curious, melancholy interest, knowing that, like the men seen in the Vision of Merza, sooner or later he would drop from sight.

So our attitude had to be one of unyielding opposition, the only alternative being the easy-going, shallow tolerance of the unconcerned.[12]

SCHOOL DAYS

Nellie L. McClung, 1935

The great event of our first three years [in Manitoba] was the building of the school — two miles from our farm, a government school, for the upkeep of which a tax was placed on each acre of land, and ten dollars a month was given as a grant from the provincial government. I would be ten years old that fall and I was deeply sensitive about my age and my ignorance. Hannah, who had been to school in Ontario and could read newspapers or anything, was willing to teach me, but I would not be taught. I was going to be a cowboy anyway, so why should I bother with an education? I could count to a hundred and I would never own more than a hundred head; all of which was a bit of pretense on my part, a form of self-protection. . . .

Great excitement prevailed when Northfield School was finished. . . . The following spring [1884] we had our first Inspector, Dr. Franklin of Portage la Prairie, and . . . I remember him with gratitude. I was in the Second Reader then, and able to read. We were reading for him the lesson called "The Faithful Dog," and when my turn came the story was approaching its heart-breaking climax, where the traveler, having shot his dog thinking he had gone mad, rides on and then suddenly remembers the saddle bags left behind in his haste, and gallops back to find them safe with the dog, who had crawled back leaving blood drops all the way, and now lies beside them, dead.

I mired down before I got that far and could not either see or speak. It was an awkward moment, and someone in the class laughed, and my humiliation was complete. Dr. Franklin reached over and took the book from me, and said, "Very well read little girl!

That's really too sad a story for a school-reader," — then to Mr. Schultz [the teacher], "Here is a pupil who has both feeling and imagination, she will get a lot out of life."

And at that I cried harder than ever.

Soon after Northfield School was built there came a new settler to our district, a Mr. Frank Kinley . . . [who] suggested that we start a Sunday school in our own school house. . . .

I don't know how it was arranged for the school room was very small, but there were four classes organized. . . . Mr. Kinley had sent for the Sunday school lesson helps and each of us was given a Quarterly with a red and white cover. Hymns appropriate to the lesson were given in these and the music, so we learned the lessons in prose and verse. In the day school each morning we read first the lesson and then the daily readings. So when Sunday came we were rooted and grounded in the scripture for that day and Bible stories flamed into reality with us. Rehoboam and Jeroboam walked with us as we crossed the prairie with our dinner pails and we had long discussions on what would have happened if better counsel had come at the call of the young king. We could see how jealousy ate up Saul and the story of his throwing the spear at David was so well dramatized one day at noon that Billy Day nearly lost an eye.

Mr. Schultz gave us composition exercises and memory work from the scripture lessons too, and the Bible became to us a living book over-flowing with human interest. . . .

Mr. Kinley was a tall thin man, with light blue kindly eyes and a hesitating way of speech. . . . Sometimes, when he reviewed the lesson at the close of the Sunday school session, in his painstaking way, the school grew restless. We had very little sentiment and he had an irritating way of saying the same thing over and over, and usually before the school was dismissed the order was lost.

One day, I heard two of the teachers discussing the situation with him. "I often wonder if the children are getting anything out of the lessons," Mrs. Ingram said, "We try so hard and yet they seem so inattentive. I watched my class today and not one was listening, they were looking out the window, fumbling their books, pinching each other, whispering. I declare, I am about ready to quit."

"Oh, no!" Mr. Kinley said earnestly, "we won't quit, I don't believe they are as inattentive as they seem. They may forget what we say now, but they will remember it in years to come. . . . Anyway . . ., we owe it to them, we, whose hearts have been touched with grace, we must not eat our bread alone."

I was about eleven when I heard this, and it opened another door for me, that gave me a glimpse of a heavenly country here on earth. If "no one ate their bread alone," we could have a glorious and radiant world here and now, a bright and happy world! There would be joy and gladness and singing in it, with plenty of work for everyone, but it would all be happy work; there would be no bad tempers, or tattlings, or scoldings, or ox beating, or ugliness. ... I saw it in a flash, in a radiant beam that shone around me in that moment, and I experienced a warming of the heart that has never altogether faded even in my darkest hours.[13]

Nellie L. McClung, 1935

There was a great pride in my heart, when I saw the cultivation of our farm increasing year by year. We had taken fields of grass and turned them into fields of grain. We had brought the seed and soil together. ...

But there was a shadow on my happiness too. From the time the grain was high enough to be eaten by the cattle, someone had to keep them out of the fields for we had no fences at this time. Before the school started, I was very glad to be the herder. It was much nicer to sit outside with good young Nap [the dog] beside me, than stay around the house, where there were always dishes coming up to be washed. But when I started to school and got a taste of learning, and swept through the Second Part and the Second Book and arrived in the Third Book, and was able to stand by Annie Adams in her blue cashmere dress and brass buttons, her hair ribbons and covered slate frame, all in the first year, how was I going to survive, if I had to stay at home and keep the cows out of the grain? But someone had to do it.

Hannah was a wizard at learning, and in two years was by far the best student in the school, and would soon be able to write for her second class certificate; she must not be held back. I knew that, I knew too, that when she got through and was able to teach she would help me. I was very proud of Hannah, as we all were. ...

But when in the morning, I saw Bert Ingram and Hannah walking up the trail on their way to school, when I set out across the creek driving the cows ahead of me to the pasture, on the school section, the darkness of the pit was in my soul. I had a little brown arithmetic with me, a slate and pencil and I would lie on my stomach on some green knoll, and work long division problems and Hannah would mark them for me at night, and tell me what [had] happened all day, but that did not dry my tears. ...

[One day] I was busy reading Collier's History, with Nap beside me lazily snapping at flies. The sky was cloudy with a promise of rain, in the northwest, where thick dark clouds were piled on the horizon. Rain would save the country, if it came now, for the grain was in the shot-blade but with the intense heat, was yellowing. Rain would bring up the pasture too, and ease the mental strain from which everyone was suffering. My people were getting edgy, and cross, with this sorry business of waiting and hoping and being daily disappointed. Today, I had been glad to get out and away by myself, and as I sat on a knoll, reading about King John and the barons, I wondered about the common people of that time, and what they were doing and thinking while King John and his nobles battled at Runnymede. Maybe they did not know anything about it, nor cared; perhaps, that was the fate of common people, to go on raising crops, doing all the drudgery, paying taxes, fighting when they were called out and, always letting someone else decide big questions. . . .

The fires of rebellion in my heart were fanned by the agitation going on now about the railways, and the men at Ottawa giving away our railway rights without consulting the people of Manitoba. . . . I knew the government at Ottawa had promised the Canadian Pacific Railway Company that no other railway would be allowed to come into Canada for twenty years. American companies were ready to come, but they could not get permission. We wanted them, and needed them. It was our country! We were doing the work, but we were powerless! We were the common people! I grew indignant as I read the history and saw how little the people ever counted, and longed for the time when I would be old enough to say something.[14]

AMBITION

Nellie's impulse toward social justice was also quickened about this time by news of the North-West Rebellion. It was on this issue that she made her first "political speech" — in support of the Métis cause — to a family gathering. "I have faced audiences who were hostile since then and encountered unfriendly glances," she recalled many years later, "but the antagonism here was more terrible, being directed, not as much against what I had to say, as against the fact that I dared to say anything."[15] (Her mother did not approve of forward young women.)

Politics wasn't the only subject which stirred Nellie's emotions. It was during her "sentence" as cowherd that she made her start in literature, with Tennyson's "Lady of Shallot." At first, the poem hadn't appealed to her: "such doings were far removed from the bright sunshine of Manitoba, and its plain people." Besides, the heroine was a milksop: "she quit too soon — she had turned up her toes and died like a young turkey!"

But when I went back to the beginning of the poem determined to squeeze out the last bit of meaning from the words I read:

> Willows whiten, aspens quiver
> Little breezes dusk and shiver

I was sitting on a bank above Spring Brook that hot July day watching that the cows did not go into the grain. The bright sun poured down on the little creek below me. Willows bent over the stream, and as the wind passed over them the white underside of the leaves were turned up. I suddenly made contact with the writer. "Willows whiten, aspens quiver." The story came alive in that moment. The lady of Shallot might have been passing below me in her barge![16]

Nellie's literary education was no sooner under way than she started to dream of writing. She would be a novelist, she decided, and, to that end, "began many soul-stirring narratives in scribblers." But fiction took too long to write — her mother was sure to find her and put her back to work long before she could reach the denouement. "By the time I was ready to return to my story, the fires of inspiration had turned to black ashes, littering the damper of my soul!"[17]

With verses, she had a better chance of success. Her sister Hannah's talents ran towards graceful lyricism, but Nellie's compositions were, for lack of a better word, unusual.

My first writings were sad and tearful obituary verses, wrung from a heart of grief. I remember one of these, a very tear-soaked one, was as follows: —

> "Four dear dogs — they died alone,
>   Nobody saw them or heard them grown,
> There they died by the drifts of snow,
>   While the wind rocked their tales to and fro."[18]

Hannah protested about this:

> She knew I never had four dogs and so naturally had not
> lost them; that I had created them merely to cut them off in
> their prime; and she said a person shouldn't lie, even in an
> epitaph, but in that contention, I found out afterwards she
> was in a hopeless minority.[19]

One of the great longings of Nellie's childhood was for things to
read. When the Sunday school was formed, the community received a
small library as the gift of an Ontario congregation, and Nellie read all
of the books. Then too, every new family which arrived in the
neighborhood could be canvassed for volumes which they were willing to
lend. (Books which mother might disallow could be smuggled into the
hayloft out to the fields to be enjoyed in secret.) Each week, the Family
Herald carried a new installment of adventure or romance, and the girl
gladly made the five-mile trek to the post office in Millford when the
paper was due, fair weather or foul. Sometimes she dawdled on the way
back, reading the story as she walked, and as soon as she came within
sight of the house, her family would hurry out to meet her and get caught
up on the plot. "An author had a chance with his readers in those
days."[20]

"No one knows what books can mean except those of us who have
been hungry for them," Nellie observed.[21] Fifty years later, she still had
the first book she'd received as a Christmas gift.

> It contains three uplifting stories about a little girl in
> pantalettes and ringlets. She was a sober child in delicate
> health and had a governess. The stories were dialogues
> between the two of them on serious themes — obedience to
> parents and respect for elders. I knew them by heart and I
> really admired little Lucy and wanted to be like her (except for
> the pantalettes). But outwardly I scoffed. Hannah and I made
> up conversations on the same high intellectual plane, filled
> with "prithee" and "forthsooth" and "but me no buts" —
> though our themes were not on the subject of obedience and
> respect for parents and elders. Ours dealt with the duty of
> parents to us, and the evil effect of potato-picking on young
> ladies of fine sensibilities.[22]

In the fall of 1884, Nellie was still preoccupied with the evil effects
of herding cows on her own education. She was aching to learn. Every

day away from class increased the weight of her desperation and desire. Even when the pasture was finally fenced, she didn't get much of a reprieve, for the rains failed, the grass was poor, and the cows had to be moved to another as-yet-unfenced field. She was at the mercy of the weather; who could say when she would be freed?

By the calendar, her schooling wasn't interrupted for long — just a few months — but it was a sad, slow eternity for the frustrated young student. Material considerations were being given precedence over spiritual growth, and she was suffering for it.

Finally the day did come when she was back in her desk, and she quickly worked her way to the top of her class — at least where academic subjects were concerned.

Nellie L. McClung, 1935

The girls at school ... were doing fancy work at noons, crocheting lace and doing wool-work for table mats on corks with pins, and I was seized with a desire to create something beautiful too. It looked quite easy and I got a hook from Lizzie and a spool of white thread and was all ready to go when I made a painful discovery. It was not easy at all. I could not get the right crook in my little finger, and I seemed to have no way of making the stitches of uniform length. The veteran fancy workers who were now doing intricate designs in Gordon braid, raised their eye-brows as they watched my frantic efforts. I put my tongue out too, which was always a sign with me of mighty concentration. But I could not make a scallop that had not a bulge and the thread soon lost its snowy hue. It was hard to take the things they said as they talked over my head. Even ... [one of the little girls] who had just started to school could do the mile-a-minute pattern. There was only one thing I could do.

I renounced all forms of handwork; and plunged into the regular work of the school with greater diligence; though my heart was sore at my defeat, I professed a great disdain for lace trimmed petticoats and drawers. Plain ones for me. Underwear should be neat but not gaudy! And how I studied my spellings, drew maps and memorized all the poetry in our readers; and recited with gestures one Friday afternoon:

"The heights by great men reached and kept
    Were not attained by sudden flight,
But they, while their companions slept,
    Were toiling upward in the night

> They did not leave their reading books
>   To fool around with crochet hooks;
> They did not slight their history-notes
>   To make lace for their petticoats;
> But step by step they did advance
>   And gave no thought to coat or pants!
> So let my steps be ever led
>   Away from wool, and crochet thread;
> And let my heart be set to find
>   The higher treasures of the mind."

I did not get clear away. The crochet squad were not deceived by my high resolves. Little Maude Adams tried to comfort me by telling me her mother knew a woman once who couldn't crochet or do any fancy work either and it was all right. She couldn't help it. Her father and mother were cousins.[23]

WOMANHOOD

It was a few years after this that Nellie began to face the issue of her sex in a more serious way.

Nellie L. McClung, 1935

My sister Lizzie's first baby died. . . .

The loss . . . was a great grief to Lizzie for she had been very happy about its coming even though she had not been well all summer. . . . I was not so sure. . . . I felt sorry that she had to be tied in with a baby. She seemed too young to have to take up life's burdens when she was only twenty-two and have to stay at home from all the parties and picnics. When a woman had a baby her good times were over!

But, when I saw the baby's sweet little wrinkled face; and heard his protesting cry, I would have given my heart's blood, if it could have saved him. I stayed at home from school and helped with the housework and all day long, as I worked in the kitchen that little hurt wail, like a spring wind mourning in a chimney, cut through me. Sometimes he slept, but even then I heard it through my ears, laying my heart wide open. It was such a little helpless cry, a complaint against a world which he had not wanted to enter.

One afternoon, when Mrs. Ingram had come to relieve mother, I went out to the bank of the ravine behind the house, where no one could see me cry, and laid my face on the earth's cold breast, and tried to make a bargain with God. I would renounce every ambition I had ever known if He would let the baby live. I would burn my books, and turn to household work — which I hated; I would carry the baby in my arms night and day. I would shelter and care for him, and find all the joy of my life in him if God would let him live.

But the clouds sailed on, wild geese flying south keened above me, a cold wind shook down dead leaves around me and the hard grass of the hillside hurt my face. . . .

When I came back to the house, the stillness of it struck me like a blow. I knew without anyone telling me that the little flame of life had gone out. . . .

After Lizzie had recovered, life settled down, and I was back at school again, sobered somewhat by what had happened; I was not quite so sure of myself, and not a little afraid. Life might take a snap at me any time. I thought of the prairie chickens off their guard, when they danced their mating dance; easy victims in their one mad delirious hour. Women were the same and for them life was as treacherous as ice. I had thought I was strong like Queen Elizabeth who kept clear of sex complications, but now I could see I was wavering. I knew that I would like to have a baby of my own sometime. I had resisted dolls all my life, not without a struggle. I had been scornful of the great trunk full of pillow shams and splashers and hem-stitched sheets that Lily Dewart had all ready. Marriage to me had a terrible finality about it. It seemed like the end of all ambition, hope and aspiration. And yet I knew now since the baby had come that a child is greater than all books and all learning and that little first cry is mightier than the cheers of ten thousand people.

I wished very bitterly that I was either one thing or the other; hard as nails, and able to do without all family connections or as simple and contented as little Mrs. Billings who had just come to Millford. She said she had never read a book in her life for after all "they only take a woman's mind off her work and maybe make her discontented," but she did like having a newspaper coming in each week because there were cooking recipes in it and besides "scalloped newspapers looked nice on the pantry shelves."

Life was a direct and simple thing for the people who knew what they wanted, I thought, reasoning from the lives of the people I knew.[24]

CHAPTER TWO
MARRIAGE OR A CAREER?

When I was a girl we either taught school or got
married. Most of us did both.

By the time Nellie was fifteen, she had decided on a course for the
future. What she wanted most urgently, in her outbursts of frustration,
was to get away from home.

Much of the girl's anger was directed against her mother, for
Nellie and her dad had always enjoyed a special, easy relationship. John
Mooney was a steady man, devout, upright, and hardworking, but what
Nellie loved most in him was his sense of fun. Father and daughter
shared an enjoyment of make-believe, dancing, and other pleasures which
the stern Presbyterian mother viewed askance. Even when Nellie was a
tiny child, before the family had left Ontario, she had spent many happy
hours entertaining him with her imitations of "the aunts," two
bagpipe-voiced old chatterboxes who sometimes came to visit. But mother
did not approve of this game, and after a while, little Nellie became
concerned. Was it wrong for her to "mock the aunts," she had asked her dad.

He stopped his work and looked over toward the house,
before he answered; his voice fell, as if he were afraid the
wind might carry it.

"Your mother thinks it is," he said, "she thinks it
shows disrespect. I do not think so. . . . ['The aunts'] are
funny, queer stiff old ladies, set in their ways and right in
their own eyes. It's no harm for you and me to have a laugh
over them, a laugh is as good as a meal or an hour's sleep.
But perhaps we had better not offend your mother. We know
that would be wrong, we'll just keep it to ourselves and not be
hurting anyone's feelings."

"What makes mother like that?" I asked after a while.

"She's Scotch," he said, "they're very serious people, a little bit stern, but the greatest people in the world for courage and backbone. The Irish are different; not so steadfast or reliable, but very pleasant. Irish people have had so much trouble, they've had to sing and dance, and laugh and fight to keep their hearts from breaking.

"I am glad you are Irish," Nellie said stubbornly.[1]

It was not that she actually disliked her mother. For all her severity, Letitia Mooney was a generous and sociable person. Nellie once described her as "a splendid type of pioneer woman."

No night was too dark or too cold for her to go to the help of a sick neighbor; her house was never too small to give refuge to a passing traveler. . . . With all her hard work, she always kept alive her own ambition and the desire for better things.[2]

Nellie's mother believed above all else in duty, service, and self-sacrifice. There was no masochism in this; rather it was an expression of her religious ideals. For her, Christianity entailed selfless service, good deeds done without hope of thanks but in the expectation of plentiful reward in the hereafter. (As the prospect of heavenly bliss has dimmed over the last several decades, this kind of altruism has lost much of its appeal. Nowadays, people tend to demand their payoff in the hard coin of this world, rather than gambling on the uncertain currency of the next.) For Letitia and many others of her day, self-forgetfulness and charity were fundamental human virtues. Not surprisingly, her children, including Nellie, shared this point of view.

"I loved my mother," Nellie recalled frankly, "and understood the working of her mind."[3] In her willing, neighborly service, Letitia Mooney was an unwitting model for the "new," socially responsible woman her daughter would champion later on.

But the affection which Nellie felt for her mother could not obscure the fact that the two were frequently at odds. The girl was adventuresome and exuberant; the older woman prudent and restrained. The youngster was subject to flights of emotion and fantasy; the mother's greatest resource was her good, hard common sense.

What Nellie complained about most noisily during her rebellious periods were the "acid little economies" of her mother's careful expenditures. If the family could now afford new blinds and carpeting, might they not have real shoe polish instead of lard and lampblack? Was it really necessary for Nellie, who had always loved finery, to wear scarlet bloomers, cut from an old dressing gown? And did she always have to turn out the lamps the instant her homework was done? Would she never be allowed an evening of reading for fun?

How I hated all this! But in my fiercest moods of rebellion I was glad of these irritations; they kept alive my ambition. I would make my escape; I would gain my independence, and every day brought me nearer. I thought of John Wesley, who, being my father's idol, was mine too. He had a nagging, uncomfortable wife, who gave him no peace at home, and perhaps that was one reason he gave himself so freely to the world. A soft chair, comfort and domestic calm might have held him to his own fireside. . . .⁴

Under cover of her more trivial complaints, Nellie was probably nursing some old grievances as well. For years her mother had scolded her for speaking out in public or acting too boldly. Why did she have to accept restrictions from which her youngest brother, Jack, was exempt? Why couldn't she ever go out without a male relative as chaperone? She had always been dubious about the limitations which her mother placed on her because she was a girl. Dubious and resentful, too.

What's more she hated the way Jack lorded over her. And her mother always backed him up unequivocally. After all, he was male!

Only years later was Nellie able to see that her mother's attitudes, conservative though they were, also reflected sincere and affectionate concern. If this youngest child had been as docile and compliant as her sisters, there would have been less reason for conflict. But she was impetuous, headstrong, a tomboy, and, in her mother's view, needed restraint for her own sake. She had a worrisome habit, for example, of chattering away in her friendly way with men she didn't know. It was unseemly; it was dangerous. Life was perilous for girls like her. Besides, Nellie was the "baby" of the family, and perhaps her mother was particularly cautious because of that.

All the same, the girl couldn't be protected indefinitely. If Nellie wanted to further her education, her mother certainly would not stand in her way.

> Looking back, I can see how unfair I was to mother. She
> was as ambitious for me as I was for myself, and never
> begrudged me money for books or necessary clothing. She
> would gladly deny herself to this end; and she knew how
> slowly money came, with eggs ten cents a dozen and butter
> eighteen. But, with the intolerance of youth, I only knew that I
> was being held down with bit and bridle.[5]

In fact, it is unlikely that Letitia Mooney really supported her
daughter's ambitions wholeheartedly — if indeed she knew about them
all — for Nellie had decided against babies, marriage, and love. She
would be free, have a career.

It could not have been an easy choice, for there was little in her
background to prepare her for an independent life. All the women in her
community lived in much the same way — as mothers and wives.
Literature, which might have offered other models, was of no help. Of
the few books at her disposal, Nellie's favorite had featured a sickly girl
who yearned for a dark-haired suitor and was willing to endure any sort
of mistreatment for the sake of love. The women in the popular
recitations and songs of the day were of the pining, mourning, and
expiring sort. Even Nellie's youthful fantasies had centered on feminity.
She and Hannah had loved to picture themselves as guests at some
glittering soirée, dressed in gowns of their own extravagant and
elaborate creation, and courted by swarms of young men.

Was it courage? rebellion? independence of mind? Explain her
decision as you will, Nellie had resolutely turned away from her
childhood daydreams. Already the idea was forming in her mind that
she had a mission "to give people release from their drab lives! This is
not all of . . . life," she declared, "this sowing and reaping, cooking and
washing dishes. There is an inner life that can be deepened and
widened."[6] Her family and most of the people she knew were preoccupied
with land and plows and gardens and barns; they had to be if they were
to survive. But with the idealism of youth, Nellie demanded more. "We
are as we think," she said, "not as we dress or eat. The world of the
spirit is the real world."[7] It seemed she had a message; perhaps she
really was destined to write. Certainly she had no time for men and the
fatal "prairie-chicken dance" of sex.

A woman had to decide early between ambition and family life:
there was not so much as a hint that one might hope for both. And so
Nellie hardened herself against the satisfactions of love.

The options that remained were very limited. "Any woman born in the sixteenth century with a great gift would have gone crazy or killed herself so thwarted, hindered, reviled, and mocked at [would she have been]," Nellie once observed,[8] and while the situation at the end of the nineteenth century was somewhat improved, it was still not enviable, especially not for a girl from the boondocks who had only a grade-eight education.

The eighties had been a decade of economic depression in Manitoba, and the Mooneys were still struggling to get by. The expense of a prolonged period of studies was beyond their resources, particularly since it would have meant leaving the province. (Manitoba did not have a teaching university in 1889.) In any case, many Canadian universities did not accept women into their professional faculties — law, medicine, divinity. Even office work was very nearly a male preserve. So, as her sixteenth birthday approached, Nellie really had only two alternatives: do housework on a neighboring farm or teach school.

As soon as she had the opportunity, she was determined to follow Hannah to Normal School. If she were a teacher, she reasoned, people would have to take her seriously. Maybe her own family would even someday forget her long list of scatter-brained misdemeanors and hear her to the end.

An early frost in the fall of 1889 ruined the Mooneys' crop and almost took Nellie's hopes with it, but, thanks to her sisters' help, she was able to leave for Winnipeg and the five-month-long teacher-training course. The next year, well before her seventeenth birthday, she was put in charge of the eight grades at Hazel School, 3 miles from Manitou and almost 100 miles from home. Already she had the freedom — anxious though it proved at first to be—which she'd been so clamorous to get.

Teaching in a one-room school was heavy work. Not only did Miss Mooney have her lessons to mark and prepare, but she had to keep discipline, and that was challenging at times. Most of the families in the school district had lived together in Ontario before coming west, and memories of old grievances were long. On the playground, the children taunted one another about scandals and disputes of long ago. What they needed, Nellie thought, were some good, healthy games to clear their minds of the past, so she bought a football with her first pay check and joined in the play herself. It worked — no more quarreling — though some of the parents grumbled that football was not a "ladies' game."

She had other duties, too, outside working hours. Would teacher sew a dress for one of her little pupils? Would she cut another child's hair? Letitia Mooney's daughter, brought up on neighborliness, was generally ready to help.

Nellie L. McClung, 1913

I was not remarkable in any way as a teacher. I liked the children, and never had any difficulty. They were very agreeable with me always.[9]

Mrs. Clarence Truman, 1977

Nellie McClung was my father's first teacher in Manitoba. I believe she was sixteen years old at the time and was Nellie Mooney. He spoke of her often as we were growing up and always held her in the highest esteem. He said that she had a way of inciting a child to try harder all the time and to achieve. She took her pupils on long hikes over the Pembina Hills and taught them the appreciation of nature — also how to get along with another person that you really didn't like, by looking for one thing in them that you really admired. She also taught them to have fun and enjoy themselves and others, but to keep Christian morals at the head of their list of priorities. Whenever my father and any member of his family got together . . ., the name of Nellie McClung and her teaching and lessons always came up. They admired her immensely and felt she had been a big influence in their early years.[10]

THE NEW MINISTER'S WIFE

While she taught at Hazel School, Nellie boarded with the family of one of her trustees.[11] Every Sunday, the whole household, teacher included, attended the local Methodist church, where Nellie and the daughter of the family were enrolled in the "Young Ladies' Bible Class."

Nellie L. McClung, 1928

. . . the new minister's wife was our teacher. She was a strikingly handsome woman, in her . . . forties, and to my country eyes, at least, beautifully dressed in seal brown cashmere with smocked yoke and cuffs and a moonstone brooch to hold her linen collar in place. She wore a velvet bonnet trimmed with folds of silk that made me think of the rosy tints of a winter's dawn, opalescent in their changing sheen; and her eyes — when looking into her eyes, I saw the browns and greens and gold of the moss in the meadow brook at home when the sunshine fell into [its] clear stream.

The lesson, I remember, was the story of the Prodigal Son, and the group of . . . [1890] flappers, with their hair in braids with the ends teased out, were not especially interested in the Prodigal Son, coming or going. So I, being a teacher myself, and having sympathy for a fellow-sufferer, fell upon that lesson with fervor. I drew lessons, expanded thoughts, asked questions, repeated the golden text and was able to tell where it was found. Indeed, I can safely say without pride, I was the best girl in the class, and though I was probably detested by the others, I saw the gratitude in the teacher's golden brown eyes, and came home in an exalted mood — quite determined to keep to this breakneck pace of proficiency.

The family at home were greatly interested when we told them that the minister's wife had taught our class. A new minister's wife is always "news." Clara did her best to describe her, but even though she described the brown dress, velvet bonnet and moonstone brooch, I felt her description lacked something, authority, or conviction, or enthusiasm or something.

"In fact," I said, "she is the only woman I have ever seen whom I would like to have for a mother-in-law."

Clara's mother checked my enthusiam by telling me the minister's wife had only two quite young boys.

I inquired their ages.

"Fourteen and ten."

Then, I pointed out that I was not quite . . . [seventeen], and what was . . . [three] years' difference in ages anyway. It would never be noticed when he was fifty and I was . . . [fifty-three]. Having put my hand to the plow, I was not going to be turned aside by . . . [three] little insignificant years.

Six weeks later, Clara's mother brought back the news from town that the minister had also a big boy — eighteen years old, who had stayed behind in the East to complete his full, qualifying teaching term.

"So you may have your mother-in-law yet," she said to me, as I helped to carry her parcels into the kitchen; "but," she added, "he has red hair."

"I like red hair," I said. I hadn't known it until that moment, but I knew then I had always liked it.

The next day when school was over, I went to town. I was dressed in my best dress, a dark green cloth, trimmed with military braid and brass buttons, hair waved by taking thought and curling papers the night before; shoes polished — lard and lampblack — my pale complexion toned up a little by vigorous application of a hard towel. Afterwards I used a rose leaf from a hat, but I didn't know that method until later. I had no business or errand that night. I went to see the boy with the red hair who was working in the drugstore. I made no excuse either, remember; I made no pretence of being the Victorian maiden who sat on the shore waiting for a kindly tide to wash something up at her feet — not at all! Having seen something on the sky-line, rocking on the current, something that looked like treasure, I plunged boldly in and swam out for it.

The red-headed boy was in the drugstore, a tall, slim young fellow, with clear blue eyes, regular features and clean skin, like his mother. I bought a fountain pen, taking quite a little while to decide, and being guided entirely by his superior knowledge — which, come to think, wasn't too bad for a beginning, considering that I was an unsophisticated country girl, sixteen years old, and had never heard of "Dorothy Dix." I paid three dollars for the pen, my last three, and I wouldn't receive any part of my salary for a month. No matter, I paid over the money with a fine air of opulence, and came home well satisfied with the evening. . . .

Shortly after the fountain pen episode, I went to the little town to spend a Saturday afternoon with a fellow-teacher, and before the afternoon ended, we went to a quilting bee at one of the big houses. . . .

Soon after our arrival, one of the women gave out the news that the [Methodist] minister's wife and another woman were going around with a petition asking that women be allowed to vote, and a general discussion arose and surged and swelled above the quilt. I gathered that the ladies were opposed to the movement, and were bitterly scornful of the minister's wife and her friend for sponsoring it. One of the ladies, whom I knew well afterwards — she was the wife of the town drunkard — said: "It's an insult to our husbands to even ask for a vote."

I wanted to speak; I wanted my friend the teacher to put them right. I knew it must be right — though I hadn't heard anyone speak of it before — but I knew if the minister's wife was for it, it must be right. To my amazement, my friend was scornful, too, and just as the conversation became embarrassingly personal, a cry arose that the ladies were coming, and a knock sounded on the door. At once the quilters took flight; up the stairs, into the kitchen and pantry they flocked, even my friend fled with the others, and the hostess and I were left.

The ladies explained their errand, while the hostess sat stonily uninterested, on the end of her chair, and the house pulsed with strange rustlings.

"We thought we would meet with your guests, Mrs. _____"
the minister's wife said, in her sweet way, "but it seems they have
gone"; at which the house seemed to fairly crackle with suppressed
emotions.

I signed the petition, mine being the second name. . . . The
hostess repeated over and over: "I do not think I care to." The ladies
went on their way. It was an embarrassing moment, when the
quilters came back, shrill with excitement and a new sense of
adventure, and stormed at the petitioners. I had to declare my
allegiance to the Cause, which I did, to about the most antagonistic
audience I ever faced. My friend was ashamed of me I know. She felt
she had harbored an anarchist. I couldn't argue — I didn't know one
reason in the whole world why women should vote, and still, she
didn't know why they shouldn't. So not being able to argue, we
parted, and I rode home on my sorrel horse, pondering with deep
agitation a world-old problem. . . . ["Why are women so mean to
each other?"][12]

POLITICS

*The more Nellie learned about the suffrage movement and politics,
the more uncomfortable questions she was forced to pose.*

Nellie L. McClung, 1935

I attended one political meeting in Manitou about this time and
would not have been there but for the persuasion of Mrs. Brown
[one of the ardent suffragists of the district]. . . . The Hon. Thomas
Greenway [premier of Manitoba] was speaking. He commented on
our appearance and said he was glad to see at least two women in the
audience. Politics concerned women as much as men, though he did
not think women would ever need to actually take part in politics.
But their influence was needed and never more so than at this time.
It was the woman's place to see that their men folk voted and voted
right and this he said (so even we could understand), meant voting
Liberal. . . .

Mrs. Brown and I had written out two questions and signed
them [in advance]. . . .

(1) Are you in favor of extending the franchise to women? If so
when may we expect to have this privilege?

(2) Are you in favor of women having homesteading rights, and
if so, will you ask the Dominion government to consider this?

There was a collection taken to defray expenses and we put our questions on the plate along with our contributions. We saw the chairman read the questions and show them to Mr. Greenway, who laughed good-naturedly when he read them and looked down at us with a sort of fatherly rebuke in his eyes! . . . Then there were more whispers, the other speaker was consulted and he took the questions, read them, and shook his head. Then the chairman put the paper in his pocket, from which it was never recovered and we were sorry then that we had given our two quarters.[13]

We stayed and listened, not greatly interested in what was said. . . . The meeting closed with feeble cheers for the premier and I think everyone was glad when it was over.

Mrs. Brown and I were not spoken to, though I saw men whom I knew, and she, no doubt, knew many. But they charitably ignored us.

We parted at the livery stable, where she too had left her horse. We were indignant at our chilly reception but undismayed and full of plans for further advances. But when I got away from Mrs. Brown my enthusiasm for political life began to wane. It was a sordid, grubby business, judging by this dull meeting with its stale air and I was uncomfortable all the time I sat in it, knowing we were not wanted. . . .

[That night, before going to sleep] I . . . brought out the "Giant" scribbler where I kept my diary and made an entry detailing the events of the day. Then I went on: "I do not want to be a reformer," I wrote, "I will do my share of the work of the world some other way. I want a big friendly house, white and glistening, under great spreading trees with a huge fireplace in the hall which will send out a welcome to the world. Inside there will be a long table set with gleaming silver and china with rosebuds and when my friends gather there to look through wide windows at the pageant of the sunset, saffron, rose and flame, and when the night comes down fading the sky to ashy gray the fireflies will stipple the purple dusk of the garden with their dots and dashes and there will be good talk and a great fellowship. No, I do not want to be a reformer and sit in a dull meeting where the air is dead and stale and everyone is wondering what I came for. . . . Agnes Wakefield, Florence Dombey, Ruth Pinch [Dickens characters] did not attend political meetings. Still I must remember that they lived a long time ago and this is a new country. I wonder what C[harles] D[ickens] would have thought of

Mrs. Brown. Well, I admire her anyway. She has stood up to life."[14]

NEW ATTACHMENTS

By this time, Nellie had chosen her own way of "standing up to life." That "big friendly house" she envisaged was not to be filled with the calls of children, but with quiet places, papers, and pens. It was when she was seventeen that she had experienced one of the surges of passion to which she was occasionally subject and which she found it impossible to deny. Her emotions often rolled over her with great power. "The happiest people in the world . . . ," she once wrote, "are the people who are easily shocked. We forget that there are shocks of beauty as well as ugliness."[15]

This time her inspirations were the novels of Charles Dickens — Martin Chuzzlewit, A Christmas Carol, David Copperfield.

> As I read and thought and marveled, a light shone around me. I knew in that radiance what a writer can be at his best, an interpreter, a revealer of secrets, a heavenly surgeon, a sculptor who can bring an angel out of a stone.
>
> And I wanted to write; to do for the people around me what Dickens had done for his people. I wanted to be a voice for the voiceless as he had been a defender of the weak, a flaming fire that would consume the dross that encrusts human souls, a spring of sweet water beating up through all this bitter world to refresh and nourish souls that were ready to faint . . .
>
> I had no words to express the deep, poignant longing that swept my soul. I remembered the lines from Milton about fame being the spur that makes people scorn delights and live laborious days. Yet it was not fame that I craved. It was something infinitely greater. I wanted to reveal humanity; to make people understand each other; to make the commonplace things divine, and when I sat on the flat stone on my way home from school, I thought of these things until my head swam and my eyes ran with tears.[16]

The greatest obstacles which Nellie saw between herself and this lyric ambition were her inexperience and lack of education, so she studied as much as she could and practiced writing character sketches about her *neighbors. People who insulted her were likely to get their secret comeuppance in her notebooks: one woman who was so unwise as to suggest that Nellie didn't look much like a teacher ended up with a fictional case of unrequited love, frustrated ambition — and rickets!*

But for the most part, Nellie's time was taken up by her duties at Hazel School. Then in 1892, on the strength of two excellent inspector's reports, she got a job teaching in Manitou. By more than coincidence, that was where the McClung family lived, and Nellie arranged to board with them. Mrs. McClung was the minister's wife who had so impressed Nellie in Bible class, and the red-haired boy was her son Wes.

> I will admit (though it would have been considered an unmaidenly confession at that time) that I was much influenced in my desire to teach in Manitou by the presence of the minister's eldest son. I felt sure Mrs. McClung's son must be the sort of man I would like. She had all the sweetness, charm and beauty of the old-fashioned woman, and in addition to this had a fearless, and even radical, mind. I had been to the parsonage quite a few times before I came to board there; and I saw the methods of training her children. Her one girl, Nellie, who was my age, did no more than one share of the work; being a girl did not sentence her to all the dishwashing and bedmaking. The two younger boys took their turn and there were no complaints from them. Wes, of course, worked long hours in the drugstore, and so he was immune from chores. On the other hand, Nellie had no special favors because she was a girl. And there was no talk of having to be accompanied by a brother every time she went out.
>
> All this I liked, and while I was still profoundly serious in my determination to travel the highway of life alone, giving myself to the world of letters, I liked this tall slim young man of twenty very well indeed, and was glad of a chance to see him at close range.[17]

The McClungs' place was to become her second home, and the elder McClungs were like parents to her. The Reverend J. A. McClung was a heavy-browed man with flashing blue eyes, and "all the conquering fire of the circuit rider."[18] For him, Christ's message was a call to action, and he exhorted his congregation to work for social reform, whether it was prohibition or the early closing of stores. His preaching wasn't popular with everyone (some of his listeners didn't enjoy being assailed with their worldly responsibilities at Sunday service) but criticism meant little to him — his faith drove him on. For him and for his wife, Christianity was personal, social, and political. That had been John Mooney's attitude as well, though he had generally been too busy to act on it, and now Nellie was having his views powerfully reinforced by her association with the McClungs.

Annie E. McClung was a capable and dynamic woman who could give a speech or deliver a baby with equal aplomb. She was also an unshakable supporter of the Women's Christian Temperance Union (W.C.T.U.). The "White Ribboners," so-called because of the little bows they wore as their badge of membership, all took pledges of complete abstinence from alcohol and promised to crusade for prohibition. Alcohol was a menace to society, for did it not contribute to crime? Did it not lead to the decline of the race, by causing mental retardation and insanity? And who could estimate its cost in moral decay? Alcohol aroused the base, physical passions of men, their violent, libidinous, unreasoning nature.

Women, of course, had no part in this. Though acknowledged to be irrational, they were by nature neither violent nor sexual. Not surprisingly, then, the sale of alcohol was perpetrated by men, for men, without thought of the gentle, blameless souls who suffered the consequent poverty, beatings, and despair. Like "white slavery," the liquor traffic demonstrated the extent to which male depravity could prey on female innocence and purity. And nothing would stop the carnage until women stepped boldly forth, armed with nobility of mind and maternal love, to set the world aright. Women were mothers, hence humane and nurturing. If they won the right to vote, prohibition would follow automatically, and the Demon Rum would vanish from the land. That was why the W.C.T.U. was one of the first and most persistent advocates of women's suffrage.

Nellie was an obvious candidate for recruitment to the temperance cause. Not only had experience taught her the evil effects of alcohol, but her mother had been "strong in her belief that liquor was one of the devil's devices for confounding mankind. . . ."[19] Her father may have felt much the same way, for the Methodist Church, to which he belonged, had a strong prohibitionist faction. (Though John Wesley had had a taste for wine, he had inveighed against drinking of "Spirituous Liquors," except "in Cases of extreme Necessity.")[20] By 1883, the Canadian branch of his church was advocating total abstinence from all intoxicants and state prohibition of their sale and manufacture. Nellie had doubtless heard this position at Sunday school and church; perhaps she had even taken the pledge to "abstain from all intoxicating liquors, and from the use of tobacco in any form, also from the use of profane language, and the reading of bad books."[21]

Whether or not she was yet a sworn prohibitionist, Nellie was certainly a temperance advocate. In fact, she had made her first tentative beginnings as a temperance educator while teaching at Hazel School. Armed with charts, statistics, and scientific explanations, she had even ventured to hold a public meeting for the adults. Everything went so well that she was ready to proclaim her victory on the spot. But the next Saturday night, when she was awakened as usual by noisy revellers, she had suffered "a great disappointment." "I lay awake a long time that night," she remembered.[22]

So, at the age of twenty, Nellie still did not have much inclination to crusade for reform. Her sights were set on an education, and at the end of term in 1893, she left for Winnipeg, to take her high-school grades at the Collegiate Institute. Fall of 1895 found her teaching in Treherne, a village of 600 or so, northwest of Manitou. As luck would have it, the McClungs had also been stationed there (though Wes had not come with them) so Nellie once again fell under their welcome influence. But their comforting presence could not settle the uncertainty about her future, as an aspiring writer and a woman, which she continued to feel.

Nellie L. McClung, 1935

When four o'clock came [on school days], and I got my desk tidied and the boards cleaned, and the last item of the day's business closed, I was glad of the period of relaxation before supper time. There was a hammock made of barrel staves, with a rope run through auger holes an each end; and covered with a blanket and plenty of pillows hung between two trees, at the northeast corner of the parsonage. And there I often lay, when the weather was fine, looking up at the clouds. . . .

Often . . . as I enjoyed that hour under the trees my thoughts ran into the future with a tingling sense of danger. I knew there was no security in life . . . . no security for women anyway. They could make such tragic mistakes . . . . I had seen it in my twenty years of life . . . . Had I any reason to think I might escape?

If I could be like Mrs. McClung — sweet, placid, serene, "whose life flowed on in endless song, above earth's lamentation," who had a gift for goodness as others have for music. But I knew that could never be! And I wanted to write, and how could I write unless I lived and felt, and sorrowed — and living was dangerous. Still, I had no desire to stand off in the side lines all my life. And besides there was Wes. I never got far in my thinking without coming to him. He believed in me; he said no one could tell a story as well; no one could be more convincing; and when he became engulfed in doubts and fears, and at enmity with the doctrines of the church, and his father's stern theology, and belief in eternal punishment, he had been helped by my exposition of the plan of salvation. I believed that when we are not asked whether or not we wanted to be born, God would not lightly condemn us to suffer forever, no matter what we had done. I had welcomed the sane theology of *Robert Elsemere* and *John Ward, Preacher.*

Wes and I had walked for miles in Manitou threshing out our beliefs, and I thought of him often as I lay watching the pageant of the sky. He had suffered in reputation from being a minister's son; not that he had ever done anything very wrong, but because he loved fun and company, and athletics, and had played cards. He had been in Toronto at college when I was in Winnipeg at the collegiate, and during that time we had written each other every week high-minded letters of theological and literary import, and I knew that a delayed letter made me very miserable.

I would not need to lay aside my ambition if I married him. He would not want me to devote my whole life to him, he often said so. He said I always called out the very best that was in him, and I knew I was filled with a great sense of well-being when we were together, for he seemed to light all the candles of my mind. We wondered if this could be love; we were disposed to think it was, but we had a sort of gentleman's agreement that, if at any time either of us found out there was something beyond all this, we would not hesitate to intimate to the other that such was so. And there would be no scenes, no recriminations; and we would go on liking each other always.

On my birthday he sent me an opal ring, which I kept in the pocket of my valise and did not wear — to save explanations. I found it always hard to speak of the things that mattered most, and when I heard girls tell of the proposals of marriage they had received, repeating conversations relating thereto, I was distinctly uncomfortable. There was a certain indecency in it, I thought, and a betrayal of confidence equivalent to the showing of letters, or listening at keyholes. So I said nothing at home of the young man in the drugstore. There would be plenty of time for that . . . and if either of us found out we had made a mistake there would be no explanations to make.[23]

FROM HER JOURNAL

Though Nellie remembered herself as having been calm and rational, at the time she didn't know what to make of her affection for Wes. One week she was flying, elated, the next week tearful and distressed. Her confusion is obvious from a diary which she began in the spring of 1895, during her last months at Treherne. That summer, when she returned home to help on the farm, and even into the winter of 1895-96, when she taught at Northfield School, she continued to make entries now and then. Her theme is always love and, sometimes, regret for her unattained goals.

Because it records her feeling rather than events, this journal is cryptic and incomplete. Still, there is plenty here to demonstrate how dizzy and troubled she felt.

Nellie L. McClung, 1895-96

Grief that can be howled away lies principally in the mouth, and does not really hurt anybody. But when you cry with dry eyes, and a quiet mouth, and a sore heart — that hurts.

You never cry that way until you are a woman and have loved.

12 May 1895   Through the dim mists of receding years we can hear the death dirges of youth, and faith, joy and love, and that wailing death song is set to the saddest of all music — the music of irreparable loss. God pity those "who lose and wish they might forget."

Not me, for I have gained. To me has been given the greatest gift on God's earth, a happy, and requited love. . . . My life, until it came was as a sleep, and with what a glorious awakening! It is higher than Happiness, it is Blessedness, and in that awakened blessedness will my awakened soul spare my darling for me! . . . I have gained by my love, I have gained a reverent and a thankful heart toward the God who gave it, and a great yearning love for that most winsome and wayward of all children gone astray — Humanity.

31 December 1895   The ghosts of my dead selves come to me tonight and with loud imperious knocking force themselves on my

vision. I see the little brown-eyed innocent young one who used to feel pain and pleasure, who loved [her dog] old Nap more than anything on earth. . . . Poor old Nap! he's dead now years since, dear old friend. I loved him then and I love him even now. . . . Little Nellie, you, too, are dead and laid beside old Nap. There is a grown-up Nellie who thinks of you tonight and drops one little tear on your grave. She has the brown eyes too, but she is so big and knows so much more she can't be you. Turn the sod back upon the grave of Nellie and Nap for my eyes grow dim and tomorrow is New Years Day.

Then comes that other so happy, careless and free, brown-eyed still, but different. So full of ambition and the desire to excel that everything is made subservient to that end. O, the high hopes, the daydreams of greatness and fame, never, never to be realized, but a merciful Father kept that hidden, and keeps it hidden now. I was to have been a great author and send my thoughts to the millions and sway the minds of many and hear the whole world ring with my praise but dear[er] than that was the hope that someday, some poor weary heavy-laden one would find something in those pages that would comfort and cheer them, and the sad eye would brighten and the compressed lips would smile and that one would perhaps steal her hand in mine and say: — "You helped me — You comforted me. You made me think better of my race." O angels who pity us in our frailties, why did you not take me then as I lay on that green bank and dreamed that my dreams had come true? Why did you not take me then, for I have never been so worthy of Heaven since.

4 January 1896   I am so very aimless and so very discontented. It's wrong and it's uncomfortable and it should be shook. There is plenty to be done.

13 May 1896   O Lord what an infernal world of heart-break it is! Bury it deep away, away from the light. . . . Laugh and be gay. Be careless and indifferent and never, never let the world know how deep the wound was and how sore it is. They will think your heart is cold, but it is only broken!

> If we'd never loved so kindly
> If we'd never loved so blindly
> Never met and never parted
> Never have been broken hearted.

3 June 1896 . . . everything is changed, badly, sadly changed. We may get it made straight and fixed over, but the marks will still be there and they are not a nice thing — Spirit has its wounds as well as body. —

10 June 1896 I've come back. Maybe you didn't know I was away, but I was. I have come back to my senses, and they seem real glad to see me. It is a rather pleasant thing to regain sensibleness, after having a vacation in the region of the brain. . . .

There is now only one cloud that maybe the dark thoughts will come again. . . . O Lord, keep us from ourselves! and from our dear friends who have our best interests so near at heart. What a heaven on earth if the people who never *meant* any harm, never *did* any.

Such is Life, dear Nellie L.[24] and the tail of the serpent is over us all. . . . Tomorrow — thank a merciful providence for that kind provision "tomorrow" . . . everything will be serene and this bitterness forgotten.[25]

MARRIAGE

And so, ultimately, all her doubts were resolved.

Nellie L. McClung, 1935

. . . I knew I could be happy with Wes. . . . I would not be afraid of life with him. He would never fail me. He was getting on too. He had the drugstore now in Manitou, and there were four little rooms above it where we could live.

Wes had come to see me in January [1896]; and to my great relief was received by my family with real enthusiasm. I had been a little bit anxious about this meeting from both sides. I wondered what he would think of my people — would they seem to him just plain country people who ate in the kitchen, in their shirt sleeves — I wondered! Or would he see them, as I saw them, clear thinking independent people, more ready to give a favor than ask for one. I thought of my mother especially — would he see what a woman she was? Fearless, self-reliant, undaunted, who never turned away from the sick or needy; . . . who, for all her bluntness had a gracious spirit, and knew the healing word for souls in distress; who scorned pretence or affectation, and loved the sweet and simple virtues. I wondered would he see all this, or would there be just a trace of condescension in his manner, of which perhaps he might be unaware.

It troubled me, for I know that was one thing I could not take, and he could not help. But these were my people, and I would stand or fall with them.

I need not have worried. The first night he came, looking so smart and handsome in a rough brown tweed suit, he settled into the family circle like the last piece of a crossword puzzle. He and mother were so enchanted with each other I thought it best to leave them, when eleven o'clock came, and went to bed.

The next morning mother came into my room before I was up and said to me, "Nellie, you have more sense than I ever gave you credit for, and I like your young man — I couldn't have picked out a finer one myself. Now, if you cannot get on, I'll be inclined to think it will be your fault — and you certainly are getting something to look at, as you always said you would."

But the next night, which was his last — for he left on the early train the next day, when I thought we might have had a little time to talk, and Jack had obligingly gone to bed early — mother announced that it was ten o'clock and time for me to go to bed —

And I went — without a word, I went!

We were married on 25 August [1896], at a quarter to eight in the morning.[26]

Letter from a friend, 1946

How times passes! I can remember as if it were yesterday meeting . . . [you and Wes] one day in the Leland Hotel and you told me you were going to be married. And I remember protesting "But you planned to be a *Writer*, Nellie" — I thought in those days that marriage put an end to every woman's outside ambitions.

But you showed us dear. You opened up new prospects for thousands of women folk and you have been a comfort to many.[27]

CHAPTER THREE
A LADY OF MANITOU

It is not so much a woman's duty to bring
children into the world as it is to see what sort of
a world . . . she is bringing them into.

The newlyweds settled into their quarters above Wes's drugstore in
Manitou, and Nellie turned her attention to keeping house. They were
down to their last few dollars, but neither of them worried much about
that. "I believe in early marriages," Nellie wrote fifty years later, "and
I believe that young people who have good health need not ever be afraid
of being hard up. It only draws them closer together. I am sorry for
young people who get married now and have everything given to them by
fond parents. I think it is great fun to save for a new set of dishes. I know
we found it so."

I am not going to say that we never had a cross word.
Two people of strong character are bound to have a clash once
in a while, and there is no harm done by a plain
straight-spoken word, but I can truthfully say this — there
never was a bitter word said or one that rankled. In our
quarrels we left no unfinished business and I have often said
that I would rather quarrel with my husband than agree with
any other man, because he was a good straight debater, with a
sense of justice and fair play that has always held my admiration.[1]

As far as one can tell, Nellie's work as a teacher was never an issue
between them. She simply left her job as a matter of course (well into the
Second World War many school boards would not keep a married
woman on staff) and even in retrospect didn't think the subject worth
talking about. Apparently she was quite content to quit; now she would
have time to study and write.

But it was not to be that simple. A magazine which commissioned her to do a feature on Manitou disappeared without releasing a single issue, and without returning the five-dollar subscription fee its eager young front-man had extracted from her. She had to spend time learning how to cook, not only to satisfy Wes but to please his two assistants, who took their dinner at the McClungs'. (One of them, her brother-in-law, teased that he liked the way she read to them at meal time, because it took his mind off the food!)

And then there came the October morning, just a few weeks after the wedding, when she woke up feeling queasy, and "a possibility not entirely pleasant suggested itself. . . ." Not even the pharmacist's wife had contraceptives in 1896. It wasn't that she didn't want a child: she and Wes had already decided on six. But so soon? Her passionate ambitions seemed more remote than ever, and she felt old at 23. She also felt sick.

> . . . why had not something been found to save women from this infernal nausea? What good was it? If it had been a man's disease, it would have been made the subject of scientific research and relieved long ago. But women could suffer; it kept them humble! I had heard about the curse of Eve, and here it was in full measure. But what useful purpose did it serve? Life at that moment looked like a black conspiracy against women. If God ordained that the race was to be perpetuated this way, why had he thrown in this ugly extra, to spoil the occasion? It was not like God . . . who paints the wayside flower and lights the evening star, . . . who tempers the wind to the shorn lamb and notices the fall of the sparrow. . . .
>
> Women had endured too much and said nothing. I certainly was not going to be meek and mild and resigned. Women should change conditions, not merely endure them, and I was positive something should be done. . . . Then suddenly I found myself crying, not for myself, but for all the overburdened inarticulate women of the world. . . .[2]

It took the soothing words of the village doctor to quiet her "raging mood."

> I do not know exactly how he did it, but I know that once again I was a member in good standing in the human family,

and more than that, he made me feel that I was one of the standard-bearers of the race, pledged to its protection and continuance. Any little inconvenience suffered by me would be small dues for me to pay for membership in this greatest of all societies.[3]

By the time her baby was born, he was as welcome as a child has ever been, and motherhood soon became one of the pivotal and defining forces in her life.

Nellie L. McClung, 1945

Our first born arrived in the gray dawn of 16 June [1897] when the scent of wild roses came down the village street, carried on the dewy breeze of morning. It was at a time of great heat but there had been a cooling rain in the night, and so the hour of Jack's arrival bore that odor which is dear to every prairie dweller — that good earthy smell when the rain has laid the dust. This bit about the scent of roses is all hearsay on my part. I was not noticing anything except the handsome young stranger who had come with the dawn; his round pink head covered with soft-silky brown hair, tight little ears and doubled up fists covering his eyes; his perfect finger nails, and his regular breathing — that was the sweetest sound I ever heard. He came with a cry of distress, but that soon hushed when he found he was among friends. There was a white and blue-lined cradle ready for him, with white blankets and a down pillow. But I wanted him beside me in his white shawl; I think that was the most exquisite moment I have ever known! . . .

I have a vivid memory of the first night we were left alone with the baby. I was all right until I heard Mrs. Law's footsteps going down the stairs. The baby was asleep in his cradle, and I assured Mrs. Law that I would get along all right. But when the darkness settled in, and the streets grew quiet, I began to be afraid. What would I do if he should suddenly take sick? He might have colic, or even a convulsion.

I pretended I was asleep. I did not want Wes to know I was frightened. Then suddenly we clutched each other's hands in the darkness. He was worse than I was. We were almost afraid to breathe. The baby slept on. He might not have been so composed, if he had known he had two fraidy-cats to take care of him.[4]

Nellie L. McClung, 1915

Women are naturally the guardians of the race, and every normal woman desires children. Children are not a handicap in the race of life either, they are an inspiration. We hear too much about the burden of motherhood and too little of its benefits. The average child does well for his parents, and teaches them many things. Bless his little soft hands — he broadens our outlook, quickens our sympathies, and leads us, if we will but let him, into all truth. A child pays well for his board and keep.[5]

Nellie L. McClung, 1928

I have never suffered from the obsession that no one can care for a child, but its mother. I believe a mother does, or at least should, understand a child better than anyone else, but, after all, normal healthy, happy children are not much of a puzzle to anyone. . . .

[Nor have I] . . . had any illusions about the real work of running a house, the baking, scrubbing and washing — I have done enough of it to know it requires patience, and skill and a gift for planning, and, knowing this as only a woman knows it who has done it, I am not an exacting mistress. If a maid burns a pan of biscuits, or breaks a dish, I remember some of my own shortcomings and am not unduly perturbed, nor do I make her feel she is a social outcast. And because I am able by my attitude to allay her ruffled feelings the affair does not assume undue proportions. After all what are a few burnt biscuits, or even broken china, in the great plan of life? Junk! just junk! and I believe it is well for us to keep always our sense of proportion. In this way, and because I am not grieved to see a maid sit with empty hands if she wishes to relax that way, I have kept house . . . very happily, and though I have not actually performed many of the household operations, they have been carefully executed. The basement is whitewashed and clean; the linen-shelves are in order, the fruit-cellar is well stocked — and the jars are not sticky either! and the meals are served with a reasonable promptness, and regularity, and the people most concerned are satisfied, I may even say, happy.[6]

"FAMILY INCREASE"

Motherhood suited Nellie well, though it was a busy life, even with capable help. By 1901 there were three little McClungs — Jack, the eldest, Florence, and Paul — all under four years old.

Nellie L. McClung, 1945

... I remembered the old rhyme which I had often heard, relative to this matter of family increase:

> "When you have one,
> You can take it and run,
> When you have two,
> Perhaps you can do.
> But when you have three,
> You stay where you be."[7]

Nellie L. McClung, 1901

16 January 1901   I found a gray hair today in my head but I yanked it out quick as possible and so have contrived to keep it dark a while longer.

1 February 1901   With three small children and a house to run you can imagine what sort of frame of mind I'm in. In fact the frame is all that is left of my mind.[8]

HOME LIFE

When, as a teenager, Nellie had decided on her career, one of her heroines had been E. Cora Hind. Cora was a phenomenon: a woman who wrote for a living. Every now and then, you could read her articles on agricultural matters in the Manitoba Free Press. *While Nellie was teaching at Hazel School, Miss Hind had come to Manitou for a visit, and Nellie had ridden into town, dressed in her best, just to catch a glimpse of the great woman as she met her friends on the station platform.*

In time, the two became acquainted, and a warm affection developed between them. "E. Cora Hind ... has been my friend and loyal supporter since the day we met," Nellie later wrote, "the sort of friend who would 'stand by' ... through good and evil, the kind one does not meet often but if you have one such you can 'get along' — "[9]

It was in 1909, three years after the birth of Horace, the McClungs' fourth child, that Cora Hind came back to Manitou, this time to stay a while with Nellie and Wes.

E. Cora Hind, 1909

It was a gorgeous day in the autumn ... when I stepped off the train ... and found waiting me on the platform Nellie L. McClung.

. . . The visit was a long promised one and with cordial greetings and merry jests my hostess carried me off to her home, a big, plain house with a mansard roof, standing in a wide stretch of garden where a row of rowan trees were ablaze with crimson berries.

I spent eight long and delightful days in that home. . . .

There are one or two incidents of that week which stand out in my memory more vividly than others; one was the morning after my arrival. Mrs. McClung was standing beside the table in her kitchen, a great sunny room, exquisitely clean and very convenient for the doing of housework. She had on a big print pinafore, trimmed with turkey red, her sleeves were rolled up and she was deep in the mysteries of cake making. At the critical time of the cake, the minister appeared at the side door of the kitchen. Might he speak to Mrs. McClung? The maid bade him enter. Somebody had failed and a meeting was without a leader for that afternoon. I think nine women out of every ten, who were in the middle of making a cake, and who were expecting company in the evening, would have promptly told the minister that he must look elsewhere for help; not so Nellie L. McClung. She thought carefully for a moment and then said, "I will do it." Off went the minister greatly relieved and she turned back to her cake with a merry little laugh, and the remark "Men are helpless creatures anyway" and that was the end of it. The cake was a success, I fancy the meeting was also, and I am sure that not one of the guests who had such a delightful time in her big, cosy sitting room that evening dreamed of what a strenuous day their hostess had put in.

Another morning we had settled down in her study. I had made a bargain that she was to read [to] me . . . while I darned the family stockings.[10] I counted twenty interruptions that morning, and among them were long distance telephone calls, a visit from the president of the Ladies' Aid who "must see her for a moment"; a committee from the Christian Endeavor that wanted advice; "Please mother can I go to Taylor's if I can be ready in five minutes" from her second boy Paul; . . . a lengthy consultation with her little daughter Florence because the girls of her class at school wanted to get up a millinery opening and could they do it all in the tent in the garden; numerous visits from her youngest boy, a dear little golden-haired chap, who called himself "Hor-Barrie-Clung" being a new and original rendering for "Horace Barrie McClung." These were a few of the things that interrupted the reading that morning.

One afternoon we had decided to drive along the famous

Pembina valley, then in all its glory of crimson and gold. We had said we would take no children with us, but at the last moment she found that to look after Horace would interfere with a music lesson which her maid-of-all-work wanted to take, so the small man was tucked in between us and we started. It was a never-to-be-forgotten drive, the beauty of the afternoon was great, but to me it was not so beautiful as the sweetness of the woman who cheerfully answered all the child's questions and who, in the various calls that we made in the valley, found something cheerful and pleasant to discuss with the members of each household. I could see that her visits were highly prized and I did not wonder at it, for she has, in a pre-eminent degree, that rare virtue, forgetfulness of self and the power to enter the lives and interests of others.

Mrs. McClung has four children, three boys and a girl. They are bright, fun-loving, mischievous youngsters, but mother's word is law. There are not too many rules, but, when a rule is laid down, it has to be adhered to. The greatest camaraderie exists between mother and children.

Someone will ask, what about her husband? I can only say that I have rarely seen more perfect sympathy between husband and wife. R. W. McClung is a big, silent man, but it is only necessary to see his eyes follow his wife about their home to realize that theirs is, in very truth, a marriage.

One of the dear delights of the year and what is in reality a repetition of their honeymoon, is to go together, leaving the children behind, to a little hunting camp, where, for a week, they see no one but each other. He shoots ducks, for he is an ardent sportsman, and she cooks the meals and the intervals are filled with long walks and talks.[11]

Nellie L. McClung, 1946

I am sure that through husband and wife developing their own individuality without impinging on each other, happiness is assured.

Mr. McClung and I are fond of different activities, and we have many happy times talking things over. In this way we never get under each other's feet — or in each other's hair.[12]

Mark McClung
Nellie's youngest son, 1975

[Without any doubt it was a happy marriage.] There were occasional disagreements about quite minor things. My father used to give my mother housekeeping money, and sometimes things didn't balance out right. And he — he was a businessman — would say, "Nellie, you must look after these things more carefully," and she would say, "It just bores me. Why don't you do it, or get somebody else to do it?" But there were no fundamental disagreements between them.[13]

Miriam Green Ellis, 1950s

One day [when I went to visit her] she was complaining about her husband who overbought the meat supply. Even by stuffing the dog she could not clear out the refrigerator. There was always a fifteen-pound roast awaiting.

But then, she admitted, "I cannot hold my hand when it comes to buying butter. I have two crocks of butter in the basement right now." She was Irish, and generous. If a caller happened in at meal time, she would ask the kids to move over and get another plate.

She had such a knack of telling a story that the whole family was rather spoiled.

They would urge her off to a lecture or a sermon. They did not go with her; they preferred to hear her account of what happened. As a matter of fact, she could throw drama into the dullest speeches that brought them to life. . . .[14]

Mrs. A. H. Rodgers, 1970

She was . . . [a person] of abounding good nature and a brilliant sense of humor. Her home was . . . like a three-ring circus — everybody witty and good-natured. They could take it, or they . . . could dish it out to each other, and it was a joy to go there. Mr. McClung was Mrs. McClung's admirer, and if she stopped . . . [in the middle of a story] or something, he'd say "Go on, Nell, tell them!" There was no keeping the women in the background in his life, at all.[15]

Nellie L. McClung, 1913

I cannot lay claim to public sympathy. I like my own folks. I get on well with my neighbors and friends. My hired help does not "sass" me. I've had my troubles like most folks — "most of them never happened." Still I've had clothes-lines break, and jelly that wouldn't "jell." But I've had a very happy time all along. My credit is good. "Himself" and I are always on speaking terms. The rent is paid. Why should I not speak well of the world?[16]

THE CRUSADING FIRE

Nellie was content and therein lay a danger. "The most deadly uninteresting person," she wrote in 1914, "and the one who has the greatest temptation not to think at all, is the comfortable and happily married woman — the woman who has a good man between her and the world, who has not the saving privilege of having to work. A sort of fatty degeneration of the conscience sets in that is disastrous to the development of thought. ...."

> I believe God intended us all to be happy and comfortable, clothed, fed, and housed, and there is no sin in comfort, unless we let it atrophy our souls, and settle down upon us like a stupor. Then it becomes a sin which destroys us. Let us pray!
>
> > From plague, pestilence and famine,
> > from battle, murder, sudden death
> > and all forms of cowlike contentment,
> > Good Lord, deliver us![17]

Nellie was saved from the snare of complacency by her association with the W.C.T.U. Though the Temperance Union's concept of womanhood may sound unenlightened to us, the White Ribboners were the radical feminists of their day, at least in rural Manitoba, where the only alternatives were the denominational ladies' aids. True, the W.C.T.U.'s philosophy was based on a double standard of feminine spirituality and masculine dross. True, they glorified motherhood: mothers were women, women were mothers, end of tale. But this did not imply that females should confine themselves to diapers and prams, for God had meant the two sexes to work together in the world. Their natures were complementary, the practical efficiency of the man balanced by the sensitivity of his mate. (Just how there came to be male artists and humanitarians the W.C.T.U. didn't say.) Women's influence was needed in public life; it was God's plan.

These ideas underlay the W.C.T.U.'s work, but nobody made much fuss about them in the early 1900s. The focus of the organization was not feminism, but rescuing mankind. These women strove to be "assertive" because they had a great and pressing task to perform. Nellie found them congenial — here was a circle in which a woman could speak her mind. And beyond that, she was drawn into the movement by the grandeur of its program for social and moral reform.

Nellie L. McClung, 1947

[The birth of her first child had kindled the crusading fire.]   I
guess I felt like a lot of young mothers, that all the children of the
world were now my children. . . . I wanted to do something about the
inequalities of the world. I wanted to make other women feel their
responsibility; organize their instinctive mother love to do away with
evils that prey on childhood, like slums, undernourishment, child
labor and drunkenness. I felt that women could abolish these if they
wanted to. That's why I started by joining the W.C.T.U.[18]

Nellie L. McClung, 1945

[The W.C.T.U.] was the most progressive organization at that
time, and I determined that I would stir the deep waters of
complacency. It could be done in one generation. These flashes of
the crusading spirit often assailed me.[19]

Nellie L. McClung, 1938

Looking back at . . . [our life in the small town] I see we owed
much to the activities of the W.C.T.U. and these initials, I hasten to
explain, stand for "Women's Christian Temperance Union," and not
"Women Continually Torment Us," as some have believed.

It was the W.C.T.U. that planned debates and spelling matches
and ran a reading-room wherein the *Review of Reviews,* and *Scribner's*
and *McClure's* magazines could be read, along with the *Family Herald,*
the *Witness* and others.

They were a resolute band of women, these early crusaders,
and I am always glad I met them and fell under their influence at an
early age.

A composite picture of the leaders at that time would show a
tall, thin woman with her hair parted in the middle and waved back
into a bun at the back of her well-shaped head, a crisp white frill
fastened with a cameo brooch, a hunting case watch pinned on her
left shoulder, secured by a gold chain around her neck; black
henrietta cloth dress, black stockings and a white handkerchief, a
white bow of ribbon, probably tied on the watch chain; clear eye, a
light hand with cakes, and not afraid of anything!

The rank and file of the sisterhood sometimes had fears! For the
W.C.T.U. was never in any danger of inheriting that "woe" which is
pronounced against those "of whom all men speak well." Little Mrs.

Durban found that out the day she joined, and went home wearing the bow of white ribbon. Mrs. Chisholm of Winnipeg had given an address in the Methodist church, and under the spell of her eloquence, Mrs. Durban had paid her dollar, signed the pledge and had the bow pinned on her.

But when she got home, her husband, James Durban, being a man of the world, engaged in the fuel business, saw danger in this innocent little white bow. He knew it might endanger his trade with the Ellis House, licensed to sell malt and spirituous liquors. Once every week Mr. Durban delivered fuel to the Ellis House, and got his money "right on the nail."

This being in the nineties when men were masters in their own house, James Durban commanded his wife to lay aside her white ribbon bow and go no more to the meetings of the W.C.T.U., and Mrs. Durban obeyed. But that was not the end. Mrs. Durban still paid her dues, still considered herself a member of the society pledged to rid the world of the curse of alcoholism, but she worked behind the lines. She made cakes for the socials; made candy for the Band of Hope; minded Mrs. Brown's two children on Monday afternoons when she led the singing at the Loyal Temperance Legion. There were other unseen members who worked quietly for peace sake, but were all part of the Maginot line of defence against the invader — the W.C.T.U. had tact as well as courage.

The W.C.T.U. trained young orators and reciters, and gave medals for the winners, and people traveled long distances to attend these gatherings.[20] They also got permission to give temperance talks in the schools, and studied charts and diagrams to make their lessons "stick." They explained the circulation of the blood, and the effect of alcohol on the stomach, and showed why athletes do not drink even mild intoxicants, and had the children figure out how many pairs of boots and little red sleighs a man could buy with the money he spends on a daily glass of beer. At the Band of Hope, they gave badges and pins, and taught the children a marching song of which the refrain was: "Tremble King Alcohol! We will grow up!"[21]

Nellie L. McClung, 1910

The W.C.T.U. is a very broad institution, with many departments of work. . . . [It] is the society that stands for doing little things, as well as big things. [The members] . . . believe that progress in moral reform must be made slowly, and for that reason they try to leave no stone unturned. . . . They have what they . . . [call] the Do-everything policy — any good work for helping . . . a neighbor, the education of a child. If any woman has a desire to help, in any way — the W.C.T.U. has a place for her. If she believes that women should vote, and will try to convince others the W.C.T.U. will make her their superintendent of equal franchise. If she does not believe that women should vote . . . and will spend a little time trying to care for and cheer the sick, the W.C.T.U. will give her a place as a superintendent of that department.

The W.C.T.U. is best described as organized motherhood — the women banded together to make life easier and safer and better for the boys and the girls — Whatever seeks to destroy our homes — whatever hurts our children — whatever makes it harder for anyone to do right — these are our enemies — these we are pledged to fight. The W.C.T.U. aims at helping every agency whereby men are made better and Christ's kingdom extended.[22]

Newspaper report, 1911

No longer does the W.C.T.U. worker feel her "homemaking" efforts lie within her own four walls. Full well she knows that the dram shop, the cigarette stand, the "segregated district," and the pool table spread their horrid snares to trap and trip her youth.[23]

Nellie L. McClung, 1910

I am a firm believer in women — in their ability to do things and in their influence and power. Women set the standards for the world, and it is for us, women of Canada, to set the standards high. . . .

The very best work that any woman can do in the world, is to bring up her children in the nurture and admonition of the Lord.[24] That is her greatest, her first work. But that is not all. The woman that is only interested in her own home and her own children is a selfish woman. . . . The woman who really loves her own children, wants to bring them up to manhood and womanhood in purity and goodness, and wants to see them have a good chance in life — is the woman that wants to see other people's children get their chance too. They want to make the way clear for the children. It is for this reason that many of the greatest problems of the world today are stirring the hearts of the women and arousing them to action.[25]

MENTAL FERMENTS

Nellie L. McClung, 1945

The first time I felt the stirrings of ambition to be a public speaker was at a W.C.T.U. convention in Manitou in 1907. . . . I had not been a delegate up to that time, but I had been a member of the organization, and I was simply thrilled when I was asked to give the address of welcome on behalf of the local unit. I began my preparations at once. I got a new dress, navy blue and white striped voile trimmed with narrow white Valenciennes lace; a white leghorn hat with red velvet flowers. I was determined to be as easy as possible on the eye. Years afterward I heard Carrie Chapman Catt [the American suffragist] say when she was not sure of her speech she always got a new dress, but if she knew she had a good speech, any dress would do.

In spite of the new dress I had some anxious moments when I contemplated the task of welcoming the delegates. What could I say that hadn't been said many times before? I had a clear idea of some of the things I would not say. I would not run into statistics like some temperance speakers I had heard, nor would I tell them how many loaves of bread a man could buy if he never drank beer. I knew vaguely why people drank. It answered something in their blood, some craving for excitement and change. Hadn't I turned round and round myself to enjoy a moment of dizziness, a blotting out of the old familiar landscape? I knew it was foolish, bad, and dangerous, and yet it had a charm.

I knew the lives of these country people, with their disappointments, long hours, and gray monotony; and I felt that we must give them something rather than take something away. We must be like the pack rats who never steal but merely make an exchange.

Prohibition is a hard sounding word, worthless as a rallying cry, hard as a locked door or going to bed without your supper. It could never fire the heather, and yet the heather must be fired. . . . We, the temperance women, would have to make our cause attractive. We must fight fire with fire.

I never doubted for a moment that this could be done, for I knew we had all the arguments. No one could deny that women and children were the sufferers from the liquor traffic; any fun that came from drinking belonged to men exclusively, and the men themselves would be the first to admit that. I saw in my easily stirred imagination, that life for both men and women could be made much more attractive with recreation grounds, games, handicrafts, orchestras, folk dances, better houses, better farms; new hopes for a new world. I was well away on the wings of fancy as I drafted out a speech of welcome for the delegates. . . .

It is quite likely that there is no person else who remembers that speech, but I remember it. I remember the effect it had on me. For the first time I knew I had the power of speech. I saw faces brighten, eyes glisten, and felt the atmosphere crackle with a new power. I saw what could be done with words, for I had the vision of a new world as I talked. I was like the traveler who sees through the mist the towers of the great city. It was not ideas I was giving them exactly, but rather ferments — something which I hoped would work like yeast in their minds.

That was a long time ago as we reckon time, but it does not seem long. I still remember that my head was lighter than my heart when it was all over, for I knew that I was committed to a long fight and a hard one. Still the vision has never faded. There is a land of pure delight ahead of us, a land of richer fruitage and brighter sunshine, even though the way may be long and hard and dangerous. That Better Country has fired man's imagination since time began.

War had no place in our thoughts then. We were too civilized for war we thought. We believed the enemies we had to fight were ignorance, greed, intolerance and boredom.

It is easy to see why we concentrated on the liquor traffic. It was corporeal and always present; it walked our streets; it threw its challenge in our faces! We were worried then about Jennie Gills who was one of our members. Jennie was "expecting" again, and her husband had celebrated the last occasion by getting roaring drunk and coming home with the avowed intention of killing Jennie and the new baby.

There were other homes too, across whose portal the shadow of the trade had fallen. In a little town the currents run deeply and we knew each others sins and sorrows. We knew about the men who cashed their wheat tickets and spent most of it over the bar, forgetting to bring home the children's shoes. . . . Oh no, there was nothing fanciful about the evils of intemperance with its waste of money as well as its moral hazards. It was ever before us.[26]

Charles Oke, 1974

About a mile or so east of Manitou, there lived ... a bache-
lor ... [who] had one failing: occasionally he would get helplessly
drunk.

He had no relatives in our area and Mrs. McClung made it
known whenever he was found in that condition he was to be taken
to her home where he was given the best of care until he recovered.
He would then apologize, cry like a child, and vow that it would
never happen again. More than anything else, he wanted to
overcome the habit that had enslaved him, but found it impossible.

He had relatives in Saskatchewan and one day he received a
letter from them inviting him to go there and spend the rest of his
life with them. He took the letter to Mrs. McClung, for he
appreciated more than anything else, the interest and concern that
she had shown in him, and the fact that she had never given him up.
He told her that he had decided to go for he felt that in a good home
and with their help he could win out, which had become the main
ambition in his life.

A few years later, [when this man died,] Mrs. McClung
received a letter from a minister in the town where ... [he] had been
living. It informed her that he had told him about his former life and
of his struggles, and that he had never failed to tell of Mrs. McClung
and what she had tried to do for him. The minister said he knew that
the man had not touched liquor since he moved to Saskatchewan
and he was writing to let Mrs. McClung know that her help and
prayers had not been in vain.[27]

Bill Wallcraft, 1977

Unless she was reading a deep book, she was out doing
something for somebody.[28]

Nellie L. McClung, 1930s?

[Minding one's own business] ... is a cheap and second rate
virtue, much extolled in certain circles, over estimated by the world
at large; in constant use as an excuse for laziness; an alibi for
indifference, coldness and neglect; the slacker's refuge; the slug-
gard's sure defense.[29]

Nellie L. McClung, 1931

The greatest thing in the world is to be a good neighbor.[30]

Mark McClung, 1973

[Her eyes] . . . were always filled with light. Whether it was the light of fun or of anger, there was always this light. She was stubborn and determined, but extremely compassionate, and whatever the situation, no matter how much she was against something, her compassion far outweighed everything else.[31]

John Mooney, Nellie's fun-loving father. (Drawing by Cathryn Miller, from a photograph)

Letitia McCurdy Mooney, Nellie's dutiful Presbyterian mother.
(Photo courtesy of Mark McClung)

Above, Millford, the town nearest the Mooney's homestead, in the 1880s. (Manitoba Archives photo)

Below, Millford's combined post office and store where little Nellie sometimes picked up the mail. On the way home she'd eagerly devour the serialized story in the weekly paper. "An author had a chance with his readers in those days!" (Manitoba Archives photo)

Nellie, aged six, as the Mooneys made their way to Manitoba.
(Photo courtesy of Weston Sweet)

Nellie as a teenager. (Drawing by Cathryn Miller, from a photograph)

Annie E. McClung. At first sight, Nellie decided on Annie McClung as the ideal mother-in-law. (Photo courtesy of Mark McClung)

Rev. J. A. McClung. Nellie boarded with the McClungs for about three years while she taught school. (Photo courtesy of Mark McClung)

R. W. (Wes) McClung in Edmonton in the early twenties. (Photo courtesy of Mark McClung)

Nellie in Toronto, December 1910, at thirty-seven. (British Columbia Archives photo)

E. Cora Hind was Nellie's teenage heroine and later a staunch friend. (Manitoba Archives photo)

Nellie with her four eldest children, in Manitou. (Drawing by Cathryn Miller, from a photograph)

It was motherhood which aroused Nellie's crusading spirit and led her into political action. (Top: British Columbia Archives photo; bottom: Glenbow-Alberta Institute photo)

CHAPTER FOUR
AN AUTHOR, AT LAST

I do not want to pull through life like a thread
that has no knot. I want to leave something
behind when I go; some small legacy of truth,
some word that will shine in a dark place.

By her thirtieth birthday, 20 October 1903, Nellie's family was well under way, and her politics had begun to coalesce under the influence of the W.C.T.U. But her writing career was languishing. There just weren't enough hours in a day for everything, and she seems to have felt that writing was an indulgence — duty came first. She did word the advertisements for her husband's drugstore, afterwards clipping them out of the local newspaper and pasting them neatly in an old silverware catalogue for safekeeping. Once she won five dollars by composing a slogan for Stearns Headache Powders. "That was a proud day for me let me tell you," she wrote in one of her notebooks. "I bought a washing machine with the money."

One bright spot in her intellectual life was the W.C.T.U., which frequently sponsored debates among its membership. The meeting of 12 March 1900, for example, considered the proposition "that women exert greater influence for good than men," with Nellie helping to argue the negative. "A woman . . . from the narrowness of her vision is inclined to hasty and harsh judgments," she claimed.

> Women have not, I say it with sorrow, the executive
> ability to successfully carry on an organization. . . . Women
> have so much individuality, such self-centered ideas, they
> cannot efface themselves for the general good. . . . Man has
> been the architect, the builder [of human achievement].
> Woman has cheered and sustained him and urged him on to
> greater and more earnest effort. . . . What a fallacy it is to
> esteem the helper above the Architect.[1]

It was good fun, no doubt, and valuable experience, but the fact remained that her serious writing was getting nowhere. There was, of course, no literary community around Manitou, no one much she could turn to for support. As one of her few colleagues rather acerbically put it, Manitoba was still a "remote prairie province, where wheat growing . . . [was] supposed to absorb all the thought and all the time of all the people."[2]

Nellie wrote little, and even that she rarely sold. Was it a sign that she had no talent, or did it really come back to her lack of time? Concentrated work was next to impossible. If she were going to write at all, she had to do it between having babies, with children perched on her desk, in the middle of her household chores. When one of the neighborhood children needed a place to practice music, Nellie invited her to use the McClungs' piano. "It'll help me think," she joked.[3] *Sometimes she even scribbled away while ironing, to the detriment, she cheerfully admitted, of her good table clothes. "I wrote feverishly, hurriedly, not very well. I got it done somehow."*[4]

That would be her method of operation for the better part of forty years, so much so that when, with her second-last book, she finally had everything right — "not a thing in the world to do but write" — her mind threatened to go blank![5]

Nellie L. McClung, 1925

When no one comes to see me and the phone is not ringing, and the children are at school and there's nothing in particular to do I write. I know this is not the proper way. . . . Someday I hope to forsake the busy streets of life. I shall take 144 scribblers and twelve lead pencils, a brown stone jar of ink, my fountain pen, the Corona, and a long blue box of paper. And I know where I shall go. North of Entrance, [Alberta] on the Canadian National Railway, in the mountains, there is a log cabin which looks out over a satin blue lake. I will go there. I have the Idea, and I know the Place. All I need is a generous slice of Time.[6]

Nellie L. McClung, 1945

The actual beginning of my serious writing began under the encouragement of Mrs. J. A. McClung, my husband's mother. It was in Manitou, soon after the birth of Paul [in 1901], when she came to visit us. One morning she came out to the kitchen where Alice [the maid] and I were at work on the weekly washing, with a magazine in her hand.

"*Colliers* had a short story contest particularly for unknown writers," she said, "and I think you should send in one. You can write. . . . It seems like a great chance."

Operations stopped while the announcement was read. But how could I ever get a story done?

"Alice [the maid] and I will look after the house if you will go right now and get at it."

"I could not do it today," I said — "there's the church tea — I have to see about Florence's dress . . ."

My mother-in-law held firm. "Trifles — all of them" — she said. "If you wait until you are ready to write, you will never write. Don't you know that conditions are never perfect? Life conspires to keep a woman tangled in trifles. Well now Alice and I are in charge — so you are free. How long do you need?"

"If I could have one free day, I believe I could write a story," I said. "I have been thinking of one."

So I went to the den. It was too cold upstairs. I think this was in November 1902.

By night I had written the first Watson story — afterwards the first chapter of *Sowing Seeds in Danny*.

The next day I re-wrote it in ink, on foolscap — the announcement said writing would be acceptable if plainly legible. The next day I mailed it, and as the months rolled on, nothing more was heard.

I began then to write short articles and stories for Dr. W. H. Withrow of the Methodist Sunday School Publications, and from him I received some encouragement, and some small cheques.

In the following March, I got one day a letter from *Colliers* — and this too arrived on wash day — I remember hastily drying my hands on the roller towel before opening it.

It said my entry had not won a prize but it was held to the last, having passed all the preliminary readers. It was rather too juvenile for their purpose — but it was "a delightful story, with humor, and originality."

Then, acting on impulse, I sent the story to Dr. Withrow, and again the waves of silence broke softly over it. In June 1905, it again came to the surface. This time a letter came from one "E.S.C." who told me he had found the manuscript in a forgotten file — read it, and been impressed by it. . . . It had "vitality, humor, and originality." The Watson family were real people, and he would like to know more of them — "You should go ahead with this," he wrote, "and make it into a book."

I shall never forget the radiance that shone around me that day. I had not a doubt in the world about my ability. Of course I could write more — now that I had this assurance. "E.S.C." was, I found, Mr. E. S. Caswell of the William Briggs Publishing Company, and he became my patient, wise, encouraging counselor. As I wrote I sent my chapters to him. . . .[7]

Letter from Nellie's "mentor," 26 April 1906

Dear Mrs. McClung,

Tonight at home I got my first chance at a good read of this story of yours — and I finished it up. I can hardly describe to you the sensations or emotions it evoked. It is a wonderful story — not a *dry* one, for humor and pathos alike keep tugging at the tear ducts. I don't know when a story moved me more than did your closing chapters. Well for me I was alone . . . for I discovered how emotional I am as the tears streamed down my face. My, my those are *wonderful* chapters, there is a deep well of pathos in them. And yet through my tears I found myself bursting into a chuckle over some of your inimitable touches of humor. . . .

E.S.C.[aswell][8]

PEARLIE WATSON

From *Sowing Seeds in Danny*, 1908

Mr. Samuel Motherwell was a wealthy farmer who lived a few miles from Millford. Photographs of Mr. Motherwell's premises may be seen in the agricultural journals, machinery catalogues, advertisements for woven wire, etc. — "the home of one of Manitoba's prosperous farmers."

The farm buildings were in good repair; a large red barn with white trimmings surmounted by a creaking windmill; a long, low machine shed filled with binders, seeders, disc-harrows — everything that is needed for the seed-time and harvest and all that lies between; a large stone house, square and gray, lonely and bare, without a tree or shrub around it. Mrs. Motherwell did not like vines or trees around a house. They were apt to attract lightning and bring vermin. . . .

Behind the cookhouse a bed of poppies flamed scarlet against the general sombreness, and gave a strange touch of color to the common grayness. . . . Sam had not planted them — you may be sure of that. Mrs. Motherwell would tell you of an English girl she had had to work for her that summer who had brought the seed with her from England. . . . She was the craziest thing, this Polly Bragg. She went every night to see them because they were like a "bit of home," she said. Mrs. Motherwell would tell you just what a ridiculous creature she was! . . .

"And, mind you," Mrs. Motherwell would go on, with a grieved air, "just as the busy time came on didn't she up and take the fever — you never can depend on them English girls. . . ."

Mrs. Motherwell felt bitterly grieved with Polly for failing her just when she needed her the most; "after me keepin' her and puttin' up with her all summer," she said. She began to wonder where she could secure help. Then she had an inspiration!

The Watsons still owed ten dollars on the caboose [which they had converted into part of their house]. The eldest Watson girl was big enough to work. They would get her. And get ten dollars' worth of work out of her if they could.

The next Saturday night John Watson announced to his family that old Sam Motherwell wanted Pearlie to go out and work off the caboose debt.

Mrs. Watson cried, "God help us!" and threw her apron over her head.

"Who'll keep the dandrew out of me hair?" Mary said tearfully, "if Pearlie goes away?"

"Who'll make me remember to spit on me warts?" Bugsey asked.

"Who'll keep house when ma goes to wash?" wee Tommy wailed dismally. [Mrs. Watson worked as a washerwoman.]

Danny's grievance could not be expressed in words. He buried his tousy head in Pearl's apron, and Pearl saw at once that her whole house were about to be submerged in tears, idle tears.

"Stop your bleatin', all of yez!" she commanded in her most authoritative voice. "I will go!" she said, with blazing eyes. "I will go; I will wipe the stain off me house once and forever!" waving her arms dramatically toward the caboose which formed the sleeping apartment for the boys. "To die, to die, for those we love is nobler far than wear a crown!" Pearl had attended the Queen Esther cantata the winter before. She knew now how poor Esther felt.

On the following Monday afternoon everything was ready for Pearl's departure. . . .

[As she walked through the countryside toward the Motherwells,] the exhilaration of the air, the glory of the waving grain, the profusion of wild flowers that edged the fields with purple and yellow were like wine to her sympathetic Irish heart . . . and it was not until she came in sight of the big stone house, gloomy and bare, that she realized with a start of homesickness that she was Pearl Watson, aged twelve, away from home for the first time, and bound to work three months for a woman of reputed ill-temper. . . .

When supper was over and Pearl had washed the heavy white dishes Mrs. Motherwell told her, not unkindly, that she could go to bed. She could sleep in the little room over the kitchen in Polly's old bed. . . .

Pearl went up the ladder into the kitchen loft, and found herself in a low, long room, close and stifling. . . . She tried to open the window, but it was nailed fast.

Then a determined look shone in her eyes. She went quickly down the little ladder.

"Please ma'am," she said going over to Mrs. Motherwell, "I can't sleep up there. It is full of disease and microscopes."

"It's what?" Mrs. Motherwell almost screamed. She was in the pantry making pies.

"It has old air in it," Pearl said, "and it will give me the fever."

Mrs. Motherwell glared at the little girl. . . .

"Good gracious!" she said. "It's a queer thing if hired help are going to dictate where they are going to sleep. Maybe you'd like a bed set up for you in the parlor!"

"Not if the windies ain't open," Pearl declared stoutly.

"Well, they ain't; there hasn't been a window open in this house since it was built, and there isn't going to be, letting in dust and flies."

"You go straight to your bed," she said, with her mouth hard and her eyes glinting like cold flint, "and none of your nonsense, or you can go straight back to town."

When Pearl again reached the little stifling room she fell on her knees and prayed.

"Dear God," she said, "there's gurms here as thick as hair on a dog's back, and You and me know it, even if she don't. I don't know what to do, dear Lord — the windy is nelt down. Keep the gurms from gittin' into me, dear Lord. Do ye mind how poor Jeremiah was let down into the mire and Ye tuk care o' him, didn't Ye? Take care o' me, dear Lord. Poor ma has enough to do without me comin' home clutterin' up the house wid sickness. Keep Yer eye on Danny if Ye can at all, at all. He's awful stirrin'. I'll try to get the windy riz tomorrow by hook or crook, so mebbe it's only tonight Ye'll have to watch the gurms. Amen. . . ."

Pearl slept the heavy sleep of healthy childhood and woke in the gray dawn before anyone else in the household was stirring. . . . When Tom, the only son of the Motherwells, came down to light the fire, he found Pearl setting the table, the kitchen swept and the kettle boiling. . . .

"Good-morning," Pearl said brightly. "Are you Mr. Tom Motherwell?"

"That's what!" Tom replied. "Only you needn't mind the handle."

Pearl laughed.

"All right," she said. "I want a little favor done. Will you open the window upstairs for me?"

"Why?" Tom asked, staring at her.

"To let in good air. It's awful close up there, and I'm afraid I'll get the fever or somethin' bad."

"Polly [Bragg] got it," Tom said. "Maybe that is why Polly got it. She's awful sick now. Ma says she'll like as not die. But I don't believe ma will let me open it."[9]

"Where is Polly?" Pearl asked eagerly. She had forgotten her own worries. "Who is Polly? Did she live here?"

"She's in the hospital now in Brandon," Tom said in answer to her rapid questions. "She planted them poppies out there, but she never seen the flowers on them. Ma wanted me to cut them down, for Polly used to put off so much time with them, but I didn't want to. Ma was mad, too, you bet," he said with a reminiscent smile at his own foolhardiness.

Pearl was thinking — she could see the poppies through the window, bright and glowing in the morning light. They rocked lightly in the wind, and a shower of crimson petals fell. Poor Polly! she hadn't seen them. . . .

After sundown one night Pearl's resolve was carried into action. She picked a shoe-box full of poppies, wrapping the stems carefully in wet newspapers. She put the cover on, and wrapped the box neatly.

Then she wrote the address. She wrote it painfully, laboriously, in round blocky letters. Pearl always put her tongue out when she was doing anything that required minute attention. She was so anxious to have the address just right that her tongue was almost around to her ear. The address read:

Miss Polly Bragg, english gurl
and sick with fever
Brandon Hospittle
Brandon. . . .

"We'll have to move poor Polly, if she lives through the night," the nurse said to the house doctor in the hospital that night. "She is making all the patients homesick. To hear her calling for her mother or for 'someone from 'ome' is hard on the sick and well."

"What are her chances, do you think?" the doctor asked gravely.

He was a wiry little man with a face like leather, but his touch brought healing and his presence hope.

"She is dying of homesickness as well as typhoid," the nurse said sadly, "and she seems so anxious to get better, poor thing! She often says, 'I can't die, miss for what'll happen [to] mother?' But for the last two days, in her delirium, she seems to be worrying more about her work and her flowers. I think they were pretty hard people she lived with. 'Surely she'll praise me this time,' she often says, 'I've tried my 'ardest.' The strenuous life has been too much for poor Polly. Listen to her now!"

Polly was singing. Clear and steady and sweet, her voice rang over the quiet ward, and many a fevered face was raised to listen. Polly's mind was wandering in the shadows, but she still sang the songs of home in a strange land:

Down by the biller there grew a green willer,
A-weeping all night with the bank for a piller.

And over and over again she sang with a wavering cadence, incoherently sometimes, but always with tender pleading, something about "where the stream was a-flowin', the gentle kine lowin', and over my grave keep the green willers growin'."

"It is pathetic to hear her," the nurse said, "and now listen to her asking about her poppies."

"In the box, miss; I brought the seed h'across the h'ocean, and they wuz beauties, they wuz, wot came h'up. They'll be noddin' and wavin' now red and 'andsome, if she 'asn't cut them. She wouldn't cut them, would she, miss? She couldn't 'ave the 'eart, I think."

"No, indeed, she hasn't cut them," the nurse declared with decision, taking Polly's burning hand tenderly in hers. "No one could cut down such beauties. What nonsense to think of such a thing, Polly. They're blooming, I tell you, red and handsome, almost as tall as you are, Polly."

The office-boy touched the nurse's arm.

"A gentleman who gave no name left this box for one of the typhoid patients," he said, handing her the box.

The nurse read the address and the box trembled in her hands as she nervously opened it and took out the contents.

"Polly, Polly!" she cried, excitedly, "didn't I tell you they were blooming, red and handsome."

But Polly's eyes were burning with delirium and her lips babbled meaninglessly.

The nurse held the poppies over her.

Her arms reached out caressingly.

"Oh, miss!" she cried, her mind coming back from the shadows. "They have come at last, the darlin's, the sweethearts, the loves, the beauties!" She held them in a close embrace. "They're from 'ome, they're from 'ome!" she gasped painfully, for her breath came with difficulty now. "I can't just see them, miss, the lights is movin' so much, and the way the bed 'eaves, but, tell me, miss, is there a little silky one, h'edged with w'ite? It was mother's favorite one of h'all. I'd like to 'ave it in my 'and, miss."

The nurse put it in her hand. She was only a young nurse, and her face was wet with tears.

"It's like 'avin' my mother's 'and, miss, it is," she murmured softly. "Ye wouldn't mind the dark if ye 'ad yer mother's 'and, would ye, miss?"

And then the nurse took Polly's throbbing head in her strong young arms, and soothed its restless tossing with her cool, soft touch, and told her through her tears of that other Friend, who would go with her all the way.

"I'm that 'appy, miss," Polly murmured faintly. "It's like I was goin' 'ome. Say that again about the valley," and the nurse repeated tenderly that promise of incomparable sweetness:

> Yea, though I walk through the valley of the shadow
> of death I will fear no evil, for thou art with me, thy rod
> and thy staff they comfort me.

"It's just like 'avin' mother's 'and to 'old the little silky one,'"
Polly murmured sleepily.

The nurse put the poppies beside Polly's face on the pillow, and
drawing a screen around her went on to the next patient. A case of
urgent need detained her at the other end of the ward, and it was not
until the dawn was shining blue in the windows that she came back
on her rounds.

Polly lay just as she had left her. The crimson petals lay thick
upon her face and hair. The homesickness and redness of weeping
had gone forever from her eyes, for they were looking now upon the
King in His beauty! In her hand, now cold and waxen, she held one
little silky poppy, red, with edges of white. Polly had gone home.

There was a whisper among the poppies that grew behind the
cookhouse that morning as the first gleam of the sun came yellow
and wan over the fields; there was a whisper and a shivering among
the poppies as the morning breezes, cold and chill, rippled over
them, and a shower of crystal drops mingled with the crimson petals
that fluttered to the ground. It was not until Pearl came out and
picked a handful of them for her dingy little room that they held up
their heads once more and waved and nodded, red and handsome.[10]

Letter to Nellie
from her father-in-law, 1908

I am just finishing *Danny* for the second time and my opinion of
both [the book and the character Pearlie] has been greatly elevated.
So far as my knowledge goes Pearlie is the finest in modern fiction
and it's because of her Christlikeness — her evangelical character if
you like. . . . I am delighted that you made *Danny* "too evangelical"
for some people. I am more than delighted that the reading public
delight to honor one who is not ashamed to avow her love for the
teachings of our great Master. My dear daughter never let the . . .
[evangelistic] be wanting in your books and stories when it comes in
as naturally as in *Danny*.[11]

Nellie L. McClung, 1945

A writer in the *Canadian Author* this month (that is October
1943), contributed a kindly biographical article dealing with my
literary work, which he entitles "Nellie McClung — Crusader." In it
he says that my didactic enthusiasm has marred my art. "Some of
her stories are sermons in the guise of fiction. There is the flavor of

the Sunday school hymn and the Foreign Mission Board in some of her work."

I hope I have been a crusader, and I would be very proud to think that I had even remotely approached the grandeur of a Sunday school hymn. I have never worried about my art. I have written as clearly as I could, never idly or dishonestly, and if some of my stories are, as Mr. Eggleston says, sermons in disguise, my earnest hope is that the disguise did not obscure the sermon.[12]

Book review, about 1908

[Sowing Seeds in Danny] . . . makes me glad to be a human.[13]

Letter to Nellie L. McClung, about 1908

Five ladies sitting in Clinton station two weeks ago were overheard talking about Seeds in Danny and one said re the authoress "I wish I could get at her and I would hug and kiss her."[14]

Dr. Mary Hallett, 1975

She was always spoken of as being western and the people who lived here thought of her that way, too. One friend of mine was telling me how she had read only English books — only books from England — and when she got Sowing Seeds in Danny and read it, she thought, "Why this is my country. Someone's talking about what I know."[15]

Newspaper report, about 1908

It is an interesting study to examine the records of the best-selling books in Canada from month to month. . . . The honor of occupying first place [this month] is accorded to a Canadian lady, Mrs. McClung of Manitou, Manitoba. The writer has been compiling this list of Canadian best sellers for six years now, and to his best recollection, only one Canadian author has ever reached the top before — Rev. C. W. Gordon (Ralph Connor).[16]

Letter from Nellie's publisher, 1908

We have been using, as you know, up to the present time the headline of a number of advertisements as follows — "A new book by a new writer which *will make* the author famous." We have now come to the conclusion that it is time to change this line . . . to read "A new book by a new writer which *has made* the author famous."[17]

RECITATIONS

Nellie L. McClung, 1945

The success of *Sowing Seeds in Danny* led me into a new field of adventure. I gave public readings from it. My mother-in-law was again to blame. She had a project in Winnipeg which needed money — the W.C.T.U. Home for Friendless Girls, called the Williard Home, and one day the possibility that people might be induced to pay to hear me read from the new book caused her to telephone me at Manitou. I told her it would never do, no one would come — but I also knew from the first second that I would do it. She had a way with her — that gentle, soft-spoken woman; she had the strength of the meek — the terrible meek, who win by sweetness and gentle persuasion and the brushing away of all arguments as only the meek can.

I got a new dress, a soft blue; I had my hair done at a hairdressers, and a manicure and facial. My first excursion into the aromatic world of Applied Beauty! I even had a little rouge to tone up my pale complexion. The operator put it on, without bothering to ask me, and I had to admit it was an improvement on the rose leaf from a summer hat, hitherto used by me for the purpose. I was learning.[18]

Newspaper report, 1910

Mrs. Nellie McClung, of Manitou, Manitoba, author of that popular book, *Sowing Seeds in Danny*, has discovered that she possesses a new talent. Mrs. McClung has become something of an elocutionist. In the aid of charity some time ago, she consented to read a little of her work at church gatherings. Her rendering of parts of *Danny* created quite a furore. Requests began to come in from all the little towns throughout Manitoba asking for engagements.[19]

Letter from Elkhorn, Man., 1910

Mrs. McClung,

I am instructed by the Methodist Ladies' Aid to write you asking if you could favor us with an evening. Would you require a choir or some music as well also terms and if you could come — whew! We would prefer to have you before the rink opens if at all. . . .[20]

Newspaper report, about 1910

Last evening Nellie L. McClung, the clever authoress of that delightful book, *Sowing Seeds in Danny*, delighted a splendid audience in ... [Brandon, Manitoba] with readings from this well-known work. Even to those who were well acquainted with Mrs. McClung's ability as a reader, her work on last evening's program was a pleasing surprise. Instead of reading from the text, she gave her numbers entirely from memory, and her interpretation of the five chapters given revealed histrionic talent of a high order.[21]

Letter from her publisher, 1910

You must have a regular picnic, a continuous picnic, going around to these small burgs [on reading tours] being lionized in the way you are, and since you are not the kind who is apt to get a swelled head you must sit back sometimes and revel in it all.[22]

Comment on a speech, 1935

It isn't what she says so much as the way she says it and her wonderful personality.[23]

Newspaper report, 1909

The popularity of Mrs. Nellie McClung ... came with a genuine western rush. A year ago she was unheard of exclusive of her intimate friends. Today hundreds of Canadians have formed acquaintance with her unique personality through reading her work. Mrs. McClung makes the welcome announcement that *The Second Chance*, a new book introducing some of the old *Danny* characters, is underway.[24]

Newspaper report, 1910

The first edition of Mrs. McClung's new book, *The Second Chance*, was sold out in a day, and it has been necessary to issue a second and larger edition.[25]

Magazine article, about 1912

Though Mrs. McClung is a famous woman now, to her former friends she is "Nellie." Her popularity has not created in her one bit of affectation. She is sweetly natural. One woman who knew her before she began to write said to me: "With all her success and fame she is to us 'The same Nellie'." What a splendid compliment! But that is the secret of her charm.[26]

CHAPTER FIVE

BRAVE WOMEN AND FAIR MEN

> I point you to a better day which will reverse the
> old order, a day of brave women and fair men.

   The real "secret" of Nellie's charm was her outgoing and cordial
self. She simply liked other people, especially other women. One summer,
for example, she attempted to hold a small garden party at the beach,
with no more than one dozen guests. In the end she invited every woman
at the lake, and there were forty of them. "I really could not draw the
line," she explained afterwards, "because I liked them all."[1]

   "It's no compliment to have Nellie McClung like you," a boastful
acquaintance was once told. "She likes everyone."[2]

   But for all the breadth of her affections, Nellie did have her
favorites. If there was one thing she could not stand, it was
pretentiousness. "I like plain people — the real ones," she confided, "and
I am glad that they like me, and know me for one of their own."[3] There
was the woman at a convention, for example, who in parting, "shook . . .
[Nellie's] hand warmly and remarked with evident sincerity, 'I will
certainly have something to tell our people when I go home. I will tell
them that I met Nellie McClung, and there was sure no style about
her!' "[4]

   "This was at the Governor's reception," Nellie observed, "and I
had on my white gloves too! But I knew what she meant, and I have been
glad ever since."[5]

   Another time, she befriended a family of picnickers at Winnipeg
Beach, letting them eat lunch on her verandah and serving them tea, "all
the while wearing the popular 'bungalow apron' of that day."

   Upon leaving the woman said, "Now to whom am I indebted
for this kindness?" Mrs. McClung told her name — "Not

the writer!" exclaimed the woman. Mrs. McClung nodded,
whereupon the woman called her daughters who had strolled
on ahead, "Come here, girls . . . and see a real live writer" —
but she said after a scrutinizing glance from herself "You
certainly don't look much like a writer!"[6]

Nellie took great delight in these incidents and stored them up to
retell at her own expense. There could have been an element of reverse
snobbery in this — the pleasure a special person gets from being
mistaken for run-of-the-mill. Perhaps there was reassurance, too, that
she wasn't exceeding the common denominator of womanhood by too
much, for there were strong prohibitions in her nature against personal
ambition and conceit. (Her mother had seen to that.) Perhaps it simply
reflected her desire to be liked, which was an important source of her
warmth.

What is certain is that she had a very great attachment to the idea
of herself as a typical small-town woman, the home-loving mother of
four. She had found peace and satisfaction in this role, and she was
happy to retain the self-image which went with it as long as she could,
even when it no longer adequately described her life.

Her world was changing. First had come her triumph as a novelist,
then success as a stage performer, and now, in 1911, she was leaving
Manitou.

The responsibility of running the pharmacy had been taking its toll
on Wes. He was afflicted with what Nellie called a "primitive
Methodist conscience" that kept him awake nights worrying. Had all the
prescriptions been filled correctly? Were the drugs locked up securely at
closing time? The strain was beginning to tell on his disposition, Nellie
recalled.

> One day when there was some unpleasantness about a
> misplaced hammer, Jack wrote a rhyming explanation of the
> episode which he left beside his father's plate at dinner. I
> remember the summary:
> > "Good old Wes would worry less
> > If he were free from the store's distress."
> And that seemed to be the situation, and I could see something
> had to be done, even if we had to live on less. I could not stand
> by and see Wes drift into a state of nervous exhaustion, and
> his fresh complexion dull down to the drugstore bleach.
> And so we sold the store. . . .[7]

Wes tried his hand at farming first, but when he was invited to join Manufacturers' Life Insurance Company, it was off to Winnipeg for the entire clan. Although the city was only a hundred miles away, the move changed "the whole tide" of Nellie's life.[8]

In 1911, Winnipeg boasted a population of 136,000 — seventeen times what it had been when the Mooneys first passed through on the way to their homestead, only thirty years before. Many of the newcomers had arrived in the crush of immigration since the turn of the century. In fact, Winnipeg had doubled in size since 1906, and only twenty-three percent of the residents were Manitoba born.[9]

The city was still predominantly Anglo-Saxon, for most of the settlers had come from Great Britain and Ontario, and municipal politics were controlled by a WASP élite of commercial ambition and wealth.[10] But this was also the era when Clifford Sifton and his colleagues in the federal Department of the Interior went recruiting in eastern Europe, trying to induce the "stalwart peasant in the sheep-skin coat," his "stout wife," and their large brood of children to take land in western Canada.[11] Many thousands did just that, but thousands of others crowded into the north end of Winnipeg, displaced, out of money, out of work.

Living and working conditions in the "foreign" quarter were dismal. The clique which governed the city were preoccupied with "making themselves — and only themselves — rich"[12]; tax money went into services for industry, not into amenities for the "shiftless bohunks."

To be fair, Winnipeg was no more neglectful of its poor than were other North American cities of the time, though the influx of immigrants had made the situation there worse. Laissez-faire was the ideology of the day, especially on what was still the western frontier. Government was deemed successful if it made the world safe for the entrepreneur. Material success was up to the individual; the "failures" could be left to charity. And so, Winnipeg got its new railway bridge, but there were no sewers in the slums, and excrement oozed out of the backyard privies into gutters along the lanes. Typhoid and smallpox were epidemic. In the stuffy, ill-kept tenements, people slept three or four to a bed; babies and children often died for lack of medical care. Workers were underpaid and ill-fed, with little hope of attaining a more comfortable life. Not surprisingly, booze, so luxuriantly available along the Main Street strip, was a release (and a problem) for some.

In comparison to this, Manitou was a homogenous and untroubled community. True, there was an occasional family which could not get ahead, but more often than not, the problem might be traced back to some man who drank. At least that was Nellie's analysis. Ordinary neighborliness and prohibition seemed adequate to meet the needs of the community; the politics of the W.C.T.U. were appropriate to Manitou.

And if the problems of the little community were relatively simple, so was its social structure. There were none of the extremes of wealth which marked Winnipeg; nor were there cultural differences. A number of families from eastern Europe had settled in southwestern Manitoba, especially after 1900, but Nellie didn't claim any of them as friends. She kept her distance, prepared to risk only a cautious tolerance. One day, for example, about 1910, she encountered a group of "Galicians" on the train.

> [They were] . . . good looking little girls with yellow handkerchiefs on their heads and [a] great scarcity of petticoats. One little lady had a broad girdle of huckaback around her slim waist, fastened with two safety pins. There were two little boys in the party. . . and the superior way the little lady with the huckaback ordered around her brothers made me feel they are very like ourselves after all. It might have been Florence Letitia instructing Paul Harper and H[orace] B.[13]

Nellie had grown up amongst transplanted Ontarians, with here and there a settler who'd come directly from the British Isles or the States. Early on, her mother had vetoed the idea of settling near Winnipeg because there were "too many jet black eyes and high cheek-bones there," traits which she didn't want to see turn up in her grandchildren.[14] Letitia Mooney was an Imperialist, a colonial, and so were most of the people around Manitou—at least most of those in Nellie's circle. When Queen Victoria died in 1901, it had sent a tremor through the community and a visit from any member of the royal family, however distantly connected, was a great event.[15]

Nellie belonged in Manitou. These were her people; the prairies of southwestern Manitoba were her homeland. She had always been a country person at heart. A walk through the fields, a period of meditation on a comfortable rock were her standard cures for worry or discouragement. She took solace from nature. That the country, preferably a farm, was the best place for children, she had no doubts. As Pearlie Watson put it in The Second Chance, farm life gave them "a *chance to grow up decent," away from the town-bred wickedness of liquorice pipes, slang, and talking back.*[16] *Nellie liked country people — after all, they had been the inspiration for her books — especially country women. They had a direct, matter-of-fact way of getting things done which she admired. She enjoyed the busy, easy sociability of small-town life. Not counting the time she had spent in and around Manitou as a teacher, it had been her home for fifteen years, and she left with regret.*

Nellie L. McClung, 1945

I remember the day we left Manitou. I looked back from the window of the train as it made its labored way up the grade past Luke Armstrong's buildings and Elijah Harmer's big barn. We had the whole family with us, except Jack, who stayed behind to write his examinations. It was a bright June day, full of greenness and beauty, the air full of the scent of pea vines and wolf willow blossom. The hush of noon-day lay on the fields for the workers had gone in for their mid-day meal. Peace and plenty lay over all and every building, grove of trees, every winding trail seemed like an old friend from whom we were parting. I knew one pleasant chapter of our lives was ending and a sudden fear gripped my heart—fear of the market place; fear of high places; fear of the strange country. If I could have gone back to the safety of the known ways at that moment, I would have gone. Tears rolled down my cheeks, which, fortunately, the children did not notice. They were too full of joy at the great adventure, and too full of plans for the beach, for we were going to spend two months at Lake Winnipeg where we had bought a cottage. I kept my face pressed to the window, trying to subdue this flood of emotion which was really downright homesickness, premature but nonetheless real. You can't go back, I kept saying to myself; no one ever gets the chance to try the other way.[17]

AT THE BEACH

Nellie L. McClung, 1911

28 June 1911   On Sunday we went away down the shore and found a sandy beach, where a big log had fallen out into the stream. On it, we walked out and soaked our feet, and were very happy.

30 June   Wes went to Manitou, Jack to Winnipeg Beach, and

the other three to Whytewold, leaving me alone. It's lonely but peaceful. I believe I can write a story today.

(After that I did get busy and write several pages. I could see things and hear people talk.)

5 August   Lots of things have happened. The principal one being we have bought a house. . . . We got 97 Chestnut Street [in Winnipeg]. We like it—especially me!

Now I'm busy writing—I need the money. Don't talk to me![18]

INVESTIGATIONS

Nellie L. McClung, 1945

The big city gathered us in when the pleasant summer at the beach was over. Mark, our youngest child, was born in October of that year, and quickly became the idol of the family, with his blonde curls, blue eyes and quaint wisdom. The other children were all at school and Jack had started at Wesley College. Every day was full of interest. I enjoyed my association with the Canadian Women's Press Club, when we met once a week for tea in our own comfortable quarters. There great problems were discussed and the seed germ of the suffrage association was planted. It was not enough for us to meet and talk and eat chicken sandwiches and olives. We felt we should organize and create a public sentiment in favor of woman suffrage.

The visit of Mrs. Emmeline Pankhurst and of Miss Barbara Wiley, also one of the British militant suffragettes, created a profound impression. The immediate cause of our desire to organize was the plight of women workers in small factories. Some of our members had visited these and we were greatly stirred over the question of long hours, small wages and distressing working conditions.

Mrs. Claude Nash spoke one day on this subject at a Local Council [of Women] meeting, and as a result of this meeting she and I were deputed to bring pressure to bear on the government for the appointment of a woman factory inspector. We decided to go to see Sir Rodmond Roblin, the premier, and if possible, get him to come with us to see some of the factories. She knew him quite well and I had often listened to him in the Legislative Assembly from the visitors' gallery. He was a florid, rather good looking man in his early sixties, somewhat pompous in manner but very popular with his party and firmly seated on the political throne by what was known as the "Machine". . . .

Mrs. Nash must have had some political standing, for I certainly had not, and we got an interview. We found Sir Rodmond in a very genial mood, and he expressed his delight at our coming. Mrs. Nash was a very handsome young woman, dressed that day in a gray lamb coat and crimson velvet hat. I wasn't looking so poorly myself for I, too, had youth on my side, and we could see that the old man was impressed favorably. . . . He balked a bit when we asked him if he would come with us to see some of the factories and tried to get us to be satisfied with one of his deputies, but Mrs. Nash and I held firm, and much to our surprise, he consented. He called his car and we set out. He looked very well in his beaver coat, and his car was the most pretentious I had ever ridden in. The cut glass vase filled with real carnations impressed my country eyes.

On the way to the first factory, the premier, who sat between us, with his plump hands resting on a gold-headed cane, gave us his views on women working in factories. He believed in work, especially for young women. There was too much idleness now, with electricity and short cuts in labor. As a boy he had worked from sunrise, and before, until the shadows of evening fell, and enjoyed it. Happiest days of his life . . . running barefoot under the apple trees. Perhaps we were over-sentimental about factory conditions. . . . Women's hearts were often too kind . . . but he liked kind women—and hoped they would never change. And these young girls in the factories whom we thought were underpaid, no doubt they lived at home, and really worked because they wanted pin-money. Anyway, working wouldn't hurt them, it would keep them off the streets. . . .

Knowing what we did, we let the monologue go on. He advised us not to allow our kind hearts to run away with us. Most of the women in the factories, he understood, were from foreign countries, where life was strenuous (that word was in the first flush of its popularity then). They did not expect to be carried to the skies on a flowery bed of ease! It doesn't do women any harm to learn how money comes. . . . Extravagant women are the curse of this age.

We conducted the premier down dark, slippery stairs to an airless basement where light in mid-day came from gaunt light bulbs, hanging from smoky ceilings. The floor was littered with refuse of apple peelings and discarded clothing. There was no ventilation and no heat. The room was full of untidy women, operating sewing machines and equally unattractive men cutting out garments on long tables. We urged Sir Rodmond to speak to some of the workers, but he was willing to call it a day at the first glance. He was shocked at the filth of the place, and asked one of the women if anybody ever swept the floor? He had to shout to drown the sound of the machines. The woman shook her head and kept on working. Then we reminded him that all these people were on piece work.

We led the premier through a side door into the foul passage where a queue had formed before a door marked "Toilet." We could see that Sir Rodmond was deeply shocked that we should know about such things but Mrs. Nash led the way, and I pushed him along from behind. We drew his attention to the fact that there was no separate accommodation for the women, and we did not need to mention that the plumbing had evidently gone wrong. We knew that he was soon going to bolt away from us, so we didn't spare him anything.

"For God's sake, let me out of here," he cried at last. "I'm choking! I never knew such hell holes existed!"

"These people work from 8:30 to 6:00, Sir Rodmond. Six days a week," Mrs. Nash told him sweetly. "But no doubt they get used to it." I am afraid her sarcasm was lost on Sir Rodmond.

When we got him up on the street again, he remembered an important interview he had promised, but we coaxed him to come to one more factory where men's shirts were being made, and all the workers were young women, and by promising him that this would be the last one, he came with us. This workroom was in rather a better building and some daylight came in from the windows. We wanted him particularly to see these young girls who were being "kept off the streets." At one machine a girl worked with a bandaged hand, a badly hurt hand and a very dirty bandage. At another one a girl coughed almost continuously. I asked her how long she had had her cold and she said she had no cold, it was just a bit of bronchitis she had every winter, but she daren't stop work for there were plenty more to take her place, and someone had to earn some money in their family, as their father was out of work. She said she had been lucky to get the job. The manager came over to speak to us, anxious to show us the fine product they were turning out. Mrs. Nash asked him how often the factory inspector came around, but he didn't seem to know anything about factory inspectors. "In fact," he said, "we hardly need one. All the girls are glad of the work. I have no trouble with them."

"How about the girl who coughs so much?" I asked. "Couldn't she be given a few days off with pay to get built up a bit?"

The manager regarded me sternly.

"The company is not a charitable institution," he said, "and makes no provision for anything like that. If the girl is sick, she can always quit!" He threw out his hands expressively in a fine gesture of freedom.

Sir Rodmond was moving towards the door, and we followed. When we got back into the car we could see that the fine old gentleman of the old school was really shocked at what he had seen.

"Now, Sir Rodmond," we said, "do you still think that these women are pleasurably employed in this rich land of wide spaces and great opportunities?"

Sir Rodmond let down one of the windows of the car and said:

"I still can't see why two women like you should ferret out such utterly disgusting things."

"Your factory inspector knows about these places," we told him. "We mailed him a list of them and described them, but he has done nothing. He takes your attitude: Why should women interfere with what does not concern them? But we are not discouraged and have no intention of allowing these conditions to continue. We would like you to appoint a woman factory inspector, a real trained social worker."

Sir Rodmond grew impatient at that. "I tell you it's no job for a woman. I have too much respect for women to give any of them a job like this.... But I don't mind admitting that I'm greatly disturbed over all this, greatly disturbed," he repeated. "I'll admit I didn't know that such places existed and I promise you that I will speak to Fletcher about it."

With this understanding we parted, thanking Sir Rodmond for giving us so much of his time.

Our investigations went on. We were only amateurs but we did find out a few things about how the "other half" lived. We made some other discoveries too. We found out that the Local Council of Women could not be our medium. There were too many women in it who were afraid to be associated with any controversial subject. Their husbands would not let them "go active." It might imperil their jobs. The long tentacles of the political octopus reached far. So one night at Jane Hample's house on Wolsley Avenue we organized the Political Equality League, with a membership of about fifteen. We believed that fifteen good women who were not afraid to challenge public opinion could lay the foundations better than a thousand. Some good work had been already done by the Icelandic women of the city, who had organized the first suffrage society many years before, and the W.C.T.U. women could always be counted on and the same was true of the Labor women.

We wanted to get first-hand information on the status of women in Manitoba, and, of course, the whole Dominion. Then it was our purpose to train public speakers and proceed to arouse public sentiment . . . . We had all the courage of youth and inexperience with a fine underpinning of simplicity that bordered on ignorance, but anything we lacked in knowledge we made up in enthusiasm.[19]

GOING ACTIVE

One day, when Nellie's own enthusiasm got the best of her, she decided on the spur of the moment to visit Sir Rodmond by herself. A single telephone call was all it took to arrange an interview, and within a matter of hours, she found herself face to face with the premier. Once again, impulse overtook her, and she boldly asked him to order the entire cabinet into his office so that they could hear what she had to say about women's suffrage.

"It does not do to put too light an estimate upon yourself or to disparage yourself in any way," she'd noted in one of her journals a few years earlier. "If the apostle Paul lived nowadays he would not style himself the chief sinner or people wouldn't go to hear him preach. . . ."[20]

But it wouldn't have mattered how Nellie had billed herself, for Roblin wasn't about to let her "preach" to his ministers.

"You surprise me," he said slowly. "Now who do you think you are?"

"At this moment," . . . [Nellie] said, "I'm one of the best advisers you ever had in all your life. I'm not asking you for a favor, I'm really offering you help."

"What if I tell you that I don't need your help?" he said severely. "And that I think you're rather a conceited young woman, who has perhaps had some success at Friday afternoon entertainments at country school houses, and so are

*laboring under the delusion that you have the gift of oratory.
What would you say to that?"*

"I wouldn't mind," . . . [Nellie] answered.[21]

In fact, nothing he said really offended her until he started to argue
that "nice women" weren't interested in voting.

> *His voice dripped fatness.*
> *"By nice women," . . . [Nellie] said, "you probably
> mean selfish women who have no more thought for the
> underpaid, overworked woman than a pussycat in a sunny
> window has for the starving kitten on the street. Now in that
> sense I am not a nice woman, for I do care. I care about those
> factory women, working in ill-smelling holes, and we intend to
> do something about it, and when I say 'we' I'm talking for a
> great many women, of whom you will hear more as the days
> go on. . . .*
> *"I'll not be back, Sir Rodmond; not in your time . . . but
> it's just possible that you will hear from me, not directly, but
> still you'll hear; and you may not like what you hear,
> either."*
> *"Is that a threat?" he laughed.*
> *"No," [she] said. "It's a prophecy."*[22]

This was not Nellie's first brush with Rodmond Roblin. Ever since
the turn of the century, he had been the bête noire of Manitoba
prohibitionists. In 1899, before Roblin became Conservative leader, the
party had swept into power on a temperance platform, and the
then-leader, Hugh John Macdonald, had immediately outlawed the sale
of liquor in the province.

"I remember being at Portage la Prairie when the news came that
the liquor act had become law," Nellie said, "and we all stood up and
sang, 'Praise God from Whom [all blessings flow]'."[23]

"Mr. Roblin at the time in an eloquent speech called upon the wives
and mothers of Manitoba to thank God, yea devoutly thank God, that
there were men in power strong enough to put such a law upon the
statute book. . . ."[24]

But a few months later, when Roblin took over as premier, his
enthusiasm for prohibition began to ebb. He could see that enforcing the
law would be a nightmare, especially since it was not popular among the
Catholics and the foreign-born. Too vigorous application of the act

would surely lose him votes. Besides, it was rumored that the Conservatives sometimes supplied an election-day swig of hooch as a reward for right-thinking voters. Campaign promises or no campaign promises, Roblin wasn't in any hurry to have prohibition in effect.

So he insisted first that the new temperance act be tested by the courts, and when it survived that challenge, he called a plebiscite to make sure that the electorate still wanted the legislation. The people of Manitoba had already made their views clear in two referenda (1893 and 1898) and in one election (1899), all of which the drys had won hands down. To register their disgust with Roblin's tactics, many prohibitionists boycotted the new tally, with the result that their side lost. The premier took this result as justification to repeal the Macdonald liquor act.

It was not that this party had forsaken the temperance cause, he piously maintained, but that the will of the people must prevail. Thus he was in the luxurious position of calling on prohibitionists for their support while doing nothing to advance their interests.

The only course left open to the reformers was "local option": the law provided that individual municipalities could go dry if the voters so wished. In theory, this was a simple two-step procedure. First a certain percentage of the ratepayers had to petition the government for a local referendum, and then the vote itself could be held. In practice, there was another, intervening step, which presented the greatest difficulties. Unless the provincial government could be persuaded to honor the petitions, the prohibitionists were stymied. Roblin seemed determined to be as obstreperous as possible. In Nellie's opinion, he treated the temperance advocates with all the deference due to an old boot.

"Every year we went to him asking to make . . . [the local option] law effective," she lamented to a reporter. "Seventy-two times he threw our petitions out on technicalities."

> *Once we had a petition in thirty-two sheets.*
> *"Oh no, certainly not," we were told, "the law says a petition, not thirty-two of them."*
> *Next year we pasted them all together.*
> *"What an outrage!" said the government, "This is a mutilated petition. How can you prove to us that John Smith, five feet or so down from the top, ever saw that heading you have? Go home and forget it."*

By this time, of course, Nellie was "in the habit of giving recitations from her books for sundry ladies' aids and such like."

"I shall be pleased to come," she wrote the astonished next applicant, "if after I conclude the recital you will allow me to discuss the political situation for the next hour."

"Sometimes they'd say yes. . . . If not, I hired the hall myself for the hour succeeding the meeting, and, when I was through with the first part of the program, I'd announce that, my contract with the ladies having been carried out, I now invited the audience to remain as my guests while we talked politics."[25]

As long as she lived in Manitou, "politics" had meant "temperance," but now that she'd moved to the city, it was just as likely to mean "women's rights." Under the stimulus of new experiences and new associates, her thought was evolving rapidly. In 1910, in an address to a women's group in Toronto, she had gently recommended that her audience look beyond their own households and try to ensure that all children get "a good chance in life."[26] By 1912, these timid generalities no longer satisfied her. Women in Manitoba, she discovered, had the legal status of infants. Mothers didn't even have a right to their own offspring. In theory (and sometimes in practice) the father could put his children up for adoption or assign them to guardians without his wife's consent. He might also sell the family home or will it away without a thought of his wife's well-being. In a country where women were toiling alongside men to turn raw homesteads into farms, this was blatantly unjust. Back in Ontario, wives had "dower" in their husbands' property — the right to a guaranteed inheritance — but this had been suspended in the West during the settlement boom. As a result, prairie women sometimes found themselves out on the roadside with half a dozen hungry children and all their worldly goods, the victims of a husband who'd sold the family home and headed for greener pastures on his own.

Though there weren't many cases as frightening as that, Nellie was moved by the true stories she heard. Too many farm wives — young women, some of them — were neglected and overworked for so long that they finally dropped dead.[27] And farmers' daughters often fared little better. Why was it, Nellie wondered, that the land always went to the sons of the household, regardless of what the girls had contributed in labor? Nellie knew of one family in which each son had inherited a full section of land. The equally deserving daughter received one hundred dollars and a cow named Bella.

"How would you like to be left at forty years of age, with no training and very little education, facing the world with one hundred dollars and one cow, even if she were named Bella?" Nellie wanted to know.[28]

Not surprisingly perhaps, given her husband's occupation, one of Nellie's pet grievances was with insurance companies which discriminated against women. A premium that insured a male in the case of death or disability often covered a female only in the case of death. The only "rationale" for this which Nellie could uncover was that women were more sensitive than men and might imagine injuries they didn't really have. "But what about the clause relating to the loss of the hand or foot?" Nellie goaded. "You would not be altogether dependent on what . . . [the women] said about that, would you? You could check them up — if they were pretending, could you not?"[29]

Surely, if women once had the franchise, they would be in a position to demand equality. The more Nellie saw of women's legal and economic disabilities, the more she learned about the international suffrage movement, and the longer she pondered the origins of women's inferior status, the more passionately she felt the justice of votes for women and the more urgently she spoke about it.

Women's suffrage was not a popular cause in Canada when Nellie and the other members of the Political Equality League took it on. In 1912, when League members set up a literature table at the Winnipeg stampede, passersby gawked at the "suffragettes" and pointed them out to one another in tones "that might have heralded the appearance of a dinosaur in the flesh."[30] For some people, influenced by newspaper stories about the British militants, the word "suffrage" conjured up images of rock-hurling maenads with a taste for chaining themselves to the railings in public galleries. For others, political rights for women symbolized a wholesale change in sex roles which went far beyond the casting of a ballot once in four years. If women entered public life, what would become of the home and family, those guarantors of social peace?

To some extent Nellie's approach calmed these fears. She was living proof that a woman could succeed in the world without giving up her feminine charms. Besides, as she never tired of reminding reporters, she had five fine children to her credit and a stable home. She enjoyed attractive clothing, especially fanciful hats. (The decision of some suffrage leaders to wear "ill-fitting masculine clothes" was "pure *affectation," she thought.)*[31] *Her ordinariness must have been reassuring to many of her listeners.*

Similarly, her ideas, taken by themselves, didn't sound particularly ominous. For all the changes in her thinking, she hadn't abandoned her old ideas and loyalties. She was just as certain as ever that political action was a religious responsibility. She still believed women to be a special order of humanity, with a mission to nurture and to serve. In many important respects, her concept of womanhood was as conventional as that of the anti-suffragists. This gave her a common ground with her audience, a place to begin, and contributed to her success as a suffrage evangelist.

"The real spirit of the suffrage movement . . .." she once wrote, "is sympathy and interest in the other woman, and the desire to make the world a more homelike place to live in. Some say, untruthfully, that suffrage for women would destroy the home. It will only destroy the narrowness of the home; it will spread the home spirit until it finds its way into every corner of the world."[32] Women do not want the vote in order to "secure the offices that belong to men," she was quoted as saying on another occasion, but "because they love their homes and their children."[33] Ever since the industrial revolution, she observed, production had moved from the home into the factory, leaving middle-class women with leisure time. It was these free hours which women could devote to social mothering. What was so frightening about that?

Nellie L. McClung, about 1914

Women have been charity workers since the world began. The Lady of the Manor (if she were a good lady), always made garments for the poor with her own white hands and at Christmas time, it was part of the celebration for her to make visits to the cottagers, bestowing blankets and coals, and warm woollen mufflers and mittens. This was a very happy arrangement; it furnished the good lady with busy work, it helped to ease the conscience of the lord of the manor, for some of the lords of the early periods had consciences, and if the cottager was sometimes disposed to wonder why he should have to work so hard and get nothing for it while the lord of the manor did no work at all, and got everything, the "blanket and coals" showed him what an ungrateful wretch he was.

So long as women are content to distribute blankets and coals, to make strong garments for the poor, to deal with the symptoms of poverty, paying no attention to the causes, all is well, all is smooth sailing. There is . . . [an aspect of] our charity that is transitory, vain, fleeting, ineffectual. Christmas dinners to hungry people is a deed of Christian charity incumbent upon all, and yet its effects are soon gone — the people are as hungry the next day as ever.

Once a kind old gentleman found a sick dog, lying by the road in the glare of the sun, the kind old man had compassion upon the dog and climbed down from his carriage and picking the dog up carried him around to the other side of the road, and laying him in the grateful patch of shade cast by the carriage, said, "Lie there, my poor fellow, where the sun's rays cannot smite you." Then he got into his carriage and drove away! feeling that he had done a kind and charitable deed.

So there was once a man who took his journey down the road from Jerusalem to Jericho, we read in the Book whose popularity never wanes, and on the way he fell among thieves, who beat him and robbed him, and treated him very badly. The priest and the Levite came, and looked at him, and said, "Dear, dear, how very distressing, I don't know what the road is coming to," and hurried away. The good Samaritan, passing by, had compassion on him, picked him up, put him upon his own horse, and took him to the inn, and generously made provision for him, actually spending money on him, —

The next day the good Samaritan had occasion to go down the road about the same place — he found another poor fellow beaten and robbed — evidently the work of the same thieves. Again he was the *good* Samaritan, and took care of the man as before, but the next day he found two poor fellows, beaten, and robbed, and while he was caring for them, he began to do some revolutionary thinking, — he hunted up some other good Samaritans, he even tried to interest the priest and the Levite, he hunted up his old shotgun, and they all went down the line, gunning for thieves. They determined to clean up the road!

Women have arrived at the same determination, in exactly the same way. For centuries they have been acting the good Samaritan by their philanthropies, their private and public charities, their homes for the friendless, for orphan children; free kindergartens, day nurseries; they have been picking up the robbed, wounded and beaten. Now they are wondering if they cannot do something to clean up the road. Investigation is taking the place of Resignation. For too long we have believed it our duty to sit down and be resigned. Now we know it our duty to rise up and be indignant. Long ago people broke every law of sanitation, and when plagues came, they blamed the Almighty, and said, "Thy will be done." They were submissive, where they should have been investigating.

This is the meaning of the woman's movement, and we need not apologize for it. The good Samaritan would not have been a good Samaritan if he had not examined into the causes of these things, and while he tried to alleviate the symptoms, tried also to remove the cause. Prevention is the highest type of reform.

The road from Jerusalem to Jericho is the world today, — here and now, and there are operating on the road as deadly, cowardly, merciless thieves as ever beat and robbed a defenceless traveler. Eighty thousand young girls are trapped every year into a life of shame, some of them sweet and pure and innocent as your daughter and mine. Hundreds and thousands of young girls and women are employed in sweated industries, where a living wage is not paid them, while rich men grow richer as a result of their unpaid toil. One boy out of every fifth family becomes a drunkard to support the legalized liquor traffic. Have you a boy to spare to keep up the revenue? We all know the liquor traffic survives because it makes money. No reasonable being defends it. Now what should be our attitude? If we sit down under these things, gently acquiescent, we become in the sight of God a partner in them. Submission to injustice, submission to oppression is rebellion against God.

So long as women are content to deal out blankets and coals and warm woollen mufflers, and provide day nurseries, all is well, but if they dare meddle with causes, they find themselves in politics, that sacred domain, where no women must enter, or she will be defiled.

Now politics is only public affairs, yours and mine, as well as other people's. You and I are affected by what goes on outside of the four walls of home, — the home has expanded now until it has become the whole state. The work has gone out of the home and women have had to follow it, — you have to be interested in things outside of your home if you would be faithful to your home's highest interests. It is said that the outbreak of scarlet fever in the fall of the year is caused by the new overcoats made in unsanitary factories and carrying the deadly germs. Does that affect the mother in the home? But she must not interfere with factory conditions for that is politics, and politics must not be entered by women. Now there is nothing inherently vicious in politics; the highest office in the state is that of lawgiver. In [the] old days God spoke by the mouth of his servants the prophets, who administered the legal as well as spiritual affairs of the state.

If politics are corrupt, it is all the more reason that a new element should be introduced. Women will I believe supply that new element, that purifying influence. Men and women were intended to work together, and will work more ideally together, than apart, and just as the mother's influence as well as the father's is needed in the bringing up of children and in the affairs of the home, so are they needed in the larger home, — the state. Men alone cannot make just laws for men and women, just as any class of people cannot legislate justly for another class. To deny women the right of law making is to deny the principle of democracy. The workingman knows what he wants better than the capitalist can tell him, — the wearer of the shoe knows where it pinches.

> "The toad beneath the harrow knows
>   Everywhere the tooth print goes,
> The butterfly upon the road,
>   Preaches contentment to the toad."

The women's point of view has been ignored in the making of our laws, and that is why we have such gross injustice in laws relating to women. Do you think if women had been consulted in framing the laws that a woman's virture would be held at the same value as a tree or shrub growing in a public park or garden, and valued at five dollars? Yet in our laws of Manitoba today it is so regarded. The abduction of a young girl is punishable by five years' imprisonment but the stealing of a cow is punished by a fourteen year sentence. Property has ever been held dearer than flesh and blood when the flesh and blood are woman's. In March of last year a drunken man turned out into the storm his wife and two children, one an infant, who later died from this exposure. The evidence showed that the poor woman's life had been a perpetual hell of abuse and mortal fear, — the man was given six months, afterwards commuted to two. In Brandon, last September, a farm laborer stole fifteen dollars and a blue silk handkerchief from a companion, and he was sent down for one year with hard labor.

This is the chivalry of the law toward women, the weaker sex!

These laws are a trace of the old barbarism, that women are

men's chattels, they belong to the darkness of the middle ages and the reason they have not been changed is not that men still value women less than cows, but because women have been so sweetly ladylike and modest that they have not protested against such injustice for fear of losing their womanly charm.

A great many women have not known that the laws discriminated against women. Now they are finding it out, and charm or no charm, they are voicing their indignation.

These laws are not upheld by all men either, men are ashamed of them, but lawmakers are slow to change them, for, to make laws regarding women more stringent is offensive to some men, and these men are voters, and the women who seek for these changes are not voters. The political heroism of one premier was expressed in these words, "No government can afford to commit suicide."

But the day is breaking, and the darkness is fleeing away. Four million women in the United States now enjoy full parliamentary franchise. Women vote in New Zealand, Australia, Iceland, Finland, Norway and China, and have some measure of franchise in many other countries. . . .

There are three classes of women who do not want to vote,
(A) The good intelligent woman who hasn't thought about it, — hasn't needed to, — the woman who has a good man between her and the world, and who has never needed to go up against the ragged edge of things. From this class, the suffragists make large additions to their ranks every day.
(B) The young woman who shrinks from being thought strong minded, the frilly, silly, clinging vine, — whose mental caliber is that of a butterfly, — the girl who wants to be attractive to men, at any cost. This is a form of affectation which many of them outgrow, just as they get over wearing college colors on their sleeves, hanging pennants in their room, and wearing their hair frizzed over their eyes.
(C) Class C is the selfish woman who does not care, — who does not want to be bothered, the cat-woman who loves ease and comfort, a warm cushion by a cosy fire, while she babbles of woman's indirect influence, and womanly charm. This woman will tell you she does not understand how the militants in England can do such things, — she can't understand and in this she tells the truth, for she has nothing to understand with. Their actions are unselfish, and heroic, willing to suffer for a principle, an idea. Of course she does not understand. Such actions and motives belong to a higher plan of

thinking than the cat-woman can ever rise to. Here is an assortment
of caps. Let each anti-suffragist pick her own. Far be it beyond me to
say to which class any woman belongs. I believe ninety-nine percent
belong to the first and second. I am glad to believe this — their case
is hopeful. An interest in the other woman, in the cause of little
children gives a broader outlook, a more beautiful conception of life,
to any woman. Let us work for the chivalry of women:

> "We are marching, marching, marching on to brighter,
>   happier days
> For the progress of the women, means the progress
>   of the race,
> No more the drudge and idler, ten who toil while
>   one reposes,
> But a sharing of life's glories —
>   Bread and roses, bread and roses!"[34]

Nellie L. McClung, 1915

The woman movement, which has been scoffed and jeered at
and misunderstood most of all by the people whom it is destined to
help, is a spiritual revival of the best instincts of womanhood — the
instinct to serve and save the race.[35]

THE CAMPAIGN

*The Political Equality League (P.E.L.) carried on its work with
meetings, suffrage teas, pamphleteering, and petitions, and Nellie
participated in many of the activities. In particular, she remembered a
public debate where she had helped argue the case for women's suffrage.
The outcome was decided by an audience vote, and Nellie's side won,
though only narrowly. Still, the P.E.L. women were elated over their
success. "About a thousand people were out to hear us, and as each of
them paid half a dollar, it did not so much matter how they voted on the
debate. I recall the keen pleasure we had in contemplating the fact that
we had gathered in so much money from people who were opposed to
woman suffrage. . . ."[36]*

*Early in 1914, the League made its first appearance before the
Manitoba Legislature. Their purpose, of course, was to request political
rights for women, but even before they went they had a pretty shrewd
idea of the response awaiting them. Roblin, that "fine old gentleman of
the old school," could be counted on to turn them down. Knowing that*

much in advance, the P.E.L. were ready with their revenge. Lillian Thomas, Winnipeg journalist and Nellie's special friend, had learned of a "mock parliament" which had been staged by suffragists in Vancouver, with women as the legislators and men as the disenfranchised class. It sounded like a good educational device and a way of raising funds. (Seven months after setting out to collect $2,000 for an organizational campaign, the League had been $60 in debt.) Though Nellie wasn't at the meeting where the plans were made, it was decided that she should take the part of premier in the "women's parliament."

When the time came for the P.E.L. to appear before the real Legislature, the theater had already been booked for their burlesque and the advertising was all arranged. The "worst" thing that could happen now was that Roblin might relent and grant women's suffrage, but for once he played right into the suffragists' hand.

Newspaper report, 28 January 1914

Premier Roblin Says Home Will
  Be Ruined by Votes for Women

*   *   *

Children Will be Left to the Servant Girls — Retrograde Step, and Can See Nothing to Commend It — Tells Big Delegation He Has Been in Politics 30 Years and Has Never Seen Anything Corrupt

*   *   *

Straight from the shoulder, Premier Sir Rodmond Roblin yesterday told a delegation of women that he is absolutely opposed to woman suffrage. . . . Sir Rodmond's argument was quite unequivocal. Woman's place was the home, her duty the development of the child character and the performance of wifely duties. To project her into the sphere of party politics would be to cause her to desert her true sphere, to the grave danger of society. Woman suffrage would be a retrograde step. . . .

Mrs. McClung's address [on behalf of the P.E.L.] was a feature of the event. It was eloquent, logical and dramatic, and drew forth high praise from the premier. When Sir Rodmond rose to reply he paid a compliment to the intelligence of the delegation, declaring, however, that the feminine culture and refinement displayed were anything but the product of woman suffrage. . . .

"I listened carefully to Mrs. McClung [Roblin said,] and found evidence in every word to prove that men have made sacrifices to the ideal of their heart, to the end that women might have the culture and accomplishments that have been demonstrated here today.

Where can you get better evidence of woman's superiority and the high place that she occupies than has been given here? I challenge anyone to produce better evidence of woman's high place. . . .

"There are two sides to every question. I could make a speech in favor of woman suffrage (cheers), although it would probably not be as eloquent as the speech made by Mrs. McClung. But I can see reasons that cause me to hesitate as to the advantages claimed for woman suffrage. Every good citizen will tell you that a fundamental of national greatness is the home. If the home life of any community or nation is not perfect there will not be and cannot be a condition of things equal to the opportunities of the twentieth century. Now, does the franchise for women make that better home? (Cries of assent.)

"The facts are against you. It has been said by . . . [Mrs. McClung] today that you want the suffrage because it has been beneficial over the line. But for every marriage in the United States there is a divorce. Will you tell me that that is in the interests of society? I am not going to meet some of the arguments that have been submitted. That chivalry which was inspired in me by my mother bars me from making an answer to some of the arguments, arguments which I am surprised have been put forward. The answer to those arguments is so manifest that it can be seen by the most indifferent. . . ."

As a parting shot . . ., when Sir Rodmond had stated his opposition to the suffrage movement [Mrs. McClung said]: "We'll get you yet."[37]

Nellie L. McClung, 1914

We went there asking for plain, common justice, an old fashioned square deal, and in reply to that we got hat-lifting. I feel that when a man offers hat-lifting when we ask for justice we should tell him to keep his hat right on. I will go further and say that we should tell him not only to keep his hat on but to pull it right down over his face.[38]

H. B. Beynon
Member of the P.E.L., 1976

I remember meeting Nellie on the street just before the "women's parliament" and she was in quite a stew about what she was going to say. Finally it came to her — "I'll just say what Roblin said to us! What could possibly be better!"[39]

Newspaper report, 29 January 1914

How the Vote Was Not Won —
    Burlesqued in Women's Parliament

*   *   *

Smiles of anticipation, ripples of merriment, gales of laughter
and storms of applause punctuated every point and paragraph of
what is unanimously conceded to be the best burlesque ever staged
in Winnipeg when the Political Equality League presented last night
at the Walker Theater a suffrage playlet showing "How the Vote
Was Won," and a woman's parliament showing how the vote was
not won.[40]

The audience, which filled the house to the roof, were held up
in the foyer and asked to sign a suffrage petition to the government,
which many of them did. Men were actively engaged throughout the
house in selling a pamphlet on "The Legal Status of Women in
Manitoba," by Dr. Mary Crawford, in which they seemed to be very
successful judging by the number of those seen in the hands of the
audience as they left the theatre chattering or laughing uproariously
over some choice bit of sarcasm which had particularly delighted
them. . . .

Mrs. Nellie McClung's appearance before the curtain was the
signal for a burst of applause from the audience who instantly
recognized the woman whom many of them had heard make such an
eloquent speech on the floor of the Legislature last Tuesday
morning. She explained that they would have to use their
imagination as political conditions were reversed and women were
in power. She couldn't see why women shouldn't sit in Parliament. It
didn't seem to be such a hard job. She didn't want to — but you
couldn't tell what your granddaughters might want to do. Her
earnest statement that they had visited the Legislature and tried to
get local color, caused much mirth. In fact, had she been a star
comedian her every sentence could not have brought forth more
continuous applause.

The curtain rose revealing the women legislators, all with their
evening gowns covered with black cloaks, seated at desks in
readiness for the first session. . . .

Petitions were first received and read. The first was a protest
against men's clothes, saying that men wearing scarlet ties, six inch
collars and squeaky shoes should not be allowed in public. A second

petition asked for labor saving devices for men. A third prayed that alkali and all injurious substances be prohibited in the manufacture of laundry soap as it ruined the men's delicate hands. . . .

The pinnacle of absurdity was reached when a deputation of men, lead by Mr. R. C. Skinner, arrived at the Legislature with a wheelbarrow full of petitions for votes for men. Mr. Skinner said the women were afraid that if the men were given the vote that [they] would neglect their business to talk politics when they ought to be putting wildcat subdivisions on the market. In spite of his eloquent appeal he could not touch the heart of the premier.

The premier (Mrs. McClung) then rose and launched her reply to the deputation, almost every sentence of which was interrupted by gales of laughter . . . [from] the audience which was quick to appreciate her mimicry. . . .

"I must congratulate the members of this delegation on their splendid appearance. Any civilization which can produce as splendid a type of manhood as my friend, Mr. Skinner, should not be interfered with. . . . But I cannot do what you ask me to do — for the facts are all against you. . . .

"If all men were as intelligent and as good as Mr. Skinner and his worthy though misguided followers we might consider this matter, but they are not. Seven-eighths of the police court offenders are men, and only one-third of the church membership. You ask me to enfranchise all these. . . .

"O no, man is made for something higher and better than voting. Men were made to support families. What is home without a bank account? The man who pays the grocer rules the world. In this agricultural province, the man's place is the farm. Shall I call men away from the useful plow and harrow to talk loud on street corners about things which do not concern him! Politics unsettle men, and unsettled men means unsettled bills — broken furniture, and broken vows — and divorce. . . . When you ask for the vote you are asking me to break up peaceful, happy homes — to wreck innocent lives. . . ."

"It may be that I am old-fashioned. I may be wrong. After all, men may be human. Perhaps the time will come when men may vote with women — but in the meantime, be of good cheer. Advocate and educate. We will try to the best of our ability to conduct the affairs of the province and prove worthy standard-bearers of the good old

flag of our grand old party which has often gone down to disgrace
but never [Thank God] to defeat. . . ."

After the deafening applause and laughter of the audience had
subsided . . . Mrs. McClung was . . . presented with a gorgeous
bouquet of . . . roses, which, it is rumored, was a token of
appreciation of the woman premier's eloquence from two members
of the Manitoba [Liberal] opposition who had . . . secreted themselves among the audience.[41]

                                                    Nellie L. McClung, no date

[After the "women's parliament," woman suffrage sudden-
ly] . . . became talked about. Debates sprang up in Epworth Leagues
and college societies, and invitations poured in on us [in the Political
Equality League] to address meetings.

In March the Liberal opposition met in convention and an
invitation was given to two of us to go and address the convention,
which we gladly did.

It was a sight to remember when the convention of thirteen
hundred men endorsed woman suffrage and put it in their platform.
The government, and their newspapers were very scornful: they said
woman suffrage was supported only by "short haired women and
long haired men"; they called it a "fad and a fancy," and sneeringly
said that the best women were not asking for the franchise.

Thus it became a straight party issue. The Conservative
government opposed it: the Liberal opposition said, "If we get into
power we will give it to you."

We accepted the challenge and went to work for the Liberal
party. The premier had told us that he was too old to change his
mind on woman suffrage, so we said that as we could not change the
premier's mind, we would try to change the premier.

It was a great campaign, lasting two months. Everybody
worked.[42]

                                                    Nellie L. McClung, 1914

I went into politics quite without apologies to anyone, neither
did I go from choice. There comes a time when one cannot do
otherwise without loss of self-respect . . . and I am there to stay, until
we get political recognition.[43]

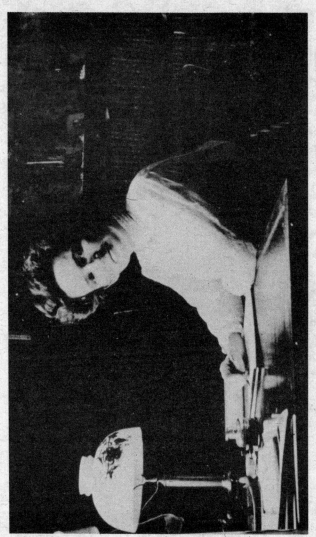

Nellie at her desk. (Glenbow-Alberta Institute photo)

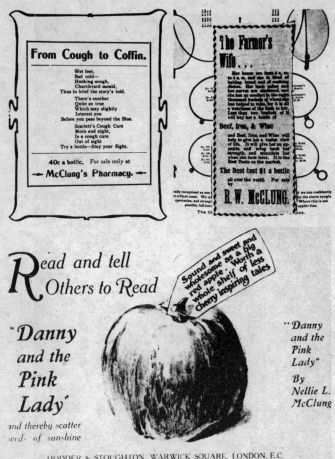

Nellie wrote ad copy for her husband's drugstore in Manitou and pasted it in a silverware catalogue for safekeeping. (Photo from the McClung Papers)

———————

Her career as a serious writer began in 1908 with the publication of *Sowing Seeds in Danny* which appeared in Britain as *Danny and the Pink Lady*. (British Columbia Archives photo)

Announcement

FALL AND WINTER SEASON, 1910-1911

NELLIE L. McCLUNG

Author of "Sowing Seeds in Danny,"
"The Second Chance"

Elocutionist, Entertainer and Reader

Mrs. McClung is prepared to arrange dates for
the coming season with Epworth Leagues, Ladies'
Aid Societies, Young People's Societies, Literary
Societies, Clubs, etc., etc.

TERMS AND OTHER PARTICULARS ON APPLICATION

Address:
MRS. NELLIE L. McCLUNG,
Manitou, Man.

The success of *Danny* sped Nellie into a career as a stage performer.
(Photo from the McClung Papers)

Winnipeg District W.C.T.U. Recital

In aid of the Building Fund
Tuesday, Dec. 3rd, 1912

———

READER .... MRS. NELLIE L. McCLUNG
VOCALIST .... MRS. GUS PINGLE
HARPIST .... MISS MABEL DOWNING
CHAIRMAN ..... DR. C. W. GORDON (*Ralph Connor*)

Programme

Introductory Remarks .... By DR. C. W. GORDON

Reading from "The Black Creek Stopping House" by the Authoress
MRS. NELLIE L. McCLUNG

Song .... "The Valley of Laughter" .... R. Sanderson
MRS. GUS PINGLE

Reading *Runaway Grandmother*
MRS. NELLIE L. McCLUNG

Harp Solo .... "Spinning Song" .... Haffellmanf
MISS MABEL DOWNING

Reading *The Return Ticket*
MRS. NELLIE L. McCLUNG

Song .... "My mother bids me bind my hair" .... Haydn
MRS. GUS PINGLE

Reading *The Way of the West.*
MRS. NELLIE L. McCLUNG

Harp Solo .... "Irish Airs" ....
MISS MABEL DOWNING

TEMPERANCE DOXOLOGY

Praise God from whom all blessings flow,
Praise Him who saves from deepest woe,
Praise Him who leads the Temperance host,
Praise Father, Son and Holy Ghost.

Recital program with annotations in Nellie's hand. These readings
came from *The Black Creek Stopping House*, published in 1912.
(Photo from the McClung Papers)

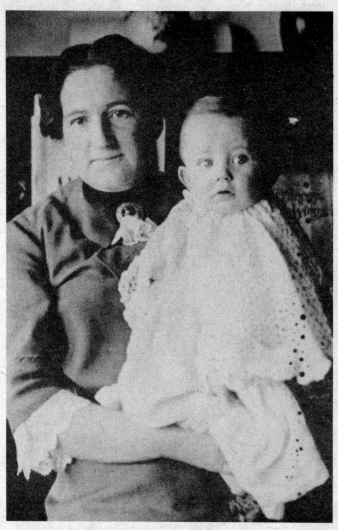

The McClung's fifth and youngest child, Mark, was born in 1911. Nellie's caption for this picture reads, "Ma, showing the stress of herding Mark." (Photo courtesy of Mark McClung)

Nellie and Emmeline Pankhurst. Nellie's admiration for the heroism of the British militants was unqualified. (Glenbow-Alberta Institute photo)

The Canadian Women's Press Club met weekly in this room. Here "the seed germ" of the suffrage association was planted. (Manitoba Archives photo)

Rodmond P. Roblin, premier of Manitoba from 1900 to 1915, became one of the suffragists' main targets. (Manitoba Archives photo)

Lillian Thomas, journalist and Nellie's special friend, proposed the idea of the "women's parliament." (Manitoba Archives photo)

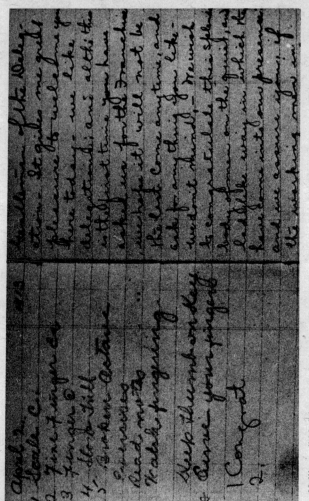

Nellie scribbled her speech for the "women's parliament" in a notebook which had been used for her children's music lessons. (Photo from McClung Papers)

CHAPTER SIX

A WOMAN ON THE WARPATH

I believe . . . that I am speaking for a long line of
women and children in this country who will
come after me, and I hope my example will give
courage to them.

*The Manitoba election was called for June of 1914, and the
Liberals contested it as the party of reform. In addition to women's
suffrage, their platform contained several planks dear to the "progressives" — temperance for one. If elected, the party was pledged to call an
immediate referendum and, assuming the results were favorable, to
introduce prohibition without delay. Roblin made a last-minute appeal
for the temperance movement's support, but Nellie, for one, was not
impressed. His offer "to do something on the eve of [the] election after
turning down the temperance forces for seven straight years was like the
man who ran to dig a well when his house was on fire," she said.[1] The
prohibitionists, newly reunited under the slogan of "Ban the Bar," put
their weight squarely behind the Liberals.*

*Compulsory education and the general reform of Manitoba's
chaotic educational system was another Liberal cause with which Nellie
sympathized. In 1914, the province's schools were a linguistic
smorgasbord, with each of the many ethnic groups using its native tongue
to supplement English as the language of instruction. What the Liberals
wanted to see was unilingual, English education. While Nellie did not
make a point of endorsing this policy, she doubtless agreed with it. In
Winnipeg, she had become associated with the All Peoples' Mission, one
of the city's few effective welfare agencies, and in this way, she had come
to know the "foreign problem" at first hand. In her encounters with
individual immigrants, she was as helpful and kind as she knew how to
be. But when she considered the "problems" which the newcomers posed,
her sympathy became tinged with condescension. Judging from some of
her remarks, she seems to have thought that the non-Anglo-Saxon*

immigrants needed to be assisted into citizenship, if not actually into civilization.

There was a "foreign" child, for example, who, upon her death, left her piggy-bank savings to the All Peoples' Mission. Nellie took this act of generosity as proof that "it is really possible to do . . . [something] for our 'foreigners'."[2]

Several years later, she wrote an article on "The Problem of Our New Canadians — and Its Solution," in which she insisted on the benefits of public schooling and English-language education.[3] And when groups of Mennonites left Canada, rather than give up the privilege of bilingual schooling, she had no regrets about their departure. Perhaps their place would be taken by people willing to conform to Canadian law, she said.[4]

Even if Nellie hadn't agreed with the Liberals' policy on education, she would have approved of the party's orientation. As she saw it, the Conservatives' priorities were all wrong: they put their emphasis on public works instead of public welfare, a position she had satirized as premier in the mock parliament. "Her" government, she had said then, (meaning Roblin's, of course) had what they called their Good Roads Policy: "Instead of insisting that little innocent children be herded together in close, unsanitary schools surfeited with decimal fractions when perhaps their parents do not approve of decimal fractions we provide their tender little toddling feet with broad sunlit country roads."[5] From this it is easy to deduce what the real-life Mrs. McClung thought of Conservative policies.

The Liberals' third major commitment was to implement direct legislation. This would mean that a specified percentage of the electorate could, by petition, force a referendum on any public issue. The vote would be binding on the government.

It was a truism in reform circles that corruption in politics originated in the party system. The political "machines" were geared to the attainment of power, by fair means or foul; too often, it was argued, this worked to the detriment of public morality and good government. In by-elections held during 1912 and 1913, both sides had been accused of misconduct,[6] but since the Conservatives had won all the contests, the case against them looked worse. Getting rid of the Roblin gang would be a first step towards clean government, the progressives thought.

Nellie shared this suspicion of partisan politics. Though she backed the Liberals, she took pains to stipulate that it was their principles which she supported and not the party itself. A few years earlier, she'd made her feelings clear in a story called "The Elusive Vote," which she billed as "an unvarnished tale" of the 1911 federal election. It revolved around one John Thomas Green, the bleary-eyed, runny-nosed town drunk, whose vote was being sought by both Tories and Grits. In the course of events, the hapless John Thomas was stuffed into a cellar by one side, snatched away in the middle of the night by a "double-agent" working for the other, locked in a hotel room, and propagandized without mercy.[7] This all made for amusing reading, but it didn't say much for party politics which could easily degenerate into a brawling free-for-all over the right to hold power.

Direct legislation, by returning political initiative to the righteous common man, would keep up the momentum of reform, progressives thought. It was fundamental to the reform movement that individual citizens could and should have an impact on public affairs. People hadn't given up on the world in 1914, nor on their ability to perfect it. Manitoba society was still comparatively simple at that time. It was possible, remember, to telephone the premier directly and arrange for an interview with him at the drop of a hat. And you didn't have to be an expert with a filing cabinet full of statistics to feel that you knew what was going on in the province. When an issue was to be viewed in moral terms, as so many political questions were, a strong personal conviction was the only qualification required.

The social gospellers were confident that "social and moral reform" was attainable, perhaps even inevitable, and that it would come easily if people could be persuaded to desire it. It was God's will that mankind should enjoy justice and harmony. And here on the western plains, humanity was being given a new start, an opportunity to get everything right. "Surely we [Canadians] were meant to lead the way to a better pattern of life," Nellie wrote.[8] The road to salvation was through enlightened debate and sound laws.

If the people of Manitoba endorsed the aims of the Liberal party — direct legislation, compulsory education, prohibition, women's suffrage — then the Kingdom of Heaven would surely be close at hand. The Liberal platform generated an enormous enthusiasm among reform-minded Manitobans, and Nellie entered the campaign with zeal.

Nellie L. McClung, 1945

That summer of 1914 ran like a torrent. Each day was full of excitement — meetings, interviews, statements, contradictions, and through it all the consuming conviction that we were actually making history. I do not think that any of us ever felt either tired or discouraged. Every day felt like the day before Christmas.

Trying to reduce all this human emotion to cold words on a page fills my heart with both joy and sorrow. I knew life had reached a pinnacle and we were standing on a high place, a place easier to achieve than to maintain. We were in sight of the promised land, a land of richer sunshine and brighter fruitage, and our heads and hearts were light. Whatever else can be said about us, one fact remains: We were in deadly earnest and our one desire was to bring about a better world for everyone. We were not men-haters as our opponents loved to picture us. Some of our most faithful helpers were men. We were not like the angry woman who cleans her house and beats her carpets to work off her rage. Ours was not a rage, it was a passion.[9]

Nellie L. McClung, 1920

I made my first criticism of the government in a little town on the Glenboro line. The elders of the church, many of whom were staunch Conservatives, forbade the minister to let me speak in the church, under pain of losing his position. But the minister was a North Country Irishman, who believed in free speech, and did not tell me of the elders' ultimatum until the next day. But the president of the ladies' aid — under whose auspices I was speaking — came to me as I sat in the minister's study, waiting for the hour of beginning, and excitedly said:

"Now — *don't* mention the government — they're bad and all that, and they have fooled the temperance people — but *don't* say anything about them. Talk temperance all you like, woman suffrage or anything, but don't come anywhere near home, for this is a strong Conservative place, and it will break up the church. They've just heard that you were going to attack the government and they're nervous about it."

"So am I," I said, "but I am going on. To take out what I am going to say about the government would spoil everything now. It would make my speech look like an *Uncle Tom's Cabin* where Eliza was not let cross the ice! We simply can't make any changes now — it all goes."

She was almost in tears. "Well, I won't introduce you," she said, "for my husband told me he would get right up and walk out if you as much as mentioned the government, and he'll do it."

I told her she must not worry about that. Most likely he would go straight home. Anyway we would take the collection first.

She went angrily out of the room.

When I began, I told them of the warning that had been given me, but explained that I must say what I thought ought to be said, and I told them I would give anyone who wished to take it, a chance to reply. I said we wanted everyone to stay. Getting up and going out, slamming the door, was a poor reply to an argument. It would be much better to stay, and slam the speaker. And then, of course, no one left. Everyone stayed it out, and we had a fine time. No one was hurt and if anyone was angry, they did not show it. And no one accepted my invitation to reply. They knew very well that what I told them was true.

That was the only time I was really frightened.[10]

Lillian Thomas, about 1915

One of the most astonishing things about Mrs. McClung's campaign . . . was that people paid for admission to her meetings to hear her talk politics. Most people, when talking politics, have felt honored when people would attend their meetings, without any inducement but their address. But . . . when Mrs. McClung began her political campaign, women's organizations all over the province begged her to go to them and give them an address . . . when they were anxious to make some money. . . . After all the expenses were paid, the proceeds of the meeting were divided between the societies and Mrs. McClung. . . .

As the campaign waxed hot, and the interest increased, Mrs. McClung decided to give addresses free, in order that every voter would have an equal chance to hear what she had to say. . . . Now . . . it was necessary for her to use her own money, and when the campaign was over, she told me that she came out about even. . . . That is, during the latter part of the campaign she spent the money she had made during the first part. . . .[11]

Newspaper report, 1914

"I never took even car fare from the Liberal party," declared Mrs. McClung. "I am a free-lance in this fight, and under instructions from no one."[12]

Newspaper report, 1914

Her presence was in demand at so many meetings during the day that the zealous friends who transported her from place to place almost took a round out of a neighbor's automobile in their efforts to

help her keep all her appointments. But they succeeded, and no
harm was done.[13]

Mrs. Nellie McClung, who ... has been following the premier
steadily around the province was criticized by the premier in a
manner which expressed intense regret that a lady should presume
so much as to approach the public platform against him. "And I am
told that she is coming here," he said [to one of his campaign
audiences]. This intimation was no sooner given than there was a
spontaneous outburst of applause which lasted for a full three
minutes, while the premier was forced to stand glumly and wait for
the storm to subside.[14]

Campaign song

"Roblin, Roblin redbreast
    O-oh Roblin dear
It was the tongue of Nellie McClung
    That spoiled your taste for beer."[15]

Newspaper report, 1914

Rumored that ... [Roblin] is bringing influence to bear
on ... [Mr.] McClung to pull his wife off from her attack on the
government. Odds are heavy against R.P.'s alleged scheme.[16]

Newspaper report, 1914

By way of adding interest to the campaign a joint debate is
suggested between Mrs. Nellie McClung and S[ir] Rodmond. An
absolutely unkind suggestion. Sir Rodmond would sooner meet —
well, anybody in Manitoba. Sir Rodmond knows a thing or two
about expedience.[17]

Newspaper report, 1914

In every town strong attempts were made to keep the people
away from her meetings. This was especially true in Killarney, where
the one rather peculiar reason given why she was not a proper
person to listen to was because she didn't know how to dress
respectfully. But all the opposition aroused seemed only to increase
the already great interest in her meetings, and they were exception-
ally successful in every way.

At Melita, where Mrs. McClung spoke on Wednesday night,
she received a great welcome. The band met her at the station, and

nearly the whole population turned out to show their interest. Here as at other places, people came from long distances to attend the meeting.[18]

Nellie L. McClung
Campaign speech, 1914

It may seem strange to many of you to hear a woman speak on political matters for the old conventions are still heavy upon us, that women and children should be seen and not heard! that women must be resigned and sweet and patient and like charity which heareth all things endureth all things believeth all things! that men must work and women must weep! quietly too, and with becoming aloofness for loud weeping is hysteria, and much to be deplored.

We have had long centuries like that. We have been blamed for all the evil in the world, and yet praised for all the good! Men have told us they understood us better than we understand ourselves; they have told us we were illogical, emotional, hysterical, patient, forgiving, not any too honest, vindictive, unreasonable and all the same! They have spoken of women in the mass; women in bulk; all women — and it has been hard for us to establish the fact that we are human beings — with hopes and fears, aspirations, and ambitions, struggles, defeats, successes just about the same as men. If you please us, will we not laugh, if you hurt us, will we not cry; we are people, just as you are!

Being people, we have been thinking, and thought is always dynamic, particularly thought without expression; we have thought of many things and learned many lessons in the school of experience. We have learned that life contains a great deal, of what for lack of a better name we call Bluff. The hand that rocks the cradle rules the world is a beautiful fiction, handed out to us to soothe us when we are restless. No one really believes it. It is intended as a sort of a bouquet. Our premier is using it a great deal in this campaign, in his opening remarks, when he says "I am glad to see we have with us this evening so many members of the fair sex, who grace this occasion with their presence. I believe a woman's intuitions are truer than a man's reasoning, and I know your intuitions will lead you to ask your husband or brother or father to vote for the government candidate and for me" — and just then some of the ladies remark "Not on your life!" It breaks the thread of his discourse and behold the scene changed, the premier forgets just what should come next, and so unfurls the flag, which is always a pretty safe bet!

The hand that rocks the cradle does not rule the world, or many things would be different. How long would the liquor traffic or the white slave traffic last if it did?[19]

Nellie L. McClung
Campaign speech, 1914

On election day, when you go behind the screen to register your vote, when you are alone with God and your thoughts, I want you to see that long line of 6,000 little boys, as sweet and fresh as any of your own, going to the bar for the first time. I want you to see these 6,000 boys, the cream of the land, turned into drunkards. I want you to see the long line of mothers, with eyes reddened from weeping and faces drawn and haggard, waiting in the night for the footsteps of the drunken father, and the little ones poorly clad and often beaten. If you back your ballot against them I will not know what to think of you. I appeal to you men in the name of your manhood that you protect our homes and our children, and I tell you women that if there ever was a time when you should be aroused it is now.[20]

Newspaper report, 1914

To those who were . . . saying she ought to be at home minding her children she sent the message that her children are all very well, thank you. . . . If her visit to a place could secure a vote against the bar, the protection thus gained for her children would far outclass the good she could accomplish were she at home rocking a cradle with one hand, holding a child on her knee, and at the same time darning a stocking.[21]

Nellie L. McClung, 1915

I wish you could see the proportion of my mail that tells me to go home and darn my husband's socks. I never would have believed one man's hosiery could excite the amount of interest those socks do — and yet, do you know, they are always darned![22]

Nellie L. McClung, 1920

It is hard for some people to understand why a woman should take part in public matters, and particularly leave her home to do it. To them it is not seemly. There must be something wrong! She must have a grievance, a grouch, a spite at someone; and many times I have been carefully questioned on this subject. "Is your husband living?" is generally the first question; thrown off casually — but steeped in grim significance. When I tell them he is, I get a very searching glance; and I know I am expected to give further details of his activities. "Yes," I say, "he is living — and he works — and he does not drink — neither does he beat me — he is quite all right. He brings his wages home . . ., and I like him well."

Even that does not entirely allay the feeling that there is something amiss. I may like him — but —

"What does he think of all this?" is then asked.

All — this — means my activity in woman suffrage, temperance and other things — my absences from home and all the rest of it. Then I try to explain, as clearly as I can, that he is rather an exceptional sport of a man, and he believes a woman has a distinct right to live her own life as she sees it, and that though he does not like to have me away from home, he believes I have a real work to do. . . .

They still seem rather doubtful. Woman's place is home — is a hard and fast rule, which must apply in all proper families.[23]

A CAMPAIGN ENCOUNTER

Nellie L. McClung, 1945

Usually I traveled in the day coach when I was moving about the country because I would be sure to meet some of our local workers there, but on one particular day near the end of the campaign, I went into the chair car so I could have a sleep. I was coming into the city from Broadview, and I had a meeting in Winnipeg that night, so I settled down gladly in a comfortable plush chair with my face to the window, glad to have a few free hours ahead of me.

The campaign was going well and my heart was warm with the evidence of an awakened electorate. I was glad to be living and having a part in a great movement. Never had I seen such loyalty and such close communion of spirit. I was grateful above all, for the loyalty of my own family, from Wes with his generous endorsement of all that I did, down to the fascinating sweetness of three-year-old Mark; Jack and Florence, aged seventeen and fifteen, and Paul, thirteen, Horace, eight, were all at school, doing well, and interested in all my activities. The household ran smoothly under the capable guidance of two good Irish girls, Elizabeth Armitage and Maggie Galway. . . .

I knew, of course, that my family affairs were the subject of much discussion. I was vulnerable in five places and I tried to guard against any grounds for criticism. The children entered into the spirit of the adventure too, and I still have a picture of Horace leading home his young brother, much spattered with mud, and one stocking at half mast, hurrying him along the lane and in through the secret entrance in the back fence, saying:

"Quick, now! It's a good thing I got you before the *Telegram* got a picture of you — Nellie McClung's neglected child!" — this with bitter scorn.

With all this background of loyalty, I was able to speak and write, catch trains at any hour, answer criticism, with a minimum of fatigue, for my mind was at ease and my heart was light, and I often quoted the words from the psalmist:

"The lines have fallen to me in pleasant places!"

It was in this mood that I sought the comfort of the luxurious chair car that lovely June day, 1914. . . . When I wakened I heard my name mentioned, evidently I was the subject of discussion across the aisle, but that was nothing. People who express their opinions in print or from the platform must expect criticism, and these people behind me were just the usual run of critics . . . and I would get along with my sleep. We were just leaving Brandon.

A man's voice boomed out above the vibration of the rails.

"Oh, you're from the East," he said, "and you don't know her as well as we do in Manitoba. Nellie McClung is nothing but a joke here and I can tell you that the government is not worrying about her or her meetings. T. C. Norris is the fellow who should worry. He is the leader of the opposition, and believe me his candidates lose votes every time she speaks."

I couldn't hear what the woman said, but evidently she was asking for more details, and he proceeded to develop the theme.

"She's a big woman," he said, "badly dressed, with a high pitched and strident voice, a regular rabble-rouser, the rough and tumble type. Irish, you know; Shanty Irish, with big hands and feet."

He nearly got me there! I thought of my dear old dad's pride in the "sparrow shins of the Mooneys" which all his girls had inherited, but I kept my feet on the foot stool and my head between the sheltering wings of the plush chair.

Another woman interrupted him at that point and said sharply:

"She must have something, all the same. Do you really know her? Have you actually heard her?"

"I certainly have not," he answered. "I wouldn't go across the road to hear her. I know all about that woman that I want to know. The way she treats her children is enough for me. She has a whole raft of them, seven or eight I should say, and she just lets them run wild! All the policemen know them, I can tell you that. My sister lives near her and she often takes them in, feeds and washes them, just sorry for the kids."

"What about her husband? What sort of a fellow is he?" the same woman asked.

"Quite a decent chap from all I hear," he said. "I think more of him since I heard he's getting a divorce. No one blames him either. I guess he got tired of being pointed out as 'Nellie McClung's husband'."

"Well, of course, that wouldn't constitute grounds for a divorce," one of the women said rather dryly, and I could feel that she wasn't much impressed with the narration of my shortcomings. "But you certainly have me interested, and I'm going to stay over in Winnipeg just to hear her. She's speaking there tonight; I saw it in yesterday's paper; I think I have it right here, and there's a picture of her too."

I could feel that she shoved the picture in front of him.

"She looks very neat and tailored to me. I wonder if you're not a little bit prejudiced. There's nothing wrong with her clothes, or her face either."

My first impulse was to turn around and "down-face" the gabby one and call upon him to name the sister who fed and washed my neglected children, but something held me back. I had let the conversation go too far for that. After all he was only repeating the gossip which I knew many people hoped was true. I knew if I turned around the women would recognize me and the situation would be a bit painful for the narrator. So I slipped on a pair of colored glasses which would make a good disguise. I could take all the chatter he could produce about myself, my clothes and the "impending divorce." I could take all that and laugh at it. But the matter of my children I could not allow to pass. I would not let him get away with that. But I wouldn't embarrass him before the women.

When they went away to freshen up before we arrived in Winnipeg, I had a word with the gentleman across the aisle. I took off the dark glasses and swung my chair around. Then I recognized him. He was one of the civil servants from the public works department, a party heeler and he knew me too.

"You said your piece very well, Mr. M.," I said cheerfully, "But it's a poor piece!"

The color went from his face. "What are you going to do?" he stammered. He looked around helplessly wondering if anyone were listening. "My tongue ran away with me, and I certainly feel cheap."

"Don't worry," I said. He was a pathetic sight as he wiped his forehead. "Just tell me one thing. Who is your sister, this good Samaritan who feeds my needy children?"

"I have no sister," he said miserably. "I heard a fellow say that, that's all. You sure have me over a barrel. You caught me red-handed."

"Oh, it's not serious," I said. "And I can afford to laugh at it. You know it's only the truth that hurts, and your conversation did not show a trace of truth. It didn't even impress the women you were talking to. You've got to do better than that if you're going to earn your expense money. I know you used to live in Alexander, and you have been sent out to oil the machine."

We sat in silence for a few minutes, and then he said:

"Are you going to tell this in one of your speeches? I know you can make me look like thirty cents."

"No," I said. "I'll give you my promise. I'll never tell it, though perhaps when I'm old and gray and have time to sit down and write my memoirs I may give it a place, for you know it has some good dramatic features, but by that time I'll be too old to remember your name. In fact I have forgotten it now. So cheer up and look out at the pleasant country we're traveling through, bright with sunshine. The Irish people say: 'It's a pity that a fine day could ever do harm,' and that's the way I feel about you. You're like a smear on the window, so I've brushed you off. When it comes to fighting fair and honest, you could learn something from the Irish, even the Shanty Irish!"[24]

Nellie L. McClung, 1928

There is one difficulty in the way of a woman having a public career, one real sore spot, and on it I am not going to dwell, for I cannot think of it without bitterness, and that is the fact that there are people mean enough to show hostility and spite to the children, when they differ from the mother politically. I could tell some tales in this regard, but I have never talked about it. It is all rather pitiful to know that people can be so cruel. That is the one part of my public life that has really hurt. You know the old saying: "He who brings children into the world gives hostages to fortune."[25]

Nellie McClung, 1915

Disturbers are never popular — nobody ever really loved an alarm clock in action — no matter how grateful they may have been afterwards for its kind services!

It was the people who did not like to be disturbed who crucified Christ — the worst fault they had to find with Him was that He annoyed them — He rebuked the carnal mind — He aroused the cat-spirit, and so they crucified Him — and went back to sleep. Even yet new ideas blow across some souls like a cold draught, and they naturally get up and shut the door! They have even been known to slam it![26]

WOMAN'S TRIUMPH

Nellie had the Conservatives, some of them anyway, running scared. They burned her in effigy in Brandon and attacked her integrity in several languages. The party's Ukrainian organ, for example, accused her of being a Liberal hack, who received twenty-five dollars a day "to insult . . . Premier Roblin throughout the province" in her "babbling story-book manner."

"The Liberals are sly. They know that whenever the devil cannot succeed a woman has to be employed."[27]

The hostility which the government directed against her personally is one measure of her influence with the electorate. In this, the "hardest fought" election in the history of Manitoba,[28] Nellie was a standout. The Liberal press hailed her as "the heroine of the campaign," "the great woman orator," "a power in the land," a "Canadian Joan of Arc," "the most noted living woman in Canada." Even the more-or-less nonpartisan Winnipeg Tribune agreed she was "the great outstanding and forceful figure of the campaign."[29]

"It is the first time that a woman has made any sort of a mark in Manitoba politics," the Ottawa Free Press noted in an article entitled "Woman's Triumph."[30] And it was a triumph, not just for Nellie but for the women who took courage from her example.

Newspaper reports, 1914

The home-coming of Mrs. McClung, fresh from her successful tour of the province, was signalized by an outpouring, estimated from 8,000 to 10,000 people, to hear her, but only one-quarter of

them found admittance to the theater. The streets in the vicinity of
the Walker Theater were alive with people, and long after the doors
of the theater were closed a crowd numbering thousands clamored
around the entrance seeking to get in . . . .[31]

The ground floor of the theater was reserved for men only, and
it was only after a strenuous fight that women were kept out and
directed to the balcony . . . . For the benefit of those who were left
outside an overflow meeting was at once started in a large vacant
space beside the theater, the audience being even greater than
within, and Mrs. McClung who had arrived consented to address
this gathering before going upon the platform. Here, standing upon a
wagon loaded with scenery she was given a wonderful demonstration of the affection and admiration felt for her by the people of
Winnipeg. She spoke briefly.

The meeting inside was full to the limit with surprising
features, and for three straight hours was carried through with a
swing and zest that kept the great audience in a constant state of
exhilaration. Mrs. McClung struck into the hearts of her audience
instantly when she prefaced her address with a personal statement.
This was to the effect that an anonymous letter had been sent to her
threatening to expose instances of her past life if she did not desist
from her platform utterances. Mrs. McClung felt very strongly on
this matter and challenged the writer to print what he had to say on
the front page of the morning *Telegram* . . . .

Mrs. McClung made a fine stage picture as she appeared before
the audience. She was simply gowned and wore a rose at her waist.
She spoke without notes and seemed absolutely at home. Her voice
throughout was quiet, calm and clear and the audience listened with
such rapt attention that every word was carried to the furthermost
parts of the theater . . . . The magnetic personality of the speaker, her
poise of body, the movement of the arms in bringing out a point, the
inflections of the voice were all used toward the achievement of a
magnificent address. Her speech for one hour and a half was filled
with bright remarks, which for clear logic and hard common sense
would be hard to excel.[32]

Mark McClung, 1975

My mother had a sense of the drama of making a public speech.
She wasn't a passive speaker. She would walk up and down; she
would gesture; she would point fingers; she would raise her hand;
she would raise both arms . . . . In a sense she was an evangelical

preacher. She wanted to move people's hearts rather than their reason, if you like. And she would raise and lower her voice and lower her eyes and then she'd raise her arms . . . . She would gesture to one side of the auditorium and gesture to the other. She was a dramatist.[33]

Newspaper report, about 1920

The secret of the success our western women have attained in public life is nothing else but the fact that they are such smooth speakers on the platform. They can talk a man blind and out-argue him at every turn, doing it in such a way that there is no come-back. Did you ever hear Nellie McClung when in good form? If not, you have missed the treat of your life. Woe betide the poor fish who interpolates a silly question. He gets his so quick that his head swims for about a week. We once went to hear this lady speak in the Grand Theater, full of amused tolerance not unmixed with prejudice. After she got through, all we could gasp to the friend alongside was, "She wins."[34]

Newspaper report, 1914

What's the matter with Mrs. Nellie McClung for leader of one of the "two great parties?"[35]

Newspaper report, 1914

As for ourselves we would as gladly welcome such a woman as Mrs. McClung to a portfolio in our cabinet as any other Manitoban we can name, and as cheerfully bestow upon her the coveted prefix, Honorable.[36]

Newspaper report, 1914

Never again will any politician in this province have the temerity to scorn women's power.[37]

Nellie L. McClung, 1945

It was a bonny fight — a knock-down and drag-out fight, but it united the women of Manitoba in a great cause. I never felt such unity of purpose and I look on these days with great satisfaction. We really believed we were about to achieve a new world.[38]

CHAPTER SEVEN

THE WAR THAT NEVER ENDS

> Women have not had much to do with *making*
> wars, though some wars in ancient times have
> been blamed on them; and as men have written
> the histories we have never heard the woman's
> side of the story. I have always wanted to hear
> from Helen of Troy.

The results of the 1914 election came as a shock and a disappointment to Nellie — the Liberals had not won. Still they had taken a big bite out of Roblin's legislative majority, and their prospects were promising. For the moment, though, there was nothing more to be done, so Nellie and the children headed for their cottage at Matlock Beach on Lake Winnipeg.

After the pell-mell rush of the election campaign, the move to the lake brought Nellie's world screeching to a stop. Life was suddenly peaceful and calm. She baked the bread for her household ("I think every woman enjoys bread making," she said) and entertained the neighborhood children by inventing stories for them.[1] In past summers she had brought the cares of the world with her to the beach; once she and her sister-in-law had hosted a "suffrage tea" there, with prizes for the woman who could come up with the best pro-suffrage arguments.[2] But this year her main object was repose. There was plenty of time to sit on the comfortable bench which she had helped to build and watch the storms come up over Blueberry Island.

Any human conflict which arose could generally be settled with holiday good humor. Nellie liked to tell the story of a black-poplar stump near her cottage which a "misguided relative" of hers had claimed "no woman could split."

> He made this remark after I had tried in vain to show
> him what was wrong with his method of attack. I said that I
> thought he would do better if he could manage to hit twice in
> the same place! And he said that he would like to see me do it,

*and went on to declare that he would bet me a five-dollar bill
that I could not.*

*If it were not for the fatal curse of modesty I would tell
how eagerly I grasped the ax and with what ease I hit, not
twice, but half a dozen times in the same place — until the
stump yielded. This victory was all the sweeter to me because
it came right after our sports day when I had entered every
available contest, from the nail-driving competition to the fat
woman's race, and had never even been mentioned as among
those present!*[3]

*Life was easy and full of laughter. "I rested body and brain," she
later recalled, "and came as near to perfect contentment as I have ever
been."*[4] *Neither she nor her lakeshore friends had an inkling of the blow
which awaited them.*

Nellie L. McClung, 1917

When the news of war came [on 4 August 1914], we did not
really believe it! War! That was over! There had been a war, of
course, but that had been long ago, in the dark ages, before the days
of free schools and peace conferences and missionary conventions
and labor unions! There might be a little fuss in Ireland once in a
while. The Irish are privileged, and nobody should begrudge them a
little liberty in this. But a big war — that was quite impossible!
Christian nations could not go to war!

"Somebody should be made to pay dear for this," tearfully
declared a doctor's wife. "This is very bad for nervous women."

The first news had come on the 9:40 train, and there was no
more until the 6:20 train when the men came down from the city; but
they could throw no light on it either. The only serious face that I
saw was that of our French neighbor, who hurried away from the
station without speaking to anyone. When I spoke to him the next
day, he answered me in French, and I knew his thoughts were far
away.

The days that followed were days of anxious questioning. The
men brought back stories of the great crowds that surged through
the streets blocking the traffic in front of the newspaper offices
reading the bulletins, while the bands played patriotic airs; of the
misguided German who shouted, *"Hoch der Kaiser!"* and narrowly
escaped the fury of the crowd.

We held a monster meeting one night at "Windwhistle

Cottage," and we all made speeches, although none of us knew what to say. The general tone of the speeches was to hold steady, — not to be panicky, — Britannia rules the waves, — it would all be over soon, — Dr. Robertson Nicholl and Kitchener could settle anything!

The crowd around the dancing pavilion began to dwindle in the evenings — that is, of the older people. The children still danced, happily; fluffy-haired little girls, with "headache" bands around their pretty heads, did the fox-trot and the one-step with boys their own age and older, but the older people talked together in excited groups.

Every night when the train came in the crowds waited in tense anxiety to get the papers, and when they were handed out, read them in silence, a silence which was ominous. Political news was relegated to the third page and was not read until we got back to the veranda. In these days nothing mattered; the baker came late; the breakfast dishes were not washed sometimes until they were needed for lunch, for the German maids and the English maids discussed the situation out under the trees. Mary, whose last name sounded like a tray of dishes falling, the fine-looking Polish woman who brought us vegetables every morning, arrived late and in tears, for she said, "This would be bad times for Poland — always it was bad times for Poland, and I will never see my mother again."

A shadow had fallen on us, a shadow that darkened the children's play. Now they made forts of sand, and bored holes in the ends of stove-wood to represent gaping cannons' mouths, and played that half the company were Germans; but before many days that game languished, for there were none who would take the German part; every boat that was built now was a battleship, and every kite was an aeroplane and loaded with bombs!

In less than a week we were collecting for a hospital ship to be the gift of Canadian women. The message was read out in church one afternoon, and volunteer collectors were asked for. So successful were these collectors all over Canada that in a few days word came to us that enough money had been raised, and that all moneys collected then could be given to the Belgian Relief Fund. The money had simply poured in — it was a relief to give!

Before the time came for school to begin, there were many closed cottages, for the happy careless freedom of the beach was gone; there is no happiness in floating across a placid lake in a flat-bottomed boat if you find yourself continually turning your head toward shore, thinking that you hear someone shouting, "Extra." . . .

We closed our cottage on 24 August . . . . Before the turn in the road hid it from sight we stopped and looked back . . . . My last recollection of it is of the boarded windows, which gave it the blinded look of a dead thing . . . . Instinctively we felt that we had come to the end of a very pleasant chapter in our life as a family; something had disturbed the peaceful quiet of our lives; somewhere a drum was beating and a fife was calling!

Not a word of this was spoken, but Jack suddenly put it all into words, for he turned to me and asked quickly, "Mother, when will I be eighteen?"[5]

Nellie L. McClung, 1917

Gay, as the skater who blithely whirls
To the place of the dangerous ice!
Content, as the lamb who nibbles the grass
While the butcher sets the price!
So content and gay were the boys at play
In the nations near and far,
When munition kings and diplomats
Cried, "War! War!! War!!!"[6]

Nellie L. McClung, 1915

When the war broke out we all experienced a bad attack of gloom. We were afraid God had forgotten us and gone off the job.[7]

Nellie L. McClung, 1945

The fall of 1914 blurs in my memory like a troubled dream. The war dominated everything. Some of my friends were pacifists and resented Canada's participation in a war of which we knew so little. Why should we step into the age-old feuds of Europe? No one profited by wars except the munition makers . . . . British peers held stocks in the Krupp Works in Germany . . . . One of the first guns captured from the Germans and set up on a village green in England with appropriate ceremonies was found to have been made in England. Was this good enough to fight for? War was a game, a plot against humanity and would go on as long as the common people could be depended on to do the fighting.

These bold utterances did not go unchallenged. Chief among

the Empire's defenders among the women was Miss Cora Hind. Her views were clear cut and definite. We were British and must follow the tradition of our fathers. She would have gone herself if women were accepted. Miss Hind saw only one side of the question and there were times when I envied her, though I resented her denunciations of those who thought otherwise.

The old crowd began to break up, and our good times were over. Troop trains were leaving the stations every week. Bands played in the streets. The heart of the people was heavy and sad. . . .

In . . . . [December] of 1914 we moved to Edmonton. Wes had a chance to go to either Vancouver or Edmonton to manage the branch for his company, and we decided on Edmonton after much discussion. My brother Will and his family lived in Edmonton, and that was one reason for our decision. Besides that, we believed that Alberta, with its mines, prairies and mountains, its newness, its incoming settlers would suit us better than the seaport city. It was a wrench for me to leave Manitoba where the other members of my own family lived, and where I had spent all my life since I was six years old. My sister, Elizabeth Rae, had just moved to Winnipeg, Hannah had lived there for some years, and George and Jack lived on the old farms at Wawanesa. Paul had spent his holidays at his Uncle Jack's each year with Harry, his cousin, and had such a good time that it was hard to get him back to the city when school opened. More than once I had to go for him.

It seemed a pity to move away from all this pleasant association and from our comfortable home on Chestnut Street and yet there were some compensations. I would get a chance to go back to my writing in a new province, I thought. I would shed all my political alliances, and go back to the work I liked best. I knew, of course, that the Liberal party in Manitoba would soon be in power, and I knew too, that the women would be given the vote and that I could be elected quite easily to the Legislative Assembly. There had been predictions that I would be invited into the cabinet, and probably be made minister of education, all of which was very exciting, and in my moments of exaltation I had great dreams of what I could do for rural education, especially among the foreign-born.

But when the McCurdy strain in my blood dominated I grew cautious because of my inexperience and the fear of high places held me down to earth. "I charge thee Caesar, fling away ambition" I quoted to myself sternly. I knew I could make a good speech. I knew

I could persuade people, and I knew I had a real hold on the people of Manitoba, especially the women, but I also knew that the whole situation was fraught with danger for if I, as the first woman to hold a cabinet position failed, it would be a blow to women everywhere. I could easily undo all I had done for I knew the world would be critical of women for a long time. If a woman succeeded, her success would belong to her as an individual. People would say she was an exceptional woman. She had a "masculine" mind. Her success belonged to her alone, but if she failed, she failed for all women everywhere. With this in mind, I hadn't the nerve to go on to the sixty-four dollar question. I said nothing to anyone, but it reconciled me to the move. I felt I was being let down over the wall in a basket.

However on the night we left on the Grand Trunk Pacific all my high thinking deserted me. All I could see was that group of kindred souls, men and women, the people I loved and have always loved. I was leaving them and my heart was desolate. I said good-bye to each of them and told them not to wait until the train left, and then I walked away without looking back.[8]

EDMONTON

It was not long after the McClungs' departure from Winnipeg that E. Cora Hind visited them in their new home, "a beautiful sunny windowed house on a quiet corner" in Edmonton.[9] Nellie was still lonely for her Manitoba family and friends, but Cora could see that her life was quickly filling up with new responsibilities.

Already she is a power in Edmonton and workers along lines of social and economic reform are leaning on her and looking to her for all kinds of assistance, and they are not looking in vain . . . . Going about the city and meeting men and women in various lines of activity, I was amazed, much as I knew her capacity for work, at the amount she has accomplished.[10]

There was something about her new hometown which Nellie found invigorating. "The whole atmosphere of the city was young, hopeful and full of surprises," she noted; "expectancy was in the air. It may have been the high altitude which stimulated me, but I never felt better or more keenly alive. I could work all day and all night. . . ."[11]

As usual, there was no shortage of things for her to do. Her reputation as a lecturer had preceded her to Alberta and the invitations she had to speak that winter "would have swamped a cabinet minister; she . . . [had] a drawer full of them which she could not accept."[12] "If she continues her strenuous platform work," one reporter quipped, "Mrs. Nellie will have to drop the C out of her name."[13] Clearly, Albertans had no intention of allowing Nellie to retire into her study and make a career of writing as she had dreamed of doing.

Her family of five — now aged three to seventeen — still had first call on her time (though, as always, she had household help, usually an immigrant girl.) Then too, she was in the thick of plans for an Alberta temperance campaign and had become an influential member of the infant Edmonton Equal Franchise League.[14] She'd joined the Women's Canadian Club and even found time to have a tea party, complete with crocheted doilies and floral centerpiece, for the local branch of the Canadian Women's Press Club.[15] One day, she turned up to inspect a school hot-lunch program, wonder aloud why it wasn't publicly financed, and leave behind a cheque for its support.[16]

Afternoon might find her at a gathering of her reading club, held in a little bookstore on Jasper Avenue.

> Quiet corners were there, where chairs were set for readers, and there we met and discussed the questions of the day, or listened while someone read. The traffic on Jasper Avenue swept past the door, and the war in Europe hung its dark cloud over every one of us, but the time we spent in the atmosphere of the little shop were hours of pure delight![17]

Nellie was also taking time to make new friends, notably Emily Ferguson Murphy. When the two women met, Emily was in her mid-forties, a beefy, graceless-looking woman, but greatly respected in Edmonton — and with reason. Equally well-known under her pen-name of "Janey Canuck," Mrs. Murphy had a considerable literary reputation for her books of travel sketches: Janey Canuck in the West, Open Trails, and Seeds of Pine.

Though not a member of the Equal Franchise League, she had long been a women's advocate. As far back as 1910, while Nellie was still living in Manitou, Emily had been battling for improvements to married women's property rights — improvements which had eventually become Alberta law.

Like Nellie, Emily had a high-minded disregard for the proprieties of minding one's own business. She was a kind of one-woman vigilance committee, forever on the lookout for injustices or irregularities, and she generally managed to be in the midst of some fight, great or small. Her crusades usually issued in success, for she was not the sort of person who would settle for anything less. In 1915, for example, several months after Nellie arrived in Edmonton, Emily led an agitation against the unnecessarily high steps on Edmonton's streetcars. According to the best medical opinion of the day, it was an ordeal for women to hoist themselves up the 16½ inches required. "There is no doubt," one prominent Edmonton physician opined, but "that untold harm is done, and many conditions of ill-health that woman has to suffer from, are aggravated by having to go through the nervous and physical strain of boarding our street cars."[18] Emily (through the agency of the Women's Press Club, to which Nellie belonged) saw to it that this hazard to womankind was removed.

The next year, 1916, Emily took on a more substantial mission on behalf of her sex, by accepting appointment as police magistrate "in and for the city of Edmonton." In all of what was then known as the British Empire, only one other woman — Alice Jamieson of Calgary — held such a post. It was a wearing and demanding position, but one which Emily filled with compassion and competence. Though without legal training, she had a precise, logical mind and a habit of authority which suited her to the bench.

Nellie's opinions on the role of women magistrates can be deduced from her short story "The Neutral Fuse." It centers on an overworked farm woman named Sadie Benton who, half-crazy with discouragement and starved for beauty, wandered into a store and started gathering up pretty things. In her confusion, she imagined herself to be in a garden of flowers. But reality coldly reasserted itself when she was arrested for shoplifting and taken to court.

> "How do you plead?" asked the judge.
> The question had to be explained.
> "Guilty," she faltered.
> "Now, there are far too many cases of this kind coming before me," said the judge, "and I am going to give each of them the limit. We will see if we cannot put a stop to this petty thieving. You admit that you are guilty. Three months. Next case!"
> (Now, by all the rules of short-story writing, this is the place to end the story, and this is the logical ending. In many cities this would have been the ending, but it so happened in

*the city of which I am writing that the ending was on this
wise)* —

"*How do you plead?*" *asked the judge.*

The question had to be explained.

"*Guilty,*" *she faltered.*

*The judge wrinkled her forehead. She was an attractive
woman, with a neat gray silk hat and a rose-colored silk
dress. Her brown eyes had grown a little weary and sad from
looking on human misery in the manifold forms in which it
came before her, but she had never grown accustomed to it,
and now her tender heart was stabbed by the hopelessness in
Sadie Benton's face.*[19]

The woman magistrate sought an explanation of the case, gave Sadie a
suspended sentence, and sent her to see a psychiatrist (another woman)
who delivered a kindly talk on overwork and saw to it that Sadie got
some rest.

By all accounts, this story contains as much fact as fantasy, for
Magistrates Jamieson and Murphy saw it as part of their role as
women to humanize the courts. Here was Nellie's ideal womanhood in
action. Small wonder that she held Emily Murphy in affectionate esteem.

Nellie also thought highly of "Janey's" literary abilities and
sometimes used her as a sounding board for stories and poems. "Are you
very busy?" she'd demand over the phone. "No! Well then listen to this!
Tell me if you think it is all right. I wrote it in church this morning when
I should have been listening to the sermon. You see it came to me red-hot
and I simply had to set it down."[20] And she'd go on to recite a bit of
verse for her friend's approval. Or she would come to Emily in moments
of discouragement, when what she was writing seemed "fribbling and
inconsiderable" and she'd decided that she could not go on with it.
"Then I," Emily explained, "Janey Canuck, withstanding her to her
face, would abuse her roundly, making remarks distinctively caustic in
character and which under other circumstances might almost amount to
an affront."[21] And Nellie would allow herself to be scolded back to
work.

By the time she moved to Edmonton, Nellie had published three
books of fiction: the two novels about the Watson family and a collection
of short stories called The Black Creek Stopping-House. All had
been written in Manitou, before Nellie's life was taken over by politics,
and all were in much the same vein — saucy, humorous, and focussed on

the people of rural Manitoba. But Nellie was no longer a simple country woman. Her world had been remade in the four years since 1911. The "Lady of Manitou" had been satisfied if she could persuade her readers to chuckle over the problems of a little boy and his pet pigeons or the adventures of a grandmother who had run away from home.²² By 1915, Nellie's concerns were more weighty by far:

> *In times like these*
> *I cannot write*
> *Sweet gentle tales*
> *Of peaceful joys.²³*

Canada was at war. What did this catastrophe mean? Nellie was of several minds about it at first. She abhorred war; it was "murder," she said bluntly, "no matter by what euphonious name it may be called. . . ."²⁴ But this opinion did no make her a thoroughgoing pacifist, for while she looked forward to the day when war would be no more, she did not wholeheartedly object to Canada's participation in the present conflict.

Still, neither did she actively support Canada's involvement in the war, at least not right away. She couldn't accept the propagandists' image of the conflict as a duel between the saintly Briton and the vile Hun. In her estimation, Britain was besmirched by permitting the liquor traffic to continue and by denying women equal rights in politics and education.²⁵ The situation was ambiguous, with wrong on both sides. She wondered how women were able to reconcile themselves to sacrificing a son to the front under such circumstances. She imagined them thinking of Abraham "when he was willing at God's command to offer his dearly beloved son on the altar" and then deciding that it had not been "so hard" for him. Abraham "knew it was God who asked it, and he had God's voice to guide him! Abraham was sure, but about this — who knows?"²⁶

Nellie had lost a measure of her assurance. For the first time, she was voicing criticism of the Mother Country, and she'd even had her doubts about God. The best she could manage at the moment was an uneasy faith that events were unfolding according to a benevolent divine plan. God must intend mankind to be purified by this struggle, for why else would He have permitted it? Perhaps people would be drawn to reflect on the forces which had brought this calamity upon them. In Nellie's view, these forces were not political but moral — materialism, selfishness, the lack of true Christianity. Eight months into the war, she wrote:

> . . . we have had before our eyes the spectacle of clever men
> using their cleverness to kill, maim and destroy innocent
> women and children; we have seen the wealth of one nation
> poured out like water to bring poverty and starvation to
> another nation, and so through our tears, we have learned the
> lesson that it is not wealth or cleverness or skill or power
> which makes a nation or an individual great. It is goodness,
> gentleness, kindliness, the sense of brotherhood, which alone
> maketh rich and addeth no sorrow. When we are face to face
> with the elemental things of life, death and sorrow and loss,
> the air grows very still and clear, and we see things in bold
> outlines.[27]

"Humanity has to travel a hard road to wisdom," she observed ruefully,
"and it has to travel it with bleeding feet."[28]

" 'Without the shedding of blood, there is no remission of sin'
always seemed a harsh and terrible utterance, but we know now its
truth. . . ."[29]

Nellie was especially concerned that Canadians turn their attention
again to her two cherished reforms: prohibition and women's suffrage.
There was a danger that people would be distracted from moral and
political battles at home by the life-and-death battles in France. In
addition, there were bound to be those who thought it was inappropriate
to raise divisive issues until after the military crisis was past. The
impetus for change which Nellie and her colleagues had worked so hard
to achieve could rapidly be lost.

But if the war posed a threat to the reformers' progress, it also
enabled them to make their case with a new intensity. Under the spell of
wartime propaganda, more people were open to the reform movement's
simplistic moral dichotomies and singleminded zeal. The hostilities in
Europe were not a mere military encounter between nations, Canadians
were being told, but an epic struggle between democracy and tyranny,
justice and injustice, good and ill. This, after all, was to be the "war to
end war." In this context, the reform movement could be viewed as part
and parcel of the war effort. Were the reformers in Edmonton and the
infantrymen at Ypres not battling the same enemy — Evil?

Nellie was quick to see that the change in social climate was a
God-send for her causes, and she lost no time in exploiting it to the full.
No sooner was she settled in Edmonton than she began revising her
speeches on suffrage and temperance to take account of the war and the
powerful (if not always entirely credible) arguments it put at her

disposal. *The result was a book published late in the summer of 1915 under the title* In Times Like These. *"Hysterical and fantastic bunkum," snapped the reviewer for* Saturday Night,[30] *but most papers in both Canada and the United States were somewhat more favorable. "Sometimes Nellie gives a woman's twist to her arguments," the* Calgary Albertan *observed, "and presents them in all the unassailable fortifications of the feminine 'perhaps' and 'because' but one forgives her lack of care when she puts forth her arguments with such bright and slangy pertness."[31]*

Review, *In Times Like These*

One scarcely need know that Mrs. McClung is forty-two years old, a vigorous efficient age in womanhood, or that she is Methodist. Something of the fiery zeal of that religious sect stamps her discourse . . . [in *In Times Like These*]. That Mrs. McClung is much in earnest, no reader can doubt, but that she feels a mild prejudice against men, their ways and their logic, when either conflicts with suffrage ideals, is equally apparent.[32]

In Times Like These, 1915

What Do Women Think of War?
     (Not That It Matters)

War is the antithesis of all our teaching. It breaks all the commandments; it makes rich men poor, and strong men weak. It makes well men sick, and by it living men are changed to dead men. Why, then, does war continue? Why do men go so easily to war — for we may as well admit that they do go easily? There is one explanation. They like it! . . .

But although men like to fight, war is not inevitable. War is not of God's making. War is a crime committed by men and, therefore, when enough people say it shall not be, it cannot be. This will not happen until women are allowed to say what they think of war. Up to the present time women have had nothing to say about war, except pay the price of war — this privilege has been theirs always. . . .

Since the war broke out women have done a great deal of knitting. Looking at this great army of women struggling with rib and back seam, some have seen nothing in it but a "fad" which has supplanted for the time tatting and bridge. But it is more than that. It is the desire to help, to care for, to minister; it is the same spirit which inspires our nurses to go out and bind up the wounded and care for the dying. The woman's outlook on life is to save, to care for, to help. Men make wounds and women bind them up, and so the women, with their hearts filled with love and sorrow, sit in their quiet homes and knit. . . .

Women have not only been knitting — they have been thinking. . . . Into their gentle souls have come bitter thoughts of rebellion. They realize now how little human life is valued, as opposed to the greed and ambition of nations. They think bitterly of Napoleon's utterance on the subject of women — that the greatest woman in the world is the one who brings into the world the greatest number of sons; they also remember that he said that a boy could stop a bullet as well as a man, and that God is on the side of the heaviest artillery. From these three statements they get the military idea of women, children, and God, and the heart of the knitting woman recoils in horror from the cold brutality of it all. They realize now something of what is back of all the opposition to the woman's advancement into all lines of activity and a share in government.

Women are intended for two things, to bring children into the world and to make men comfortable, and then they must keep quiet and if their hearts break with grief, let them break quietly — that's all. No woman is so unpopular as the noisy woman who protests against these things. . . .

I cannot help but think that if there had been women in the German Reichstag, women with authority behind them, when the Kaiser began to lay his plans for the war, the results might have been very different. I do not believe women with boys of their own would ever sit down and wilfully plan slaughter, and if there had been women there when the Kaiser and his brutal war-lords discussed the way in which they would plunge all Europe into bloodshed, I believe one of those deep-bosomed, motherly, blue-eyed German women would have stood upon her feet and said: "William — forget it!" But the German women were not there — they were at home, raising children! So the preparations for war went on unchecked, and the resolutions passed without a dissenting voice. In German rule, we have a glorious example of male statecraft, uncontaminated by any feminine foolishness. . . .

The Kaiser has done a few things for us. He has made us hate all forms of tyranny and oppression and autocracy; he has made us hate all forms of hypocrisy and deceit. There have been some forms of kaiserism dwelling among us for many years, so veneered with respectability and custom that some were deceived by them; but the lid is off now — the veneer has cracked — the veil is torn, and we see things as they are.

When we find ourselves wondering at the German people for having tolerated the military system for so long, paying taxes for its maintenance and giving their sons to it, we suddenly remember that we have paid taxes and given our children, too, to keep up the liquor traffic, which has less reasons for its existence than the military system of Germany.... We despise the army of the Kaiser for dropping bombs on defenseless people, and shooting down women and children — we say it violates all laws of civilized warfare. The liquor traffic has waged war on women and children all down the centuries. Three thousand women were killed in the United States in one year by their own husbands who were under the influence of liquor.... We shudder with horror as we read of the terrible outrages committed by the brutal German soldiers. We rage at our helpless fury that such things should be — and yet we have known and read of just such happenings in our own country. The newspapers, in telling of such happenings, usually have one short illuminative sentence which explains all: "The man had been drinking." The liquor traffic has outraged and insulted womanhood right here in our own country in much the same manner as is alleged of the German soldiers in France and Belgium! ...

And yet there are people who tell us women must not invade the realm of politics, where matters relating to the liquor traffic are dealt with.[33]

Nellie L. McClung, 1917

In the quiet old days of peace perhaps there was some excuse in women saying all was well, the world was going along quite nicely without their help, but in these days of terrible destruction, of desolation and loss, of pillaged homes, orphaned children, broken hearted women, I cannot see how any woman who has any red blood in her heart can sit idly at home comfortable, warm, fed and clothed and say that all is well.[34]

Nellie L. McClung, about 1916

When the war is making such inroads on the manhood of Canada, there is a mighty call to the women, and it isn't the drinking women, nor the cigarette-smoking women, nor the immodestly dressed women who will hold the candle for suffering humanity.[35]

Nellie L. McClung, 1918

We are calling out the last reserves of civilization; if the women
cannot save the world we are lost. Because we cannot call the angels
down from heaven, women are the last we have.[36]

A SEASON OF TRIUMPH

Under wartime conditions, the campaign for women's suffrage took
on a new urgency. In February of 1915, when Nellie appeared before the
Alberta Legislature as part of a large suffrage delegation, there was an
edge of impatience in her speech.

> Our plea is not for mercy, but for justice. I ask no boon,
> no favor, no privilege. I am just asking for plain,
> old-fashioned, unfrilled justice. A man considers himself
> honest if he pays his debt the first time he gets the bill. This is
> the second time you have got it. Therefore, in view of the fact
> that you are honest men, you must recognize the justice of our
> claim, and there is nothing for you and your colleagues to do
> but come across.[37]

The first time Alberta suffragists had presented their "bill" to the
Legislature had been the previous year, when the Edmonton Equal
Franchise League and the Calgary Local Council of Women delivered a
12,000-name petition. The Liberal premier, A. L. Sifton, had been
decidedly cool. Where did the rural women stand on the issue, he wanted
to know.

In 1915 the question no longer pertained, for the delegation that
year included representatives of the United Farm Women of Alberta.
Sifton had little choice but to be somewhat more forthcoming. He still
wasn't ready to "come across" with a franchise bill, as Nellie demanded,
but then she hadn't really expected him to. What he was prepared to
offer was more than any of the suffragists had counted on. "The matter
would come before the Legislature" early in 1916, he announced; "it
would be up to the women to buttonhole the members of the Assembly
and so impress their opinions on the legislators as to leave no doubt as to
what would happen when the vote came to be taken."[38]

The temperance movement was gaining momentum as well; there
was a tide for reform in Alberta, indeed across the West. Of special
significance to the Alberta prohibitionists was the Direct Legislation Act
of 1914. Under the provisions of this law, they had been able to force the

*government to call a referendum on the liquor question. If the "drys"
should win on this plebiscite, the Legislature would be legally compelled
to bring prohibition in.*

*The vote was called for 21 July 1915, and Nellie did not spare
herself in the six weeks of propagandizing which preceded it. As in
Manitoba a year earlier, there was the hectic excitement of a vigorous
campaign:*

> *She was whisked from county to county per auto, she was
> starred in churches, in town halls, in lodge rooms, and under
> the blue-blue sky of Alberta, just then enjoying its annual
> pour. . . . Every yellow-journal, purple-scream method was
> used to its last lone limit — buttons, badges, babies, and
> parades.*[39]

*The most impressive demonstration was saved for last, a "monster"
parade in Edmonton. The Edmonton Journal put the number of
marchers at 10,000: "Demonstration For Temperance Through Streets
of Edmonton Is Greatest In History of the City," the headlines
declared.*[40] *The women's section of the parade was led by Nellie and a
Mrs. Howard of the W.C.T.U.*

> *There were some of our own people who were rather
> timid about marching in a parade [Nellie recalled]. It was not
> done! It was not dignified — Surely we could win without
> parading! Riding in a car, in the procession, was not so bad
> — if it should be a nice day — and it was — but walking
> right in the middle of the street — it couldn't possibly do any
> good — and besides, two miles was an utter impossibility!*
>
> *I never knew before how sorely the average man and
> woman is afflicted. Talk about military inspection — and the
> imperfections it revealed — a parade brings to light a
> shocking condition of pedal infirmities — fallen arches —
> weak ankles — corns — ingrowing toe-nails — rheumatic
> joints.*

*But at last the parade was lined up, and the march could begin — "that
wonderful demonstration of men and women and children, who swept
through the streets that glorious sunshiny day, carrying their banners
and singing*

> *A Better Day is Coming —*
> *A Morning promised long,*
> *When girdled right with holy might*
> *Shall overthrow the wrong . . .;*

and the groups of children, with their glowing faces and unspoiled young hearts, carrying a banner which said 'Give us a Chance — Clear the Road for us! Old King Alcohol no friend of Ours!' "[41]

On the day the vote was taken, each of Edmonton's ninety-three polling booths was staffed by six women, "and out in the country the ladies spread free lunch under the trees for all voters, and no questions asked.

"That night the results began to come in, and when the cheers subsided the net figures showed a two to one majority for the drys." [42]

Farewell, King Alcohol!

Meanwhile, events had been going on apace in Manitoba as well. The Roblin government had been toppled by a patronage scandal, and new elections were called for early August, little more than two weeks after the prohibition referendum in Alberta. The Manitoba Liberals appealed to Nellie for help in the campaign. "Most essential that you give us your assistance," one telegram ran; "people are asking for you all over the country." [43] *"Everybody clammering for your appearance to top off campaign properly," another read.* [44] *And so Nellie set to work again.*

On the evening of 7 August 1915, she was with the other Liberal party workers at the offices of the Manitoba Free Press, watching the returns come in. Early indications were for a Liberal victory.

> *As the evening wore on and the success of the Liberal party was shown to be more overwhelming than was even at first indicated, the enthusiasm of the crowd . . . [which had gathered outside] the Free Press office likewise became more pronounced, and soon there was an insistent demand for speeches.*
>
> *The appearance of Mrs. Nellie McClung at the window was the signal for a great outburst of cheering while hats, handkerchiefs and walking sticks were waved aloft. The scene was a unique one, and will live long in the memory of those who witnessed it. The demand of the crowd had to be acceded to, and the Hon. Edward Brown stepped on to the balcony to announce that Mrs. McClung would address the vast assembly.*

> *As Mrs. McClung stepped forward a chorus of ladies'*
> *voices were heard above the cheering, shouting "Liberator —*
> *Nellie McClung."*[45]

The Liberals' victory meant that prohibition and women's suffrage
were more or less guaranteed in Manitoba. Back in Alberta, Premier
Sifton was quick to see the handwriting on the wall. Women's suffrage
was coming to the prairies and his government had no intention of
lagging behind.
In September 1915, he improved on his promise to bring the subject
up for discussion in the Legislature. Now he pledged to introduce it as a
government measure which was certain of passage.

Nellie L. McClung
Newspaper report, 1915

Thanks of Women of Alberta Are
Due to Premier Sifton

In the good old days of chivalry, when fair ladies received a
proposal of marriage, they always said blushingly, "This is so
sudden." But in these hard prosaic days, when so much of the color
and romance has gone from life, under similar circumstances, it is
said that many times the lady exclaims, "Well, it is about time!"
That's the way I feel about the proposed woman suffrage legislation. . . .
This spring, our hearts were cheered beyond measure when the
Edmonton city charter was amended so that all people over
twenty-one could vote; we took this as the foretaste of better things
to come.
The better things are here! . . . Perhaps no man can quite grasp
how pleased the women will be when they are forever taken out of
the "lunatic — idiot — criminal" class [of those who cannot
vote.][46]

Nellie L. McClung, about 1916

Things are coming our way! Without any noise or fuss or
trouble, woman suffrage is arriving! and is going to happen just as
naturally and quietly as Monday becomes Tuesday, and we are so
glad, it is hard to write about it.
And we didn't have to fight for it at the last, and we didn't have
to knock anybody down and take it away from them! It is going to be

handed to us, with kindest regards and best wishes, hoping that we are enjoying the same. . . .

We are so glad that we do not have to fight any more — we are tired of war — tired of campaigns and petitions, and signatures and interviews!

We rejoice particularly for the sake of the many unknown and unnamed workers who, against the greatest discouragements, tried to do their little bit, and were many times ridiculed, criticized and misjudged by the very people they were trying to help, that is, other women.

We are doubly glad for the sake of the noble women who fought so bravely long ago, and who had to pass out of life without seeing their hearts' desire. And we hope that God in his goodness will let them look down over the balconies of heaven and see what is happening in Manitoba and Alberta, and know this good work for their own.[47]

Nellie L. McClung, about 1916

. . . it is up to the women [of Alberta now] for the eyes of Canada will be upon us. It will be ours to demonstrate that we can cast an intelligent vote, and still do business at the old stand.[48]

Nellie L. McClung, 1916

The first work undertaken by women [voters] will be to give help to other women, particularly mothers of families. . . .

When the fire broke out in the Parliament Buildings of Ottawa and the lights went off accidentally, darkness added greatly to the horror and danger. It . . . [became] necessary for someone to reach the switch, but no one could make way through the choking, blinding smoke with any hope of return. So they formed a chain — a human chain, by clasping hands. The man who went first was sustained by the warm handclasp of the man behind. In this way, the switch was reached in safety and many lives were, no doubt, saved. Women are going to form a chain, a greater sisterhood than the world has ever known.

[We need] . . . to institute a system of rural nursing, which will bring help and companionship to . . . [isolated] women in their hour of need. . . . Already the women of Alberta are working out some such plan. . . .

There is another plan applicable to the more populated districts which is being worked out by two of Calgary's progressive women.

It is to establish in Alberta a system of nursing as free and accessible as education in the public schools. . . .

More and more the idea is growing upon us that certain services are best rendered by the state, and not left to depend on the caprice, inclination, or inability of the individual. . . . As it is now many a man, woman, and child suffers agony, or perhaps becomes a menace to their family, because medical aid cannot be afforded. Why should a child suffer from adenoids, which make him stupid and dull in school, and give him a tendency to tubercular trouble, just because his father cannot afford to pay the doctor's fee, or maybe does not know the danger?

The free school clinic is a beginning and has been so successful it has opened the way for greater reforms along this line.

Women all over the West are thinking along such lines as these. . . .[49]

Newspaper report, 1916

At a meeting held at the home of Mrs. Nellie McClung [soon after the women's suffrage bill received second reading] . . . it was moved by Mrs. Edwards and seconded by Mrs. East that the persons present . . . consider the best method of forming a committee to consider the bills desirable for the Women of the Province of Alberta to bring before the Legislature at the next or ensuing Sessions . . . [on such matters as] a Woman's Interest in Her Husband's Estate; Equal Parental Rights; Red Light Abatement; and Proportional Representation. Carried.[50]

Nellie L. McClung, 1917

. . . if the advent of women into politics does not mean that life is made easier and safer for other women and for children, then we will have to confess with shame and sorrow that politically we have failed! But we are not going to fail! Already the angel has come down and has troubled the water. Discussions are raging in women's societies and wherever women meet together, and out of it something will come. Men are always quite willing to be guided by women when their schemes are sound and sane.

In New Zealand the first political activity of women was directed toward lowering the death-rate among children by sending out trained nurses to care for them and give instruction to the mothers. Ours will follow the same line, because the heart of woman is the same everywhere. Dreams will soon begin to come true. Good dreams always do — in time; and why not? There is nothing too good to be true![51]

PRIVATE JACK McCLUNG

There was, in fact, one dream which stubbornly refused to come true, and that was that the war would end. The McClungs' first-born child, Jack, turned eighteen in the summer of 1915, old enough to enlist. Nellie recorded her feelings in a book of stories and essays called The Next of Kin.

Nellie L. McClung, 1917

When I saw the first troops going away, I wondered how their mothers let them go, and I made up my mind that I would not let my boy go — I was so glad he was only seventeen — for hope was strong in our hearts that it might be over before he was of military age. It was the Lusitania [in the spring of 1915] that brought me to see the whole truth. Then I saw that we were waging war on the very Princes of Darkness, and I knew that morning when I read the papers, I knew that it would be better — a thousand times better — to be dead than to live under the rule of people whose hearts are so utterly black and whose process of reasoning is so oxlike — they are so stupidly brutal. I knew then that no man could die better than in defending civilization from this ghastly thing which threatened her!

Soon after that I knew, without a word being said, that my boy wanted to go — I saw the seriousness come into his face, and knew what it meant. It was when the news from the Dardanelles was heavy on our hearts, and the newspapers spoke gravely of the outlook.

One day he looked up quickly and said, "I want to go — I want to help the British Empire — while there is a British Empire!"

And then I realized that my boy, my boy, had suddenly become a man and had put away childish things forever.

I shall always be glad that the call came to him, not in the intoxication of victory, but in the dark hour of apparent defeat.[52]

Nellie L. McClung, about 1917

It was a shivering cold December morning when the boys went away. . . . We [mothers] were all there, [at the C.N.R. station] and we had promised each other that we would not shed a single tear, not one. The boys would remember us gay and smiling.

The morning is a poor time to be brave. It is so cold, and shivery, and your throat is so full and chokey, and the sun is not up at eight o'clock in December. I think they might have waited for sun-up, but I didn't say so. . . .

The train went out right on the stroke of eight, and we bluffed it to the last.

— Then we came home through the quiet streets . . . and the blinds were still down on the stores, horrid shirred things . . . [that] reminded me uncomfortably of the lining of a coffin.[53]

Nellie L. McClung, 1915

When we came home I felt strangely tired and old though I am only forty-two. But I know that my youth has departed from me. It has gone with Jack, our beloved, our first born, the pride of our hearts. Strange fate surely for a boy who never has had a gun in his hands, whose ways are gentle, and full of peace, who loves his fellow men, pities their sorrows, and would gladly help them to solve their problems. What have I done to you, in letting you go into this inferno of war? And how could I hold you back without breaking your heart?[54]

Nellie L. McClung, about 1917

Although there are so many of us we do not seem to be able to help each other. We are so helpless! We can co-operate for hatred, death and destruction, it seems, but not for love and helpfulness. Money is going now, free as the wind that blows, to carry on the work of destruction and bring suffering and death to other human beings. Surely this is a mad world, hypnotized with hatred. I keep wondering if women felt this way all down the ages, when their sons went.[55]

Nellie L. McClung, 1917

There is a psychological reason for women knitting just now, beyond the need of socks. I know how these women feel! I, even I, have begun to crochet! I do it for the same reason that the old toper in times of stress takes to his glass. It keeps me from thinking; it atrophies the brain; and now I know why the women of the East are so slow about getting the franchise. They crochet and work in wool instead of thinking. You can't do both! When the casualty lists are long, and letters from the front far apart — I crochet. . . . It is a sort of mental chloroform. This is for the real dark moments, when the waves go over our heads. .... We all have them, but of course, they do not last.[56]

Nellie L. McClung, 1917

A Prayer For the Next of Kin

O Thou, who once Thine own Son gave
    To save the world from sin,
Draw near in pity now we crave
    To all the Next of Kin.
To Thee we make our humble prayer
To save us from despair!

Send sleep to all the hearts that wake;
    Send tears into the eyes that burn;
Steady the trembling hands that shake;
    Comfort all hearts that mourn.
But most of all, dear Lord, we pray
For strength to see us through this day.

As in the wilderness of old,
    When Thou Thy children safely led,
They gathered, as we have been told,
    One day's supply of heavenly bread,
And if they gathered more than that,
At evening it was stale and flat —

So, Lord, may this our faith increase —
    To leave, untouched, tomorrow's load,
To take of grace a one-day lease
    Upon life's winding road.
Though round the bend we may not see,
Still let us travel hopefully!

Or, if our faith is still so small —
    Our hearts so void of heavenly grace,
That we may still affrighted be
    In passing some dark place —
Then in Thy mercy let us run
    Blindfolded in the race.[57]

WAR MEASURES

The war years were an emotional maelstrom for Nellie. She suffered from despair as she had never known it before. Civilization had been shown to be a fraud. Europe was in flames. Her gentle-hearted son had been turned into "a man of blood."[58] At the same time, she had moments of real exaltation. Women's suffrage and prohibition had triumphed across the West, and she could see that it was partly due to the social climate of war. More and more it seemed likely that the bloodshed was God's way of saving humankind. "By the time we have emerged from the furnace of war, the clear, sacrificial fire may have purified us, burned away the dross and prepared us for plainer living and simpler pleasures," Nellie trumpeted.[59]

Meanwhile, her career as a public personage was ascending a new crest. By the fall of 1915, her fame had spread to British Columbia, where she headlined a temperance rally, and to Ontario, where she went on an extended tour.

This was the second time she'd visited the province of her birth; the first time, in 1910, she'd gone to promote her Pearlie Watson books. Toronto had cowed her then (she remembered feeling like "a raw, green girl from the country") and she'd allowed herself to be told how to behave and hurried off to the hairdresser's to have her hair done "right."[60] But by October 1915, when she returned, she was raw and green no longer and certainly not in need of advice. The surest cure for nervousness, she had learned, was to have something important to say and concentrate on getting it across.[61] Since Ontario had neither women's suffrage nor prohibition, she wasn't likely to be left searching for words. The "backward" East could stand to take a few lessons from the "progressive" West.

Ontarians seemed more than willing to be taught, for they turned out by the thousands to hear Nellie speak. The largest halls and churches could not accommodate the crowds. At one church which seated 2,500, 3,000 people had to be turned away:[62] "the vestibule was a solid mass of humanity and women leaned over the railings to hear the woman speaker. Many women remained in this stifling atmosphere standing until they were finally compelled to leave owing to faintness. . . ."[63]

Her lectures in Ontario recapitulated the themes of her earlier suffrage speeches and of In Times Like These. "Greatest Insult Comes at Marriage," the headlines announced. " 'Who Giveth This Woman' Gets Rap From Mrs. Nellie McClung"; or "Get Off Your Pedestals . . . Women Should Get Away From Old-Fashioned Idea They Are Frail and Protected."[64]

What eastern journalists found most attractive about the visitor was her energy, which they took to be quintessentially western. "One daren't take one's eyes off those Easterners for an instant," Nellie complained. "If you do they will load you down with some 'lure' and 'charm' bunk. I want a message that will carry itself and that will influence people by the force of its own appeal to their inborn sense of righteousness."[65] If she was "bright, breezy, brimming with optimism," as one reporter found her,[66] she was also unmistakably in earnest.

> The brisk, business like manner of this pioneer in women's reform in the West clothes all her speech with a Yankee-like directness. Perhaps it is that which makes it so forcible for even in casual fireside chat Mrs. McClung's words are said as though they are meant. She has no time for idle phrases uttered simply to fill up the pauses of a conversation, and, women's suffrage being the subject nearest her heart just at the present, she spoke eagerly about it.[67]

Nellie was at her passionate and charming best. One man, who admitted that he had been sceptical about her before, reported simply: "Mrs. McClung has been here. She has spoken and we are all converts."[68]

The only real nastiness Nellie ran into on her tour came from an unexpected source — the Ontario Equal Franchise Association, for whom she had agreed to give a benefit lecture. The deal was that she would pay half of the expenses and receive half the gate; the other half was to go to a patriotic fund. This arrangement was made with a great show of friendliness, but Nellie later concluded that some of those who slapped her back in apparent good fellowship had really been "looking for a soft place to drive in the knife."[69]

The problem was that the franchise association had underestimated Nellie's drawing power. When the proceeds turned out to be greater than expected, some of the members decided that she should be content with a smaller fee. One woman even dispatched an anonymous letter promising to make Nellie's name "stink in the nostrils of the Ontario people" if she didn't comply.[70] It was no idle threat, for soon the eastern newspapers had been informed that she was demanding more than the agreed-upon share.

What followed was a "thoroughly unpleasant experience," Nellie admitted.[71] "Anonymous letters poured in on me, the liquor interests rejoiced and the newspapers they controlled revelled in what they called

'The Suffrage Meeting Scandal'. If I had robbed a collection plate, or rifled a baby's bank, they could not have said more.''[72] She did have her defenders (including the president of the franchise association and several western newspapers) but the damage had been done and not only to her reputation in the East. "I lost something . . . ," she reflected. "I was never quite so sure of people after that.''[73]

"So far as I can see the truth, and I do try to see it, there was a queer streak of cheerful imbecility in me up to a certain period in my life. I believed easily, I trusted people: I grew sophisticated at last, but it came the hard way.''[74]

The next year, 1916, Nellie had a more pleasant time as a lecturer for the National American Woman Suffrage Association. Her first appearance in the United States had been in May of that year at a large suffrage convention in Minneapolis. The meeting was very dull — speech after yawn-inducing speech. "Then," in the words of the local paper, "something big happened. Somebody seemed — not to have opened the door — but to have taken out the side out of the house, and a west Canadian breeze blew in. . . . If it had been Harry Lauder on the stage instead of the Canadian woman with her Scotch-Irish burr, there could not have been more enthusiasm.''[75]

Nellie was such a hit that she was invited back for a six-week, forty-city tour late that fall. This time there would be no disagreements about pay; she was to get $200 a week plus expenses. Six weeks was the longest her political work had ever kept her away from home, but she assuaged her conscience by getting her mother-in-law in to keep house and taking seventeen-year-old Florence along.

Nellie had more going for her with American audiences than her high spirits and wit. She appeared before them as a leader of a successful suffrage movement, and her listeners were eager for information about proven tactics like the "women's parliament.''[76] They were also intrigued by the fact that Nellie had a son at the front, for the U.S.A. had not yet entered the war. "Somehow I feel very differently towards the war since I saw you," a Missouri suffragist confided. "Knowing that you have a son at the front gave it a horrid reality the magazines and newspapers had not been able to do.''[77] When Nellie returned for a second U.S. tour in 1917, after the States had declared war, her audiences were anxious for advice on sending "comforts" to the "boys." By that time she could claim to be something of an expert on the subject, having had a son in the trenches for two years, so she told them about her parcels of underwear and boots, toiletries and chocolate. Knit a band or two of bright color *into socks for the soldiers, she suggested, but not red — "they see too much of that."*[78]

By August 1917, the war had dragged on for three numbing years. Events in Europe were never far from people's minds.

> War maps hung on kitchen walls and were dotted with
> black-headed pins as we followed the course of battle. We
> raised money for the Red Cross and the Patriotic Fund in
> every conceivable way from autographed quilts at ten cents a
> name to personal subscriptions which sometimes ran into high
> figures. The newspapers printed many extras, and hardly a
> night went by without one at least. The boys sold them all
> over the city. When the first cry of "Extra! Extra!" punctured
> the night, lights appeared in upstairs windows, and front
> doors were hastily opened as we rushed out for copies.[79]

All other priorities were put aside for the duration of the conflict. Nothing was too sacred or too trivial to escape alteration in the interests of victory. Even the national anthem had been tampered with: there was now a verse which began "God save our splendid men, Send them safe home again."[80] At meetings of the Canadian Women's Press Club in Edmonton, lunch had been cut back to sandwiches and one kind of cake in September 1917 and was down to brown bread and butter by the next spring, in order to conserve food for Europe.[81] Vacant lots in the city were being cleaned up and planted to spuds.[82] Thousands of women, urban and rural, did volunteer work for the Red Cross. In one year, the Edmonton branch sent off a thousand boxes of clothing and bandages valued at over $63,000.[83]

As the casualties mounted in Europe and more and more men were drawn away from office, factory, and farm, women stepped in to replace them, either as volunteers or for a patriotically low wage. Along with their new activities came new styles in dress. The "Latest Thing Out" in 1917 was overalls: "overalls of chambray, overalls of soft cotton, overalls in stripes, white, blue, of khaki and of black sateen — but overalls not the less. . . ." "Some of my women neighbors approve," one overall-fancier reported, "while others say it is dreadful, but women must talk!"[84]

Some women even donned military uniforms and formed themselves into a corps ready "to serve the state in any capacity should occasion arise."[85] Members were trained in first-aid, marching, and use of firearms, and when seven members of this Women's Volunteer Reserve took on seven returned soldiers in a target-shooting match, the women won by a score of 475 to 387.[86]

As pleased as she was by the new importance of women during the war, Nellie never warmed to the idea of female soldiers. Nothing had happened to shake her belief that women were instinctively nurturers. Though women might reluctantly concede the importance of winning the war, now that the men had started it, their contribution to victory should come in distinctive and womanly ways.

"I like the picture of women in Red Cross work," she said, "making bandages, making comforts. Everywhere they are doing this work; it is typical; it is women's work. . . ."[87] In her mind, everyday acts of compassion and caring contributed to the war effort, for this was "a holy war . . . a war for the restoration of our Lord's ideals."[88] The woman who adopted a war orphan or worked as a frontier nurse was helping to win the real war, she thought, the "war that never ends" against callousness, materialism, and sin.

Nellie did her bit by working as a volunteer lecturer for the Red Cross and by helping to find jobs for women who were out of work. An unemployed girl would write to her, and Nellie would try to find some "kind, motherly woman" who needed a maid.[89] It was this sort of plain, old-fashioned neighborliness, not murder and bombs, which would remake the world.

Nellie was steadfast in her conviction that the underlying causes of the war were spiritual. "Wrong thinking has caused all our trouble," she wrote, "and the world cannot be saved by physical means, but only by the spiritual forces which change the mental attitude."[90]

> We know that the people of Germany have been led away by their teachers, philosophers, writers; they worship the god of force; they recognize no sin but weakness and inefficiency. They are good people, only for their own way of thinking; no doubt they say the same thing of us.[91]

Nellie wasn't always able to maintain this kind of lofty idealism and tolerance. She was, by now, determinedly partisan, fully committed to the Canadian and British cause for which her son was risking his life. Night after night the papers were full of propaganda about German atrocities, and what alarmed Nellie the most were reports of the rape and murder of civilian women. In one angry outburst she exclaimed that "the worst man in our armies would have cheerfully stood up and been shot, rather than do the cruel things . . . [the German] men did by command. . . .''[92] She wasn't particularly comfortable with these emotions (in another context she had defined "the world's disease" as the "withering, blighting, wasting malady of hatred, which has its roots in the narrow patriotism which teaches people to love their own country and despise all others") but she sometimes experienced them nonetheless.[93]

Her animosity towards the enemy colored her opinions on certain domestic issues, as well. In 1917, the federal government passed a Wartime Election Act which extended the Dominion franchise to women, but only to those with close relatives in the armed services. At the same time, Parliament disenfranchised most men who had come to Canada from "enemy" countries, the idea of both moves being to manufacture an electorate which could be counted on to support conscription. Nellie had no real quarrel with the purpose of the bill, but she did object to its provisions on women — it discriminated against those who had no male relatives of military age, she said. Significantly, though, she had no kind words for the disenfranchised "aliens." For some time, she had been concerned about the changing "moral tone" of the Canadian electorate.[94] Increasingly, the public-spirited English-speaking men had enlisted, leaving the indifferent "foreign" element behind. Late in 1916, when the prime minister, Sir Robert Borden, was visiting the West, Nellie had taken the opportunity to buttonhole him and urge that, as a war measure, he advance the federal franchise to British and Canadian women in order to right the balance in the electorate.[95]

The idea of a partial suffrage for women, excluding the foreign-born, was an about-face for Nellie. Not so long before, during the provincial suffrage campaigns, she had insisted upon universal female suffrage. When anti-suffragists raised the cry that including "foreign" women would add to the "unintelligent vote," Nellie had rebuked them for "blind egotism."[96] "We have no reason to be afraid of the foreign woman's vote," she had argued then. "I wish we were as sure of the ladies who live on the Avenue."[97]

Francis Marion Beynon, a friend of Nellie's from the Political Equality League and women's editor of the Grain Growers' Guide, was quick to identify this inconsistency. In an editorial, she lambasted Nellie for giving up on democracy when the going got tough.[98] That wasn't really the case, Nellie wrote in reply — she had never intended the limited franchise to outlast the war. In any case, she said, she was willing to withdraw the suggestion for the sake of harmony in the women's movement.[99] (There is no reason to doubt the sincerity of this offer, for Nellie was astute enough to know that united effort ranked *above individual expression if you wanted results.) Interestingly enough, though, the law which Parliament finally passed was in line with what Nellie had originally proposed.*

By February 1918, Nellie had another suggestion for the government in Ottawa. She was annoyed by the inefficient way in which women's energies were being deployed in war work. Talented, well-educated women were frittering the hours away with knitting — a task which could be better done by machine — and at a time when hundreds of rural schools were closing because of a teacher shortage. By Nellie's estimate, 20,000 children would go untaught in 1918,[100] a particular calamity, she thought, in "foreign settlements where already there is a strong anti-British feeling."[101] And while this "poison plant" of illiteracy was being allowed to grow rank in the land, there were countless women yearning for a "real full-sized woman's job."[102] It was ridiculous; it was short-sighted; it was insulting. If the government were sincere about the importance of women's contribution to the war effort, one would have expected them to manage it more carefully, Nellie thought.

Emily Murphy agreed, so the two women took it upon themselves to write Prime Minister Borden with the idea of "mobilizing" women to meet the labor shortage in schools, fields, and farm homes.[103] If the men could be registered (even conscripted) for battle, surely the women could be registered for service on the home front. The politicians apparently already had some such scheme in mind, for within days of receiving the McClung-Murphy letter, the government began telegraphing invitations to "representative women from all parts of Canada to confer with [the] war committee of cabinet on plans for [the] wider participation of women in necessary war work, including national registration, increased production, commercial and industrial pursuits, conservation of food, the further development of [the] spirit of service and sacrifice among the Canadian people, and other war problems in which women are particularly interested."[104] Mesdames McClung and Murphy were both included in the Alberta delegation, so off they went to Ottawa to give their advice to the federal cabinet.

Nellie was intent on laying two issues before the conference — the shortage of teachers for prairie schools and the need to control the use of grain being exported to Great Britain. Prohibition had not come to the Mother Country, and in her more fiercely moralistic moods, Nellie argued that the continuation of the liquor traffic in Britain was God's reason for prolonging the war. "The Peerage and the Beerage and the church refused to move" on this issue, she lamented. "Great people, but slow."[105]

Sitting on the Ottawa-bound train, the Alberta delegates to the Women's War Conference prepared a resolution on this question. It was to be moved by Nellie, seconded by Emily Murphy, that all grain destined for Great Britian be milled prior to export so that it couldn't be distilled when it got there.[106] To the noisy dismay of two eastern newspapers, which "characterized this resolution as foolish, impractical and worse," it was carried by the conference. "The torrent of ridicule has come from papers carrying liquor advertisements," Nellie noted gleefully, "and that, in itself encourages us to believe that it is not the insanity of the resolution but its sanity, which has caused them to be annoyed over it. The hit dog is the one that howls."[107]

Though this was the most controversial resolution passed by the conference, it was not the most down-to-earth. The delegates also called for free technical training for women so they could play a greater role in agriculture and skilled trades. They wanted equal pay for equal work and a minimum wage for women, and they advocated a permanent lobby of women's organizations to advise the government.[108] The idea of registering all civilians for national service was accepted, though with the proviso that service for women would be voluntary. The institution of daylight saving time as a conservation measure and the creation of a federal department of health were also endorsed.[109] In sum, the women left no shortage of ideas on which the government could act.

Whether or not the women had really accomplished anything, Nellie recognized the conference's significance. It was the first time the federal cabinet had consulted with women and, as such, was another dramatic indication of the advances women had made during the war. By the war's end in October 1918, Nellie could rejoice that women had finally come into their own. Still, she knew as well as anyone that the territory, once taken, would have to be held.

Nellie L. McClung, 1919

More has happened in the last four years and a half than in the four hundred years that preceded that time. The earth and its people have been turned 'round and 'round, and today there has come to pass what before that time was not even dreamed of.

Women, who for years battled, sometimes gently, sometimes stormily, for their proper place in the world only to be repulsed, have been invited, coaxed, bribed, to come in and take it. The doors have not only been opened, but the footmen stand there to bow the ladies in.

Women are at last admitted to every department of labor. The very voices that cried "Home is your place — you must stay in it!", have changed their slogan to "Come out of the kitchen — your king and country need you!"

And the women came!

Forty thousand of them marched behind Mrs. Pankhurst through the streets of London under the banner "For men must fight and women must work."

Women have gone into factories, offices, munition plants, everywhere that there was work to be done and even the bitterest critic has had to admit that they have made good! More than that, they have been housed better, fed better, and their children better cared for than before.

The state has seen to that. Needing the woman's labor, it became necessary to keep her in good health. A sick woman is an economic loss. So factories have been re-built to suit her, seats have been made, levers have been shortened, cloak rooms, toilet rooms, mirrors, have been installed to make her happy. Then, to keep her from wearing her strength out doing her housework after hours, communal laundries and kitchens have been opened where the baby has been cared for, for in these days of hideous wastage every human atom has increased in value.

All this has been done in the warring countries to conserve woman power for the state. It has not been done for sentimental reasons, it has been done for stern necessity, but the important thing is that *it has been done*. Under the stress of war conditions it has been demonstrated what co-operation can do to lighten the load, and the result has been marvellous.

And now the war is over and people are anxiously asking, "Will women go back?" Is it reasonable? After you have used an electric washer, will you go back to the washboard or the two flat stones in the running stream? After you have driven your own car, will you be content to drive an ox in a Red River cart?

(Time is given here for reflection). All right then, you won't! That is settled.

Now then, how is it going to be managed? The bars are down, the bombs of war have blown them to atoms, the walls of prejudice have been crumbled by the shells of necessity. But let no one think that human nature has been regenerated and that the prejudice against women has completely died away. There are many men who were glad to employ women to help them to fill their contracts who are hoping that when the men come home, they can give the women the blue envelope, and let them go. You were not employed because you were wanted, ladies, but because you were *needed*, and there was nobody else! They are hoping that you will go back to your home and split your time into a hundred odds and ends of occupations; cooking a little, sewing a little, washing, ironing, financing, teaching, social work —

But you won't — for you know better. You know now, for you have seen it, what can be done by co-operation and you will concentrate on one job and do it well.

Women have won as great a victory as the battle of Verdun! But the day of settlement is upon us and that is the time of danger. Armies win battles, nations must win wars! The women who have achieved success in the various fields of labor have won the victory for us, but unless we all follow up and press onward, the advantage will be lost. Yesterday's successes will not do for today!

Women must claim the place they have won. They must take it. Men's hearts are softened and tender to women now. They still feel the touch of soft and skilful hands; they see white linen women with red crosses on their foreheads in their dreams. They say in their speeches, "Without the women we could not have won."

Now is our time! We must claim our place in this new world that has been bought with such a price. It is ours. It always was ours but we had not taken out our papers. We were too shy, or too careless, or too contented, or too miserable, or too much afraid — or something. Anyway, we didn't!

But today the World Titles Office is open, it is Ladies' Day, and we must go in and file our claim. There is blood on the door and the way is marked with bones, some of them not even whitened, but we must enter. We owe it to the men and women and children who have perished that we will claim the world with all its labor, all its undertakings, all its problems, all its burdens, all its councils, all its sorrows, all its joys, to have and to hold, to think for and work for, to comfort and cherish, world without end. Amen.

This is the new citizenship.[110]

Nellie in 1914, the year she entered politics in earnest. (British Columbia Archives photo)

O. I. SAY
TOWN HALL
To-Night
JULY 7th   8 p. m.

Will be the scene of the greatest rally to hear

NELLIE McCLUNG

ever experienced in Macleod

She is acknowledged Canadas greatest entertainer and oratoress and will be heard in her best form on the much discussed **Drink Question**

You can't afford to miss hearing
NELLIE McCLUNG
COME EARLY AND SECURE A SEAT

By 1914, Nellie had begun adding temperance and women's suffrage to the program at her performances. (British Columbia Archives photo)

DO NOT FAIL TO HEAR
Mrs. Nellie L. McClung
LECTURE
On Woman Suffrage, Temperance Issues and Things Political.

AN OPEN DISCUSSION IS DESIRED

Mrs. McClung is acknowledged to be one of the foremost platform speakers in the west to-day.

THE TOWN HALL, KILLARNEY
THURSDAY, JUNE THE 18TH
AT EIGHT O'CLOCK SHARP

Reserved Seats 35c.   General Admission 25c.

Plan of Hall at Evans' Drug Store.

Poster for a political meeting, probably during the Manitoba election campaign of 1914. (Photo from the McClung Papers)

FRAMING THE FREAK PLATFORM WHICH MR. NORRIS TERMS THE POLICY OF LIBERAL PARTY

Conservative cartoonists liked to picture Nellie as a hatchet-wielding harridan. (British Columbia Archives photo)

HE SEES THE POINT OF THESE JOKES

Once Nellie was caricatured as a mosquito. "TCN" was Manitoba Liberal party leader T. C. Norris. (British Columbia Archives photo)

Mark and Nellie at the McClungs' first Edmonton home. As a joke, Wes coached Mark to recite, "I am a suffragette's son and never knew a mother's love." (Photo courtesy of Mark McClung)

Portrait of Nellie, 1910-1918. (Glenbow-Alberta Institute photo)

Emily Murphy, second from right, shown here in her role as police magistrate, was an important influence on Nellie after 1915. (City of Edmonton Archives)

Nellie, with Alice Jamieson of Calgary and Emily Murphy, on the day women's suffrage came to Alberta, 1916. Since they couldn't very well celebrate the victory with a drink, the women had their picture taken instead! (British Columbia Archives photo)

The war expanded women's place in Canadian life. Though Nellie did not like the idea of female soldiers, she did hope that women's gains in the economic and political spheres would outlast the crisis. Above, the Women's Volunteer Reserve, Winnipeg. (Manitoba Archives photo)

====== CHAPTER EIGHT ======
THE MEMBER FOR EDMONTON

> . . . if women ever get into politics there will be a
> cleaning-out of pigeon-holes and forgotten
> corners, on which the dust of years has fallen,
> and the sound of the political carpet-beater will
> be heard in the land.

*Nellie's plea that women hang onto the gains they'd made during
the war was lost in the shout ordering them out of the way. Work had to
be found for the returning soldiers, and an insistent cry went up for
women to quit their wartime jobs and go back home. Even confirmed
feminists joined the chorus. Louise McKinney, white-ribboner, suffragist, and (after 1917) Alberta M.L.A., argued that if women tried to
maintain their "new-found liberty and wider sphere" they would simply
"contitute one more of the already numerous after-the-war problems."[1]
Women who only a few months earlier had allowed themselves to be
coaxed away from domestic life by a national exigency now permitted
themselves to be chased back into the kitchen on the same grounds.*

*In the final analysis, Nellie wasn't particularly alarmed by
women's retreat from commerce and industry (like Louise McKinney,
she expected the "average woman" to be "instinctively" drawn to "home
life")[2] but she was deeply concerned about any withdrawal from public
affairs. Predictably, she believed that women could be "the greatest
factor in rebuilding the world" after the war, if only they could be
persuaded to take on the task.[3] By this she didn't mean that women
should enter politics en masse; the times weren't ripe for anything like
that. Instead, as she explained in 1919:*

> *The most important thing that the average woman can do at
> the moment, beyond caring for her own home, is to help make
> public opinion. (Talk is fluid — it fits into every angle of life
> — its effects are imperishable.) Every reform has begun in
> talk — the great international council of talkers sits every*

day, and in every place, and turns out its grist of conclusions.

Here is the place we can all take part, if we will lay aside gossip, slander, spite, and foolish trifles, and really begin to talk. Let us talk about the minimum wage. Let us tell the people we meet, that there are girls working in our cities for six and seven dollars a week. Let us spend a little time figuring out what a girl can live on in decency — we will find it more than double that sum. Let us visit some of these brave girls who are struggling to live on their scanty incomes and hear their stories. It is heart-interest stuff all right, and it will make an impression on the most complacent. It is quite time that the wage-earning girl had a few advocates, for up to the present, they have had none, and while everything else in the business world has advanced in price, the girls' wages have not, and for that, I hold, we older women are to blame.

It is all part of the misconception regarding women and their needs, and the vaguely comforting notion that women are always able to get along someway.

If the women begin to talk about living conditions for working women, there would soon be a minimum wage law that would bring a happier heart to many of the girls who are now burdened and apprehensive, ill-nourished and sad.

One quality is needed to make conditions improve, and that is Imagination.[4] It is fundamental to national safety. It should be taught in schools, even at the expense of history or grammar, or Latin roots! Imagination is the quality the German people lack. It is sometimes called Spirituality — it is the lack of Imagination which allows the terrible inequalities of life, and it is inequalities which cause storms, in nature as in society. A stratum of air becomes excessively heated, expands and rises. The surrounding air rushes in to fill the space, and then the trouble begins, and the air is filled with fragments of houses and trees and windmills, and we call it a cyclone.

We are about due for one in our present state of society, and nothing but a quick change of spirit can prevent it.[5]

The immediate post-war period was an unsettled and, in Nellie's view, a dangerous time. "There is a tendency and a very real reason for discontent," she observed. "People are nervous, tired, depressed and troubled."[6] Organized labor had a legacy of grievances from the war years, when working-class men had been forced by law to risk their lives in battle but capitalists hadn't been deprived of the windfall profits from defense contracts. Then, as the Canadian economy made its very disorderly transition from war to peace in 1918-19, high rates of unemployment and inflation added to people's bitterness and discouragement. The widening gap between rich and poor had Nellie alarmed. On the one hand there were people who could live "with no thought but pleasure," partying on rare and expensive food and wearing dresses which represented a working man's wages for six weeks. And while they loafed away the hours at the "afternoon dansant" in some smart hotel, a woman might be heading home outside, hurrying through the wintry streets "with her day's wages tightly held in her bare hand."

> She enters a butcher shop and asks the price of beefsteak — it has gone up again — she buys a pound; at the grocers, she gets a bottle of milk and a loaf of bread. Counting her money, she then finds she has not enough for the baby's boots; so buys a sack of oatmeal and a pound of tea. When she passes the hotel, the afternoon dansant crowd are getting into their cars, and she listens just a minute to the fragments of conversation which float out on the perfumed air. It fascinates her, it breathes such a spirit of comfort and luxury — What do they know about prices, and what do they care? She thinks of the cold, bare room which she calls home, of the ragged children who await her there, and with bitterness in her heart, she watches the luxurious cars which swing out from the archway into the storm, with their gaily chattering occupants.
>
> With a curse, she turns shivering, and begins her long walk to the place she calls home.
>
> It can't last![7]

While there were many who agreed with Nellie's conclusion — "It can't last!" — not everyone shared her enthusiasm for talk, imagination, and legislation as the vehicles of reform. Many labor leaders, for example, were much more interested in the tactics and rhetoric of the Russian Bolsheviks. In 1919 there were demonstrations of working-class power and solidarity in many parts of the world, including Winnipeg, where the labor movement called a general strike for 15 May. Nellie went to see for herself the "strange things" that were going on, and in the process, as it turned out, she clarified her own political philosophy.[8]

Interestingly, several of the prime movers behind the Winnipeg strike had been colleagues of Nellie's in the Manitoba reform movement before 1914, but they had taken a more radical turn during the war. Now, she concluded, they and the other strike leaders seemed "to have hypnotized themselves into the thought that nothing short of a social revolution and the overthrow of constitutional authority will save the world."[9]

> "This system cannot be patched up, [one of them told her;] it has to be blown up. We will do away with all private capital and all money, as we understand it now. The dollar is the wrong basis of exchange. . . . There should be no private ownership of anything and no working for profit, and there should be no basis of exchange but the hour's work."

At this point, Nellie interrupted with an objection:

> "One man's hour is not equal to anothers" . . . I said. "Some men study for years to be able to do certain things, and then minutes of their time is worth a month of another man's unskilled labor."
>
> "The state will train all" . . . [the strike leader] said loftily, "according to their several gifts."
>
> "Who will decide the several gifts," . . . I said, "I know people who think they have several gifts, —"
>
> He silenced me with a look — "That is a minor matter," he said. "All will be taken care of by the state. All will work for the state, and there will be enough for every one."
>
> "It looks like a great day for lazy people," . . . I said.[10]

But while Nellie had philosophical differences with the strike leadership, it was their tactics which offended her most. "The first two days of the strike were a perfect success from the point of view of the strikers," she reported.

> Every newspaper except their own was suppressed; water pressure was reduced to thirty pounds, for that is enough to bring it to one story buildings, and the Western Labor News stated that it is in one story buildings that the

> *"workers" live, the inference being that it did not matter whether the other people lived or not.*
>
> *Delivery wagons were gone from the streets, except a few which ran "by permission of the Strike Committee"; restaurants were closed, except a few which bore the same card. No news was let out of the city without being first submitted to Mr. Ivens, the editor of the Western Labor News, and any sentence that did not appeal to Mr. Ivens was ruthlessly struck out. The Central Committee had sent a statement out to gasoline dealers, telling them to whom they might sell. ... It seemed the only thing people could do without permission was to die, and even at that, they could not be buried, for the grave diggers were out, and at one time there were several hundred corpses awaiting burial. ...*
>
> *There was something so despotic and arrogant about all this, that even indifferent citizens rallied to the call for help.*[11]

Nellie's sympathies aligned her with the Citizens' Committee of 1,000, a group of middle-class and business people who organized to provide essential services which had been disrupted by the strike. It was the "selfishness" of the strike to which Nellie particularly objected. Unlike the women's movement which, she believed, would ultimately benefit all people, the general strike was intended to assist one group — the workers — at the expense of everyone else, and that is why she condemned it.

Still, she wasn't without sympathy for the labor movement. The hysteria of deportations and jail terms with which the government quashed the general strike left her cold. She could see that, historically, strikes had helped the "working man": without them "he might still be working twelve hours a day."[12] And she was quite willing to concede that the workers had real grievances. But the general strike was no solution. It was just another manifestation of the "hoggishness" which was threatening the world; it showed the "grab spirit" of the Bolsheviks.[13] "What then is the remedy?" she asked.

> *Certainly not a return to the old system whereby a firm of textile manufacturers may make seventy-two percent on their capital, (as announced in today's paper) and quite frankly rejoice over their handsome profits and disclaim all responsibility of the high price of clothing, which now prevents many a*

man and woman from clothing themselves in decency and
comfort. There is no doubt that the high cost of living has
driven the working man to desperation, and the government
can no longer ignore the conditions which have brought this to
pass.

The new social order which Nellie envisaged is what we know
today as the "welfare state." We take it for granted now — are even
inclined to grumble about it — but in 1919 this was visionary talk:

> There are many things that the government can do to
> relieve the situation. There is the taxation of profits, the
> fixing of all prices, supervision of crops, so that there may not
> be overproduction of some things and under production of
> others. Better and cheaper housing, state care for the sick, so
> that a family who are so unfortunate as to have sickness, will
> not be further penalized by having to pay for it; old age
> pensions to relieve the minds of our people from the fear of
> want.
> The government should, and probably will do all these
> things and many more. Even so, the trouble will not be over
> unless something else happens. Legislation is not enough — it
> is not new laws we need, it is a new spirit in our people — it
> is sometimes called a change of heart. No law or set of laws
> can bring peace to a world of grabbers.[14]

Nellie's dream ran like this: if people's hearts could once be
touched — if their imaginations could be kindled to the suffering of their
fellows — if they opened themselves to the love which was true
Christianity, then they would put aside their selfish ways forever. They
would begin to demand that the state use its power to keep everyone
healthy and happy and good: rich and poor, young and old alike. The
strong would care for the helpless, the lucky for the unfortunate, the
individual for the collectivity. This was the liberalism of the "greatest
good for the greatest number" suffused with Christianity. People would
live in harmony and contentment, governed by the Golden Rule. And it
was the women, with their gentle spirits, who could bring this about.

"Reformation does not need to be revolution," Nellie maintained.
"We women have in our hands that weapon which will gain for us our
desires, if we use it intelligently and unitedly."[15] "That weapon," of
course, was the right to participate in politics and to vote.

Nellie thought that women's great asset in entering public life was their independence: they were free to view the issues from a fresh, humanitarian point of view. Unlike the men, they were not fettered by allegiance to either of the political parties, and she urged them to keep it that way. If women merely lined up with the Liberals and Conservatives, the only effect of their enfranchisement would be to double the voters' list, she pointed out. A separate women's party was not the answer either. "We could have . . . very easily . . . [organized one], and with some cause," she later admitted, "but while we would have had a glorious time doing it, we would have merely succeeded in dividing the progressive force of the country. . . ."16

What Nellie proposed instead was that women should form a pool of active but nonpartisan voters who would study the issues in their own way and then vote as a bloc. She foresaw "a great body of intelligent, thinking, investigating, open-minded, unprejudiced women, who weigh matters carefully, gathering up evidence, listening to all sides, with patience, with understanding, with charity; slow to think evil, ready to accord to each man his measure of praise and then acting fearlessly, courageously, without flavor of favor."

"Then," she concluded, "would we truly become a terror to evildoers, a praise to them that do well."17

In her own political work, Nellie continued to make an issue of her independence from party ties. In the Alberta provincial election of 1917, she had again agreed to campaign for the Liberals, not because she was a party adherent but because the Liberal government had brought in women's suffrage and prohibition. By doing so, the party had earned women's votes, she thought. But she wasn't willing to plead their case on the hustings unless it were clear that no one — not even the premier — would have any control over what she had to say. As in the Manitoba campaigns of 1914 and 1915, she insisted on being "free-lance" in the fight.

The only one who was discomfitted by her unorthodox stance was the lone Conservative candidate for whom she spoke. He deserved to be elected, she told the audience at one of his campaign meetings, because he had supported temperance and the equal franchise, but she couldn't recommend the rest of his party. So, right there, in the middle of a Conservative rally, she went on to promote the Liberal cause.18

For all her protestations about being nonpartisan, Nellie had by now been associated with the Liberals in three election campaigns. Why did she continue to hold herself aloof? As late as the mid-1920s, she was still claiming, in a strangely ingenuous tone, that she was "not real sure" about her "politics." "I know I am not a Conservative," she said, "but very few of them are — so that does not tell much. We have not many Conservatives in Canada now. We haven't the sort of air that produces Conservatives. We are the kind of people who will try anything once."[19]

One event which must have done much to settle Nellie's political allegiances was the emergence of William Lyon Mackenzie King as leader of the federal Liberals in 1919. As the years passed he was to become something of a hero to her. Only a year younger than Nellie and, like her, Ontario-born, Mackenzie King shared her commitment to social justice as a religious ideal. "Love Humanity" was his youthful credo, and he was the kind of person easily moved to tears by religious sentiment or human misfortune. At the age of twenty-one, he had been working to have the use of "sweated labor" in the garment industry outlawed. At twenty-five, he had begun to earn a national reputation as a labor conciliator; in 1908, at the age of thirty-five, he had entered the cabinet as minister of labor to push for such measures as the eight-hour day and workers' compensation.[20] Nellie first mentioned him in 1919 when she referred to his "fine book,"[21] Industry and Humanity, in which he argued that the interests of the "community" ought to be protected, by the state if necessary, during industrial disputes. Like Nellie he was a reformer, but like her too, he wasn't interested in change at the expense of public order and harmony. Both of them put their faith in conciliation, compromise, and good will. It is not hard to understand why Nellie became a Mackenzie King devotee.

Still, she didn't really throw her lot in with the Liberals until the provincial election of 1921 when she ran as one of the party's candidates in Edmonton. Even then she made it clear that, if elected, "she would reserve the right to use her own judgment as a member of the Legislature . . ."[22]

The decision to allow her name to stand for nomination had not come easily. Since the end of the war, Nellie had slipped happily back into private life. There had been general family rejoicing when Jack came home, troubled and withdrawn, but alive. Then too, she was pleased to have time to write again. Fans had been pestering her for another Pearlie Watson book, one in which the heroine would be properly married off, and Nellie obliged with Purple Springs. Published in 1921, it was her first novel in eleven years. One reviewer described it as "a rather melodramatic piece of moderately good fiction,"[23] while another, a little more charitable, called it "a sweet story for fifteen-year-olds."[24]

For Nellie, writing Purple Springs must have been like a holiday

— a chance to get reacquainted with the Watsons and return to the sunny mood of Manitou. She also managed to relive the excitement of the Manitoba suffrage campaign by getting Pearlie involved. In Purple Springs, it was Miss Watson who played the premier in the "women's parliament" and with even greater effect than Nellie had had in real life. In the novel, it took only another week for the suffrage party to gain power. "The night of the election, women paraded the streets, singing and cheering, mad with joy," Pearlie reported; "it made my eyes blur to see them."[25] Nellie's eyes must have blurred too with the joy of reliving her triumph.

Writing fiction was her first love. How could she give it up for politics? "Could it be that she [like Pearlie] was being called of God to be a leader in a new crusade against injustice? Was it her part to speak for other women?"[26] Yes, perhaps it was. She ran for election, she said, only after "very careful and reluctant consideration, because she could foresee a chance of serving women more than in the past."[27] Her two main issues in the campaign were the familiar ones of prohibition — she wanted to see the liquor legislation more tightly enforced — and women's rights.

When the last vote had been cast on 18 July 1921, Nellie L. McClung, Liberal, was among the winning candidates. But the results were not all satisfactory. Her party had been turned out of office by the upstart United Farmers of Alberta, who would form the new government. Nellie would sit in opposition with thirteen other Liberals. Any hopes she may have had of picking up where she'd left off in Manitoba, by moving into the cabinet, were gone and, as it turned out, gone for good.

Still, she had won a seat in the Alberta Legislature, something only three other women had ever accomplished. At the age of forty-seven, she was launched upon a new career.

Letter from a friend, 1921

It certainly speaks well for your powers of electoral fascination that you can transplant your political successes within a period of a few years, from Manitoba to Alberta.[28]

Agnes C. Laut, 1921

. . . when I heard she was likely to go into political life, I wanted her to go into the federal arena rather than the provincial. I considered she was needed more in the federal arena than the provincial. . . .

I talked this . . . over with Mrs. McClung. She would not hear of going into the federal arena. Do you know why? Because she said her first duty was to her home and she could serve in Alberta and not leave her home, when she could not so serve in Ottawa. She did not want to leave home while her youngest boy still needed a mother's constant care and love.[29]

Nellie L. McClung, 1928

I wish to say that I believe I have spent more hours in my own home than the average women, for I do not play bridge, I am not a habitual attender of teas or dances, and I rarely go out in the evening. But still I get 'phone calls like this: "Is that W4717? Is Mrs. McClung home, by any chance?" To which I reply: "She is at home, though it is not by chance, it is by deliberate design, and what can I do for you?" It's good fun to hear the sudden scamper to cover; they seem to think I come home only when every place else is closed.[30]

Mark McClung, 1975

My mother used to pay a great deal of attention to me. I was, I think, thoroughly spoiled and loved every minute of it. . . .

Well, now, what was daily life like [around 1921]? When I came down to breakfast in the morning, I would find my mother and father there, at the table. They were very much early to bed, early to rise people. My father would be making his way through a great big breakfast, but my mother wasn't eating. She was reading the daily paper to him — the morning paper. . . . And my mother wasn't content to read the news, she proclaimed the news, she declaimed the news, she exclaimed the news. . . . It was always politics. She never paid any attention to the sports pages, or the social pages . . . [unless they] had to do with women. . . . But she would talk about whatever was happening in Edmonton politics, Alberta politics, Dominion politics, the League of Nations, whatever it was. And . . . she really poured it out with great conviction. She would rattle the paper . . . with indignation or with pleasure, and those tiny hands of hers were very expressive. She would make them into fists and she would shake them when she was really moved. So, you know, you started the day with the feeling of participating in the world. I can't think of a better way to express it to you. This was my mother, and I thought that all other small boys in Edmonton were growing up in the same sort of home. Of course, they weren't.

I don't want to leave you with the impression that my mother was always in high emotional gear. She certainly wasn't. So I'll go on from breakfast to lunch. When I came home from school again, my mother and my father would be at the table. After lunch, [and] this was not an occasional thing, it happened almost all the time . . . my father would stretch out on the chesterfield, and my mother would read to him. This was in 1921-23 and I was just between ten and twelve, so I didn't pay too much attention to what was going on.

Back to school. Then I'd come home, after three or four o'clock, and I'd find different situations. Because my mother was then a member of . . . [the Legislative Assembly], she had a secretary. She always had a voluminous correspondence but now she had to have a secretary. These women were always friends of hers from the different women's groups. Some of them were civil servants, some of them were stenographers, and some of them, sometimes, young women from my father's office who were supporters of hers. . . . Well, she'd be dictating, and when I came home from school, she would always stop. "How did school go? How is everything going?", with this warmth of welcome. She had a den on the second floor of the house with a natural fuel fireplace in it. It was a very cozy room — books on three sides, filing cabinets and always a rocking chair.

Or, I would find my mother, seated at the dining room table, with other women, and books and files and newspaper clippings and all other sorts of things. I would be brought in and introduced to these women. I was carefully disciplined in how to greet these people, none of this "Hiya babe, how are you?" nonsense for my mother. I always had to be perfectly polite and proper and correct. Then I would run off to play. Again we came to dinner. After dinner, there was always family prayer. And my father read from the family Bible, which I now have. It was always a chapter or a psalm or something like that. . . . And then, we would say The Lord's Prayer, and there was my father at the head of the table. . . .

I said that my mother was a person who liked repose. When after dinner and after prayers and so on, time would come for me to go to bed — well you can imagine what the inducement was. "Go to bed and mother will read to you." Oh, she read everything you should read to a child. Fairy stories, Robert Louis Stevenson's poems . . ., all sorts of Bible stories, adventure stories, Kipling, and so on. So, off I would go to sleep. . . .

Life was not entirely sweetness and light, and I disappointed my mother on at least two occasions, and confession being good for the soul, I'll tell you about [one of] them. I used to earn an allowance by performing certain chores. My two chief chores were to look after my dog, Pal, and make sure that he had his food at noon and his water . . . [dish] filled up. My mother then had quite a big dish pan (it was like a baking pan) that she put out in the back on 123 Street. It was a kind of feeding station for the birds, and I was to keep this filled up. Well, one day I was going out the front door of the house, and I heard my mother's voice say, "Mark, have you looked after Pal and the birds?" Well, the devil spoke to me, and he said, "Tell your mother that you have." I did, and I knew that I had told a big lie, not a little white lie, but a great big black one. Then the devil said to me, "Run around the house. Look after the birds and look after the dog and your mother won't be any the wiser." Well, the devil did not reckon with my mother — this tiny figure — up on top of the steps. "You lied to me." This was it. "You lied to me," her face was white. There were tears in her eyes, and she gave me the soundest homily you could ever give to any person on the importance of truth telling. I can't recall a single word — and my record for veracity is not unblemished, by any means — but at least I had the right doctrine to begin with. Years later, when I was reading philosophy in university, I read an essay, celebrated among philosophers, by the great Immanuel Kant, called, "On a supposed duty to tell lies from benevolent motives." Well, my mother, I am sure, never read a word of Kant, but she had it all in her, and out it came. Then it was all over. No punishments, nothing at all, no thrashing at all, but I'd had it with this display of anger. . . .

This is my mother. This diminutive creature totally aroused over some moral issue. It really was a formidable spectacle, I can assure you. I can understand why people didn't particularly like to encounter her on the public platform when she was in full spate. . . .

My perception of my mother was strengthened [at this time] by her taking me to the Legislative Assembly. I used to sit up in the gallery and I could see my mother down there with all these men. She would get up and bow to the speaker, and she would say something and there would be a little applause from the little Liberal rump that was left. Not much applause from the other side, of course. But I was much impressed — that was my mother down there. So, you know, gradually, it was brought home to me that there was something very special about my mother.[31]

IN THE LEGISLATURE

Nellie L. McClung, 1945

Dr. J. S. State, who sat for a small constituency in the north was my left-hand neighbor in the seating arrangement [in the Legislature]. He was one of the oldest members in the House and had served the scattered population of his constituency for many years. He was not a believer in having women in public offices, and I found out that he was very angry at having been placed beside me; to have to sit beside a woman was something he thought he would never be called upon to do so he had gone to the assistant clerk of the House demanding that his seat be changed. Mr. Andison persuaded him to try it out for a day or two; someone had to sit beside me, and I might not be so bad. Then the tactful Mr. Andison told me many things about the old doctor, his devotion to his people, and mentioned casually that he was a masterhand at puzzles. I did not know anything about his objections to sitting beside me, but I wondered why Mr. Andison spent so much time building him up. I acted upon the suggestion regarding the puzzles and the old man and I became friends over a problem of making squares with matches. When he found out that I was interested in puzzles the whole problem was quickly solved, and I was careful not to work the puzzles too quickly for I knew he would like me better if I were slightly dumb and honesty compels me to add that I did not need to do much pretending for the old man had some tough ones.[32]

Nellie L. McClung, 1945

I was not a good party woman, and I'm sure there were times when I was looked upon with disfavor. I could not vote against some of the government measures which seemed to me to be right and proper, and I tried to persuade my fellow members that this was the right course to pursue. I believed that we were the executive of the people and should bring our best judgment to bear on every question, irrespective of party ties.[33]

Newspaper report, 1926

...if there is one member...who has consistently sounded the chimerical slogan of "keep politics out of the Legislature," that member is Mrs. Nellie McClung.[34]

Nellie L. McClung, 1945

I enjoyed the five years I served as a member of the Legislative Assembly; but looking back at it now I cannot see that much remains of all our strivings. Mrs. Irene Parlby, of Alix, was a member of the cabinet and I was in the opposition, but we united our forces when questions relating to women were under discussion.[35]

Newspaper report, 1922

Women Legislators Are Aroused Over Suggestion That Wives
    Should Not Displace Workers in Need of a Job

Dr. Stewart [Conservative, Lethbridge] raised the question of allowing married women whose husbands were earning a good living wage, to take positions [of employment] . . . except in times like the war when other labor was scarce. He cited cases where women in these comfortable circumstances lived in suites and held positions when married men with families were out of work.

Mrs. Parlby was plainly incensed at the suggestion and declared in protest that women were being recognized as on an equality with men in regard to laws, and in a free country no man should be allowed to legislate in such a discriminatory way against women. She thought if male legislators of the past had given more thought to the right of women workers such an act as the . . . minimum wage measure [then before the Assembly] would have been in effect long ago.

"It is strange that in spite of the progress of the last few years the impression still exists among men that every woman should be a housekeeper," remarked Mrs. Nellie McClung (Liberal) Edmonton, the other lady member of the house. . . . "Let women follow the calling they desire for I venture to say that ninety percent of the women want to be housekeepers. But if a woman likes to teach school in preference to housekeeping and her conditions permit, then by all means let her teach school."[36]

SOCIAL ISSUES

Nellie had always insisted that it was women's responsibility to see that spiritual welfare kept pace with material development, and she was correspondingly selective about the issues she took up as M.L.A. Her male colleagues could quarrel for days about highways or game laws or freight rates and seldom provoke her to speak. But as soon as a question of social policy came up, she was quick to take the floor.

Although she was elected to represent Edmonton, Nellie defined her constituency as women and children throughout the province. She had a special sympathy for those in remote areas. For them she wanted more traveling libraries and "nursing housekeepers" who would come into the home during childbirth or serious illnesses. (Obviously, she hadn't forgotten what it was like to be a pioneer.) She was also concerned, as ever, about the "unfortunates": there should be occupational training for female prisoners, she said, and payment for male inmates who worked, so they could help support their families while in jail.[37] She resisted government attempts to reduce the allowances paid to needy widows and deserted wives who were raising their children alone. If anything were to be cut, she suggested on more than one occasion, it should not be the already skimpy welfare allocations but the M.L.A.'s stipend of $2,000 a year.[38] Needless to say, she didn't get far with that, though she did get the government to promise that the mothers' allowances would not be reduced.

If anyone had cared to make the attempt, it would have been easy for them to predict when Nellie would speak up and what position she'd take.[39] She objected to the minimum wage act, for example, because it didn't provide for women on the administrative board and criticized a plan to deprive widows who remarried of pension benefits earned by their first husbands.[40] She wanted equal pay for male and female magistrates — it turned out that the women's wage was only one third of the men's![41] And no one could have been surprised when she supported a bill permitting unmarried mothers to sue the father of the child for maintenance,[42] nor when she championed revisions to the dower act on behalf of women who had "trouble with their husbands." (At that time, any woman who left her husband automatically lost all claim to the matrimonial property, regardless of her reason for moving out.)[43] On this last issue, as on most of the others which she took up during her term of office, she was not successful.

Many of the causes which Nellie espoused as M.L.A. were seven-day wonders. She'd become interested in something — whether it was dower law reform or a government plan to stop sponsoring the Women's Institutes or an act to raise the age of consent for marriage from fifteen to sixteen — burn and seethe over it for a while, and then let it drop.[44] That was the way the game was played. Questions cycled through the House until they were defeated or passed, and that was that.

There was only one subject which came up during her term of office which Nellie was not content to leave to the Legislative routine, and that subject was the repeal of prohibition. Scarcely had she taken her seat in the Assembly in 1922, before Bob Edwards, the newly elected Independent from Calgary, was proposing that the sale of beer be legalized, not in order to kill prohibition but to make it work, he said. "The only wealthy people today are the bootleggers," Edwards told the Legislature; "they drive around in a big 'whiskey six' and are rolling in money. Whiskey is not hard to get hold of because good beer is hard to get hold of. No sane man would drink bad whiskey if he could get good beer, and if the government would allow this, the liquor laws would be obeyed."[45]

The Legislature laughed appreciately at Edwards's wit, but Nellie was not amused. Yes, she knew that the liquor law was not well enforced. But this didn't mean it was a bad law; it simply meant that the government was not wholehearted in its attempts to catch lawbreakers. And it certainly didn't mean that people should be allowed to drink beer. Did the Legislature want to be held responsible for mortalities from "beer heart"? Alberta might go the way of Munich, Nellie warned, where one-sixteenth of the population was said to die of this beer-drinkers' disease.[46]

The failure of the government to police the liquor act effectively was alarming. "If a law is bad the way to bring about its repeal is to enforce it, — the way to make a good law unpopular is not to enforce it," and Nellie could see that the violations were souring people against prohibition.[47] But she also insisted that, even allowing for the offenders, prohibition was a decided success.

> The greatest improvement is seen, of course, in the home of the man who drank. Now, he brings his wages home, and comes home himself. Crime has decreased eighty percent, arrests for drunkenness have practically disappeared, jails have become empty, and inebriate farms have been sold because there were no inebriates to be cared for. . . .
>
> The greatest increase in trade has been in the departments of women's and children's clothes. Butchers also state that they sell more meat, even under advanced prices, than they did before, which suggests a pleasant picture of a whole family enjoying a good dinner, instead of one member leaning over the polished bar, and hearing the gentleman bar-keep say "What is yours, Sir?"[48]

Or, as she put it in another article, prohibition might be "quite hard on a few of the men, but the women and children are not saying a word against it!"[49]

When the United Farmers government was elected in 1921, Nellie had not been downhearted, even though it had meant the defeat of her own party. The U.F.A. had a reputation for being "strong prohibitionists" and had come to power partly on a platform of better law enforcement. "It is the general opinion that the thirsty ones, or they who would turn thirst into money, have nothing to hope for from the Farmers," Nellie had reported in an article about the election results.[50] Her opinion seemed to be confirmed in 1922 when the government appointed a clergyman to oversee the liquor act and laughed off Bob Edwards's beer-sale proposals.

But the next year, she began to have doubts about the United Farmers' sincerity. Towards the end of January 1923, the Legislature received a 51,000-name petition sponsored by the hotelmen, asking for a referendum on the licensed sale of beer in Alberta. Operating under the banner of the Moderation League, the anti-prohibitionists had attracted followers by posing as the defenders of the family. People were being forced to drink in private, in their homes, the argument went, where women and children could become corrupted. Basically, their line was the same as Bob Edwards's had been: by legalizing the sale of beer the government would do away with the illegal, clandestine consumption of bootleg liquor.[51]

The effect of this argument was augmented by mass frustration about the "unenforceable" liquor law and a shift in the public temper since the war. People were no longer in the mood for high-minded moral crusades. As Nellie put it, there was a "tendency in the people toward more liberty and disrespect for law." It was a "defiant age."[52] Under these circumstances, the "wets" had no trouble at all in gathering more than enough signatures to force the government to hold a referendum on the beer-sale question. They were preparing to use the same Direct Legislation Act under which prohibition had been brought in.

After a committee of the Legislature had studied the petition and come to the conclusion it was in order, the government apparently thought it had no choice but to acquiesce. Nellie was horrified: the first "huff" from the liquor trade had left the government in collapse. But Nellie and her temperance allies were made of sturdier stuff: they were passionately determined to sabotage the hotelmen's scheme. If it meant checking every single one of the 51,000 names on the petition for irregularities, they were prepared to do so.[53]

Newspaper headline, 1923

MRS. NELLIE M'CLUNG
FINDS MANY HOLES IN PETITION[54]

Nellie L. McClung, 1923

The Monster Beer Petition lies in state, in its cool, chaste, gray casket, in the Executive Council Room, secured with a brass pad-lock. Each constituency has its own petition neatly encased in a folder of buff paper with the name typed on a white slip, pasted on the edge. Everything on the outside is neat, clean, orderly, and business-like; —

A closer examination reveals much of human interest. . . . We gather from . . . [the petition's] world-weary appearance, that it has lain on restaurant tables and barber's chairs and furnished a resting place for the transient fly; tea has been spilled on it. It has been used to wipe up soup, and other liquids. Some pages are even blood-stained, opening to the imagination a whole series of thrilling, creepy episodes with the true western atmosphere. . . .

It deserves special attention too, because of its national character. Although it is an Alberta petition, it has enlisted the sympathy of many who dwell beyond our borders. Well-wishers from Manitoba, and Saskatchewan, one or two from Vancouver and Ontario, have set their hand to it, and their names have been duly counted as electors of Alberta, and the obliging canvasser takes oath at the bottom of some of the pages that he was present, and saw the signature put on, and they are all genuine. — Indeed the canvassers have done even more than we have any right to expect canvassers to do. They have in many cases written the names of the petitioners, whole pages of them, telling in perfect form, their occupations and address, and doing it all with charming frankness, untainted by duplicity, or deceit. There is no low attempt at disguised handwriting.

The canvassers have evidently had a free hand, not only in writing the names but also in circulating these petitions; and they suited their appeal to suit the individual case, which is really the vital element in good salesmanship. . . . When approaching temperance people, the petition was presented as a temperance petition, a simon-pure, bone dry movement, to put the bootlegger where he belongs: — This was especially used for women, and if they still hesitated about signing, an appeal was made to them to "Save the boys!" — which always brought results. . . .

From all we can learn, no copy of the act, was carried by the canvassers. . . . They showed great wisdom there, too, for there are certain clauses in the proposed act, such as the one providing for bar-maids, that might create unfavorable discussion, and discussion is always more or less dangerous on these questions.

The clerk of the executive council, who is also the clerk of elections, gave it as his opinion that only pages with a proper petition heading, should be counted, and he was especially emphatic in saying that the usual heading on a page of a hotel register does not constitute a legal heading even though it asks for the name and address, and number of room in which the guest reposes, and also the hour at which he desires to be called. This ruling, if followed, would throw out almost every petition for not more than one-quarter of the pages had the proper heading; —

The committee of women who undertook the gigantic task of looking over the petitions made copies of more than half of them, and sent them back to their constituencies to be examined locally, and the reports were all of the character. The petition showed names of minors, visitors, strangers, dead men, absentees, non-British subjects, duplicate names, fictitious names, illegible names. Of course, there are good names mixed with these. In every case it was reported back that many signed believing it to be a temperance act, as it claims to be. . . .[55]

Newspaper report, 1923

As a prohibitionist, . . . [Mrs. McClung] felt it would be a good thing to let the measure go to the polls, for she felt sure it would be defeated and would thus tie up the beer question for another three years. But the petition was so irregular that for the house to allow it to go to the country would be subversive of law and order, claimed Mrs. McClung.[56]

THE "DESOLATE PROPOSITION"

It was all to no avail. Nellie stood alone in the Legislature. The other members could not be persuaded that enough of the signatures were questionable to invalidate the petition. The number of names was far in excess of what was required under the Direct Legislation Act. On the Edmonton lists, for example, three-quarters of the names might have been rejected and still have left a surplus.[57] *No sensible politician would consider throwing the petition out on a technicality when it obviously had massive public support.*

If Nellie was upset that a vote was to be held, she was even more alarmed by the wording of the ballot. Instead of asking the people for a verdict on the licensed beer bar, as the hotelmen had asked, the government was offering four options: prohibition, the licensed sale of beer, government sale of beer for private consumption, and government sale of all hard liquor plus licensed sale of beer. Here was a government which had always made a big fuss about its opposition to the liquor traffic offering the enemy more than it had asked! The ballot was "a desolate, deadly, ghastly proposition," Nellie warned, but no one heeded her.[58]

The plebiscite was set for the summer of 1923, and by May, Nellie was already gearing up for the battle. "We are tired of campaigns," she confessed to a Women's Institute convention held that month, but she was in good form all the same.[59] There were three classes of people who wanted the liquor laws changed, she told one of her audiences — the drinking men, the liquor profiteers, and those who believed that "the sale of beer and wine would lessen drunkenness, drive the bootlegger into insolvency, cause the law to be upheld and peace and happiness to dwell with us once more."

> I do not doubt the sincerity [of the latter] but I seriously question their intelligence. — How they can believe that a freer sale of intoxicants can lessen intoxication, — grows more strange, the more one thinks of it. — Bernard Shaw, in desperation, declared in one of his speeches that he believed the other planets were using this one, as their insane asylum; — and the fact that there are still people who light a fire with gasoline seems to argue for the contention. But what can we say of people who believe that a fire can be put out with gasoline? — That the remedy for drunkenness is more liquor, freely accessible for everyone, is much the same quality of reasoning.[60]

Nellie was in fighting trim, so she must have been disappointed when events prevented her from playing an active part in the referendum campaign. On the day of the vote, she was in Banff nursing Wes, who had fallen seriously ill. "It was a case where duties conflicted," she later explained, "and I chose the one which was the nearest and highest."[61]

As things turned out, it was also a prudent choice, for Wes recovered under her care, but nothing could have saved prohibition. It wouldn't have made a bit of difference if she'd lectured and crusaded night and day. No one could have stemmed the tide. In 1915 the men had decided to turn off the taps; in 1923 the men and the women together chose to turn them on again, and Nellie allowed herself to grieve.

Nellie L. McClung, 1924

I find it hard to be a pessimist but by no jugglery of words can we claim to have gone forward in the matter of liquor legislation. We have slipped — we have failed — we have gone back and no one who has made an intelligent study of the question, and can see the question without prejudice, can have any feeling but sorrow. . . .

Here is a case where we have to start again at the beginning. We thought we had a sound foundation; the sincere kindness of the human heart, the instinct which is in the strong to protect the weak, but apparently we were too optimistic. We will have to begin again to cultivate in the young the social conscience. We may get another chance, I do not know. The nation which deliberately chooses the path of self indulgence and appetite does not always get a second chance, Babylon, Rome, Greece laughed at the "sore heads" who warned them that they were pursuing the path which would lead to destruction. I do not profess to know God's plans for the race but I do know that when one nation fails to accept the challenge of life the opportunity passes to another. We cannot read history without getting this pretty well pounded into us. . . .

As for the prohibition people; our way lies plain before us. We are not downhearted and we are not beaten. There will come a great change in public sentiment in a very few years. Wait until our people see what it means to have liquor with all its deadly fascination easily accessible. The heart of humanity is still tender. It will not be content to let the powers of evil reign. NO! We are not downhearted.

We will summon to our hearts the grim courage which the old Highland Warrior cried out for in his hour of seeming defeat.

> "And will you fail?" Sir Andrew cried;
> "Come on my merry men.
> We'll lie us down and bleed awhile
> And then we'll fight again."[62]

A SECOND DEFEAT

Nellie did not allow herself to "bleed" for long. By the time the 1924 session of the Legislature opened she was ready to fight. One of her first official acts after the Assembly began was to lay into the United Farmers for their "fair weather advocacy of prohibition." A dry Alberta was bound to come again, she prophesied, but in the meantime, the "black hand" of the liquor traffic would be at work throughout the province and all because the Farmers had given in without a fight. "She regretted that the government had failed to carry out its convention promises to prohibition, and warned them that in adopting a [new] liquor act they were paying too great a price for political success."[63]

The only member of the government whom Nellie exempted from her condemnation was Irene Parlby, who had worked hard for prohibition during the referendum campaign, but Mrs. Parlby did not appreciate the compliment. It was she who rose to defend the government from Nellie's bruising attack. "I know quite well that the gentlemen on this side of the House will be too chivalrous to answer Mrs. McClung as they would answer a man who had ventured to make such bitter statements," she said icily.[64]

"I wish to say that I do not claim any exemption from criticism in this house," Nellie replied in her next speech. "We are on an exact equality here, and if I spoke unfairly, or made a criticism which the members of the government can answer, I beg of them not to suffer it in silence. Remember Job and speak out!"[65]

Nellie recognized that there was not much scope for a prohibitionist like herself in the drafting of the liquor control act, but she made a few suggestions nonetheless. Of the four options on the referendum ballot, the voters had chosen the most liberal — government sale of liquor and the licensed sale of beer. That meant that in addition to beer bars, Alberta would have government-run liquor stores. These retail outlets should be run on a nonprofit basis, Nellie maintained, because any earnings would be "accursed money," but the proceeds from the sale of liquor permits ("clean money") should go toward welfare and old-age pensions.[66] In addition, she asked the government to put some of its profits into providing temperance education right in the barrooms and liquor stores. "One of the great difficulties about temperance education is that it is so hard to get it over to the people who need it . . . ," she told the government. "The people who need it will not come to a temperance meeting; but they will go to your stores. Will you tell them there by advertising on your walls the scientific truth about alcohol and its effect on the user?"

"If you want my services," she pledged, "I will gladly agree to write your posters for you free of charge as long as I live in Alberta and the government stores exist."[67]

Most of all, Nellie wanted the Legislature to outlaw liquor ads. "The foaming schooner of beer in seductive advertising had even tempted her to fall, on blazing hot days, she admitted."[68]

Nellie's views carried virtually no weight with the government, which opted not only to run the stores at a profit but to legalize liquor *advertising. These decisions gave her "the jolt of her life," for they proved to her satisfaction that the government was in the liquor business simply for the money.[69] It paid no attention to her pleas that the ill-gotten revenue be spent on treatment centers for drunks and for their offspring, amongst whom Nellie expected to find a high proportion of "feeble-minded."*

If the government seemed to have sold out its principles, Nellie stood resolutely by hers, whatever the political costs. When an election was called in 1926, she again ran on a platform of women's rights and prohibition. By this time, she, Wes, and their younger sons had moved to Calgary (the older children had left home for employment, marriage, or university.) Once again, Nellie was following the demands of Wes's career rather than her own. "When the big decisions had to be made about what was going to be done," Mark McClung recalls, "where we were going to move and so on, these were always . . . [dad's] decisions. After all, he worked for the Manufacturers' Life and when they said you're going to move from Winnipeg to Edmonton or Edmonton to Calgary or Calgary to Victoria, that was it. My mother went along. There was no objection."[70] The move to Calgary had meant that Nellie was home only on weekends; now it forced her to contest the 1926 election on an unpopular issue and on unfamiliar ground — with predictable results.

If Nellie blamed herself for her electoral defeat, she didn't admit it in public. An entry in one of her notebooks sets forth her position on self-reproach: "Last night I wakened up remembering things I had forgotten and broke out in a perspiration of remorse and self-condemnation. I did feel so mean, but I gathered myself together, and reasoned it out that I was doing as well as I could and running to capacity. More important than keeping friends with the neighbors is to keep friends with yourself. I will not put the hard word on myself."[71] And so she was able to bear her setbacks with a certain measure of grace.

Nellie L. McClung, about 1926

I have read, with deep interest, of how great men have received the news of defeat — in their own homes surrounded by a few friends. Silent, dignified, serene, uttering no word of regret or dismay. Faces just a trifle pale, yet lightened by valiant cheerfulness — and at a late hour, when all hope was dead, and the wires of condolence began to trickle in, growing suddenly tired of it all, the great man bids his friends an affectionate good night, and goes heavily up the broad stairs, the light from the upper newel post falling full on his noble face, and showing the lines of care — and the friends below disperse quietly, murmuring something about one of whom the world was not worthy.

And so to bed!

We did not do it that way.

We all gathered in the committee rooms, which the night before had echoed with our laughter, our foolish boasts, and idle words, and before us on the wall a great blackboard bore the leering figures — that lurched and staggered before our eyes, changed every few minutes by one of the campaign managers. We were all frantically cheerful, but it was about as merry as an empty bird-cage. With sickly smiles abounding, seen and unseen, we sang "See him smiling" and "There's a long, long trail," and speeches were made, and everyone did their best, but there is no denying the fact that there was an outcropping of gloom in the exercises of the evening. By ten o'clock we knew that one of our members was elected, one was defeated; and I was hovering between life and death. We knew that the counting would take all night, and some of the faithful ones were determined to see it through, but I was ready to call it a day about eleven o'clock, and leaving my political fate in the hands of the scrutineers, I came home, and slept until I heard the clip-clop of the milk man's horses, and the clinking of bottles on the back step, and through the open window I could see the crystal dawn leading in another day. Then I remembered the unfinished business of the night before and before consulting the telephone, I looked out of the window for a while. It was so dewy green, and pleasant, and peaceful, with the shadows of the big trees making black lace medallions on the lawn.

The voice in the telephone was announcing the names of the elected candidates.

No! mine was not among them. There were five elected. I stood sixth. Just for a moment I had a queer detached sensation, a bewildered, panicky feeling, and in that dizzy fragment of time, it came home to me that for all my philosophy and cheerful talk, I had never really believed I would be defeated — but now . . . now . . . the boat had actually sailed — without me.

But just like David in his grief, the mood quickly passed. Why should I go mourning all my days. My political hopes had died in the night! What of it? They were not the only hopes.

My family behaved admirably at breakfast, even the youngest one, who is at the age when it is rather embarrassing to have a mother of any sort, and particularly so, to have one that goes out and gets herself defeated.

Thinking of the many women who would be disappointed, and men too, was the heaviest part of my regret. I knew how hard many of them had worked. I told myself over and over again that I did not mind. I suppose it does not require much fortitude to accept a stone wall . . . Anyway I made a fine show of cheerfulness, and felt it too.

But though I went about quite light-heartedly and gay, telling myself and others how fine it felt to be free, and of how glad I was that I could go back to my own work with a clear conscience, there must have been some root of bitterness in me, for I was seized with a desire to cook, and I wanted the kitchen all to myself.

No woman can be utterly cast down, who has a nice, bright, blue and white kitchen facing the west, with a good gas range, and blue and white checked linoleum on the floor (even if it is beginning to wear on the highways and market roads), a cook book, oil cloth covered and dropsical with loose-leaf additions, and the few odd trifles needed to carry out the suggestions.

I set off at once on a perfect debauch of cooking. I grated cheese, stoned dates, blanched almonds, whipped cream, set jelly — and let the phone ring!

It could tear itself out by the roots for all I cared. I was in another world, the pleasant, land-locked, stormless haven of double-boilers, jelly moulds, flour sifters and other honest friends who make no promise they cannot carry through. . . .

I am ashamed to have to tell it. But I got more comfort that day out of my cooking orgy than I did from either my philosophy or religion. . . . I think I could not have endured it if my biscuits had been heavy, or my date trifle tough, or the pie crust burnt on the bottom. Nothing failed me. And no women can turn out an ovenful of flaky pies, crisply browned, and spicily odorous, and not find peace for her troubled soul! . . .

The next day I wanted to get out. I craved free life, and fresh air; open fields and open sky. I wanted to look away to the mountains, blue in the distance, with the ice-caps on their heads. So I went to Earl Grey golf course, and played all morning. . . .

The game was not entirely successful. I was too conscious of the Elbow Park houses below me; some of them vaguely resentful; some overbearingly exultant; and others leering at me with their drawn blinds, like half closed conservative eyes. I tried to concentrate on the many good friends I have there, but someway the wires were crossed, the notes were jangled, and not a gleam of friendliness could I raise.

I got on better, and did some splendid driving by naming the balls, and was able by that means to give one or two of them a pretty powerful poke.

I played each morning, and at the end of three days I saw that my spiritual health was restored — I was able then to dispassionately discuss the whole matter. . . .

I know how it happened that I was defeated. Not enough people wanted to have me elected! So there is no mystery about it — nothing that needs explanation.

But just why I thought I would be elected is a human interest story:

I believe every candidate, who ran, believed in his own success. Hope springs eternal, and friends see to it that it does. Prior to election day, friends fairly bubble with enthusiasm. They haven't a doubt or a fear in the world! They tell you the enemy concedes your election! The bets are all on you! . . .

. . . a few friends full of enthusiasm can create quite an impression. Mine appeared like an army with banners. I should have remembered that there was nothing remarkable, or significant, about this. Everyone has some friends. The blackboards, in front of the filling stations carried a wise word the other day. They said, —

"Even cotton stockings have their supporters!"

I might have known the liquor interests do not forgive the people who oppose them. Temperance people will forget their friends, and cheerfully forgive their enemies at election time, but the liquor people are more dependable. Some of them spoke to me about my stand on prohibition, and told me quite frankly that if I would put the soft pedal on the liquor question they would vote for me.

And I didn't. And they didn't! And there are no hard feelings between us. . . .

But far more bitter and unyielding was the opposition of the conservative element (my own party is not entirely free from it), that resents the invasion of women. Public offices, particularly those that carry emoluments, they believe to belong, by the ancient right of possession, to men. They are quite willing to let women work on boards, or committees, or indeed anywhere if the work is done gratuitously — but if there is a salary, they know at once that women are not fitted by nature for that! And God never intended them to be exposed to the dangers and temptations incident to such a post.

The dangers and temptations incident to office-cleaning at night, which is done by women, and the lonely homeward walk, in the early morning when there are no cars running, is not so bad, for the work is sufficiently ill-paid to keep it quite womanly.

And the curious part of this is that women can be found who will support this view. Not many — and not thinking women — just a few who bitterly resent having any woman go farther than they are ever likely to go.

Another feature, which works against any woman who runs for public office, is the subconscious antagonism of men who don't want to work with women. Men are subconsciously afraid of women! Afraid they will not play fair! No individual man is to blame — it is a racial trait, and will take a lot of working out. Men will work their fingers to the bone for women — but not with them.

And then, of course, opposing me were many wives! No one should criticise the wives! And I won't! I saw many of them on election day. One told me quite sweetly — "I don't know anything about this, but Charley is frightfully keen and told me to give out these cards, and say 'I hope you will vote our ticket' — It's all a beastly muddle to me — and bores me to tears!"

I thought of Mrs. Pankhurst and her heroic followers going to jail, and suffering the agonies of social ostracism, as well as physical cruelty, to win for women like these the right to vote, and with a less worthy emotion I thought of some of the efforts we had made here. I was like the young chap of five who denounced his one year old sister, when she displeased him, in these scathing words: "I am sorry I ever prayed for you!"

Oh, well!

Life has compensation for all of us. When one door shuts — another opens.

Basil King told us once, that the day he met with the accident that made it impossible to carry on his work as a clergyman, he bought a typewriter. I didn't need to buy one. All mine needed was a new ribbon.[72]

Nellie L. McClung, 1933

We learn by experience, but the best lesson we learn from either joy or sorrow is to pass on. . . . Take the minutes as read, and get on with the next order of business.[73]

CHAPTER NINE

OUR PRESENT DISCONTENTS

*. . . there is no use sitting by the dead ashes of
yesterday's fire. There are still battles to be
won — or lost.*

In 1926, the year of her defeat at the polls, Nellie turned fifty-three. "When I go back to Manitoba," she'd admitted a few years before, "one of my friends there always says — 'Nellie — you're getting stout!' Then hastily adds, knowing the tender sensibilities of those of us who go past a thirty-eight bust — 'But you're neat with it!' "

"So in this way," Nellie concluded, "I can bear up against the encroachments of age —"[1]

In fact, she had not yet begun to feel her age; in her estimation she'd barely entered "the middle years."[2] Her schedule of club work was as hectic as ever, with the Authors Association, Women's Press Club, Local Council of Women, Women's Canadian Club, and Woman's Missionary Society. She led a large Bible class at Wesley United Church and helped run a girls' club there. She'd organized a current-events discussion group for women. The W.C.T.U. and the Liberals still looked to her for help. Mackenzie King even wrote to suggest that she run in the 1930 federal election, avowing that he would rather see her "enter the lists" than find himself "secure in the next parliament by an acclamation arranged for by the two leaders."

"It would be a fine thing to have you in Parliament," he coaxed.[3]

The flattering warmth of King's invitation wasn't enough to lure Nellie into the fray. She was intent now on her writing. For a decade, events had conspired to keep her from her desk. There had been war work, prohibition campaigns, meetings, rallies, and finally politics. But Nellie was used to dealing with distractions, and she had managed to keep her hand in at fiction in spite of everything else that was going on.

("Interruptions do not matter unless we let them turn us aside from our purpose," she once explained to a friend.)[4] *It had sometimes been possible to snatch an hour and sneak off to the Legislature library or some other quiet corner where she could scribble away at a story. The result had been three books,* When Christmas Crossed "The Peace" *(1923),* Painted Fires *(1925), and* All We Like Sheep *(1926).*[5]

If any one piece of her writing could be considered the "typical" or "essential" Nellie McClung, it would have to be When Christmas Crossed "The Peace". *Like most of her stories, it was inspired by personal experience, in this case a speaking engagement in the Peace River Country. Wherever she went, she soaked up material for her books. "Life is full of stories," she enthused; "I see them every day, and wish I could write them all!"*

> *I am always coming home with bubbling enthusiasm over some new setting for a story that I have found. Just today, I thought of one, and when I outlined it to a male relative of mine — (not really a blood relation — just a connection by marriage) — he coldly remarked "If you did not spend so much time gathering settings for stories, but hatched some of those already gathered, it would be better for you."*[6]

Nellie sometimes maintained that she didn't have to "hatch" her stories at all: she just wrote down what she'd seen and heard, sometimes "smudging" things a little with her pen "to make it sound true."[7] *She was a natural-born listener, the kind of person whose manner invited confidences, and people were forever pouring out their life sagas for her sympathetic ear.*[8] *"I have a fatal gift for starting monologues," she once wrote in mock complaint. "If there is anywhere in my vicinity a vein of idle ore I will tap it as sure as fate with some innocent word. . . ."*

> *I can't take in the daily supply of ice from a perfectly new iceman without in some occult way opening up a conversational viaduct over which come heavy cargoes of domestic or social happenings! And the awful part of it is that, every time, when I find myself cut off and smothered in someone's tale of woe, I can see that I brought it on myself! Mine was the hand that struck the Match!*

"I know where my lost years have gone," she said, "and the manner of

their going! They have been talked away. . . ."[9] But in fact, as Nellie knew well, her years of talk were not lost time at all, for they had given her stories to tell.

In many cases, the material she gathered served only as a point of departure for her imagination. "I start my characters off and then watch them — and write it down."[10] That certainly seems to have been the case with When Christmas Crossed "The Peace". Scarcely more than a pamphlet, the little book contains all the characteristic elements of her fiction: feminism, temperance, and politics, together with plenty of surprises, an outrageous plot, and even zip and good humor to do a book twice its length. The heroine is a frontier nurse, "a quiet little golden-haired beauty," who, by masquerading as a policeman, manages to coerce the local bootlegger into spending his Christmas-cheer fund on goodies for the pleasure-starved women and children of the district, instead of on liquid refreshments. Everything ends happily, with a warm glow of satisfaction in the bootlegger's heart and the prospect of marriage between the nurse and a suitably charming policeman.

Some such happy or uplifting ending is an unvarying feature of Nellie's books. This was a matter of principle with her:

> I think a writer should above all things faithfully portray life, and because there are more decent people than the other kind, it is keeping nearer to the truth to write of those who go right, — rather than of those who go wrong — it is taking a mean advantage of the inoffensive reader to spring on him a story which depresses him or saddens him without purpose, weakens his faith in his fellowmen. — The reader can get enough of that in life — he does not need to buy a book to get it. A writer should play fair with the public.[11]

In her view, "it is a serious thing to put pen to paper. To have grace with words carries a responsibility" to instruct, to inspire, to amuse.[12] She had little patience with writers who disagreed with her on this point, for she knew from her own gloomy experience what it was like to read a depressing book. One day, for instance, while riding the train from Edmonton to Calgary, she'd labored over a "sordid, ugly tale" of small-town life. The contrast between the book and the real world had struck her so forcibly that she'd recorded her reactions in verse:

> . . . suddenly I turned against this vapid, empty lie,
> Which made of life a dismal thing; for, bold against the sky
> All blue and white the mountains stood, in silent majesty.

*All blue and white against the sky, the Rocky Mountains
stood,
A blush of green about their feet, where stands the ancient
wood.
I looked and thrilled, and knew again, that Life is always
good.*[13]

Of Nellie's own books, the one which sets out most energetically to
prove that "Life is always good" is Purple Springs, her 1921 offering
and the last of the Pearlie Watson stories. The problem of the novel is to
bring about Pearlie's marriage to her childhood idol, Dr. Clay. But the
doctor has just learned that he carries a mysterious, terminal disease and
gallantly refuses to burden young Pearl with a dying husband. Nellie
manages to get around this obstacle by inventing the magical springs of
the book's title, which offer a guaranteed cure for any and all ailments.
In the end, author and heroine can merrily chirp out a duet of "nothing
is too good to be true."

Painted Fires, which followed five years later, is much less
saccharine. All the same, its plot is difficult to take seriously. What can
one say about a book in which the villain is struck dead by lightning just
in time to prevent the hard-pressed heroine from doing him in? And that
is only one of the melodramatic coincidences which Nellie arranges to
ensure that events turn tidily and justice triumphs in the end.

What this novel, like Nellie's other stories, does have going for it is
its energy and strong female characters. From Pearlie Watson on, the
McClung heroines have had little in common with the sighing, insipid
ladies of Nellie's childhood storybooks. Painted Fires, for example,
centers on Finnish-born Helmi Milander, a resourceful and down-to-
earth young woman who brings her dignity with her through all the
vicissitudes of the plot. And poor Helmi does have her difficulties —
everything from unfair imprisonment to unemployment and single par-
enthood!

Nellie's purpose in writing Painted Fires had been to give a
sympathetic retelling of Canada's "immigration story": "I wanted to
portray the struggles of a young girl who found herself in Canada
dependent upon her own resources with everything to learn, including the
language," she explained.[14] It was a story she'd come to know at first
hand, in her own kitchen. Of all the maids the family had while Mark
was growing up, he could remember only one who was Canadian-born.
The others had come from Ireland, England, Norway, Finland, Sweden,

Hungary. Nellie treated them "like daughters," Mark recalled. "Two of them got married from our house in Calgary."[15]

During the pre-war settlement era, when unschooled immigrants were arriving by the boat load, most Canadians (Nellie included) had viewed them as a threat to social unity. Then, when war broke out, newcomers from enemy countries were subjected to additional suspicion as potential traitors. But away from the special conditions of the settlement period and the war, Nellie quickly set her misgivings aside. In succeeding decades, she would become an eager promoter of multicultural festivals. And in the forties, when Doukhobors and Orientals came in for public abuse, she was one of very few to plead with the public for tolerance.

Nellie recorded with pride that she had taught English to five of her immigrant housekeepers, and reporters loved to tell about the time she'd turned down a prestigious speaking engagement in order to take her new maid, Helga, to the Calgary Stampede.[16] On Sundays she willingly drove her helpers to church. ("I don't think any one of these girls ever said to my mother, 'I don't want to go to church,'" Mark admits. "I don't know what would have happened if she had."[17]) The McClungs' "girls" had the use of the parlor and a key to the front door, rights which were not often extended to the household help. "Little privileges like this help a girl to know that she is a person of importance with the protection and dignity of a family and a home."[18]

Nellie was convinced that housework had become unattractive to young working women because the conditions of employment were generally so poor. "Housework should be the most respected and valued of all the avenues open to women," she wrote in an article on "The Domestic Help Problem." "It is the real genuine simon pure woman's sphere that we hear about. . . ."[19] If women took themselves seriously, they would think well of those who did "women's work." Instead, many women treated their maids with callous contempt, refusing them the use of the family bathtub, exhausting them with busy work, cheating on their pay. Nellie diagnosed this as another sign of women's persistent lack of sympathy and respect for their own sex.

In the five or six years following her political defeat, Nellie put most of her writing energy into fiction. Her short stories, which she merrily produced at the rate of one a week, eventually filled two plump volumes, Be Good to Yourself (1930) and Flowers for the Living (1931). But now and then she took time to write something in a more reflective and analytical vein, as often as not about women and their failure to "live up" to their enfranchisement. Since her disillusionment *with "the wives" — and more particularly since the collapse of prohibition — she had watched her most radiant visions of the future fade and disappear. What had gone wrong with women? What had gone wrong with the world? It was a problem which would trouble her for as long as she lived.*

Nellie L. McClung, 1939

When I think what I expected from women's suffrage, I blush. . . .[20]

Nellie L. McClung, 1938

When women were given the vote in 1916-17 on the North American continent . . . we believed that enfranchisement meant emancipation. We spoke glibly of freedom. We were obsessed with the belief that we could cleanse and purify the world by law. We said women were naturally lovers of peace and purity, temperance and justice. There never has been a campaign like the suffrage campaign. It was a clear-cut issue. You were either with us or against us. We had all the arguments, and mixed with our zeal for public righteousness there was a definite content of animosity for those who opposed us. We did not think much of them. We saw them as obstacles to be removed. . . . We rejoiced over their discomfiture when victory came to us.

But when all was over, and the smoke of battle cleared away, something happened to us. Our forces, so well organized for the campaign, began to dwindle. We had no constructive program for making a new world. Even the church did not see that there was a great volume of power ready to be used. Indeed, the hostility of certain sections of the church to women's advancement drove many women away from religious organizations.

So the enfranchised women drifted. Many are still drifting.[21]

Nellie L. McClung, 1927

Some women are foolishly studying ten thousand ways of appearing busy, but not having great success. Bridge absorbs some, but even those who sit in a game five afternoons a week are conscious that bridge does not make a real heart-warming, soul-consuming, life-work. Intensive child culture is a popular occupation for some, and if the child — (there is usually only one) — is strong enough to endure the mother's perpetual vigilance and care,

she — the mother — can feel she has an occupation for some
years. . . .

But a great many women . . . are wandering in a maze of
discontent and disillusionment. Idle hands, and empty minds make
an explosive mixture. Having little to do they do nothing; and doing
nothing they miss that sense of work well done which sustained their
grandmothers.[22]

Nellie L. McClung, 1930

Man cannot live in idleness and grow,
I wish he could. I wish it might be so.
I'm sure when Adam lived in Eden's bowers
Wooed by the birds, and comforted by flowers,
He wished it too, and liked the way of getting
All that he wanted without toil or fretting.
That was the life! No worry, toil, or sorrow;
No thinking of that tiresome thing — tomorrow.
Too bad it did not last; the serpent came
And Adam fell, and great has been his blame.
I'm not so sure! Perhaps the snake was wise;
The fall of Adam may have been his rise!
The only creatures that can live in ease
Day after day, and not be hurt, are these:
The long-haired Persian — and the Pekinese![23]

Nellie L. McClung, 1931

That there . . . [have] always been some idle, self-indulgent men
and women, we all know. That that class has increased in numbers
in the years following the war, we may as well admit also; and for
that increase everyone has a theory. I believe the increase can be
traced to a lack of religion and the abuse of social drinking.[24]

Nellie L. McClung, about 1925

. . . a month ago . . . I went to speak to a Parent-Teachers'
Association. . . . I knew before I went in what my audience would be
like. We know now not to expect many of the smartly dressed young
women, mothers of one. They had passed me, as I came, in their cars
on the way to the tea dansant at the hotel. They have not thought of
joining a P.T.A., just as they have not thought of joining a plumbers'

union. It simply does not interest them. The women who attended that afternoon, were serious minded, kind, motherly women, middle aged, mostly church women driven by a sense of duty. They enjoy the work, too, in a sort of high minded detached way. . . .

After I had spoken there was the customary vote of thanks, and then the principal spoke. He was a gray little man, in tweeds, with a scholarly stoop, and thick glasses. He liked what I said. But there was one fear in his mind. Women's organizations were being overdone. The home was the thing! and it was being neglected. The deeply set gray eyes, behind the thick glasses, foresaw dangers — late meals, milk bottles not set out at night, clocks not wound, salt-cellars not filled, slippers not warmed and placed, empty houses and wandering women. Didn't he see the results every day? He had one girl in his room whose mother belonged to too many organizations. Women were forgetting the function for which they were created . . . Let the home come first!

I meekly replied that I thought more homes were being neglected for social affairs than for organizations, for these meet only once a month.

The gray little man shook his head, and I could see many of the women were distressed by his words, and wondered if after all they should have stayed home and made tidies for the living room chairs.

I thought of the dazzling, silk lined company who were dancing the afternoon away at the hotel, carefree, unconcerned. The "one child" had come home at four to find an empty house, or a totally unconcerned maid, and had wandered out into the street again to find his own pleasure.

The little gray man had no reproof on his lips nor in his heart for these mothers who were so frankly taking their pleasure. . . . The women, who pursue their own way, taking no responsibility for anything but their own amusement, slip through life very easily. . . . But any woman, who attempts to improve any department of life, is fair game for the critics.[25]

Nellie L. McClung, 1930

It seems that the hostility to women in public life is not lessening; but rather growing. . . .[26]

Strike breakers in Winnipeg during the General Strike, May 1919. Nellie's sympathies aligned her with opponents of the strike, though she did not approve of the heavy-handed way in which it was quashed. (Foote Collection, Manitoba Archives)

Nellie, probably in the late twenties, when the Persons Case was being resolved. (B.C. Archives photo)

Emily Murphy (top left), Henrietta Edwards (top right), Louise McKinney (bottom left), and Irene Parlby (bottom right). Together with Nellie, these four Albertans opened the Canadian Senate to women. (Photos from City of Edmonton Archives, Glenbow-Alberta Institute, Alberta Archives, Glenbow-Alberta Institute)

A ceremony honoring the "Famous Five." Nellie, far right, is shown with William Lyon Mackenzie King. (British Columbia Archives photo)

Old age caught up with Nellie in the thirties and forties. She suffered from arthritis and a heart condition which forced her to curtail her work. (British Columbia Archives photo)

Nellie and Wes at their Victoria retirement home, Lantern Lane.
(British Columbia Archives photo)

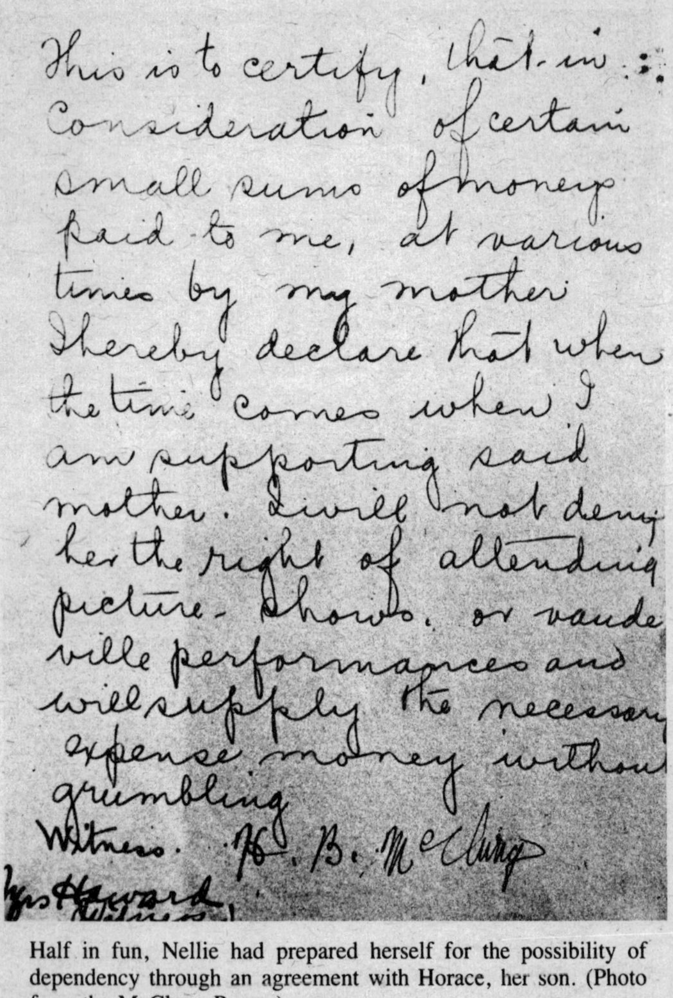

This is to certify, that in
Consideration of certain
small sums of money
paid to me, at various
times by my mother
I hereby declare that when
the time comes when I
am supporting said
mother. I will not deny
her the right of attending
picture shows, or vaude
ville performances and
will supply the necessary
expense money without
grumbling
Witness. H. B. McClung
Mrs. Howard
Nellie Mooney(?)

Half in fun, Nellie had prepared herself for the possibility of
dependency through an agreement with Horace, her son. (Photo
from the McClung Papers)

As a member of the board of governors of the Canadian Broadcasting Corporation, Nellie took a special interest in programming for women. (Glenbow-Alberta Institute photo)

Nellie at a C.B.C. Board of Governors' meeting. (British Columbia Archives photo)

Nellie in the forties, when she was about seventy years old. (British Columbia Archives photo)

Horace, Nellie, Mark, and Wes, 1940. As she had during World War I, Nellie reconciled herself to the fighting. (Photo courtesy of Mark McClung)

The McClung clan gathered to celebrate Nellie and Wes's fiftieth wedding anniversary in 1946. Though in failing health, Nellie lived until 1951. (British Columbia Archives photo)

Nellie L. McClung, 1935

Women are enfranchised, but not emancipated, and there are still a few rivers to cross. The greatest and widest, and deepest and muddiest of these is prejudice, and by that I mean, not other people's prejudices, but our own. Women do not yet trust each other.

The long years of subjection have taken their toll on us all, either directly or indirectly — and it will take time to remedy what time has done. I do not mean that time alone will bring anything right. It won't. Time has no curative quality. Everything has to be worked for. If women were really sure of each other, and ready to believe in other women's sincerity and ability, we would have women representatives in our local governments, and more than one in the Dominion.[27] Let us not blame the men for this lack. It has been very comforting to have someone to blame, but the days of that alibi are over!

Women in days gone by, when matrimony was the only course open to them, saw in every other woman a possible rival and that attitude does not die overnight, but now there has come a new day when all labor, theoretically at least, is open to women and we are no longer rivals but partners.[28]

Nellie L. McClung, 1929

The advancement of woman has been a dramatic happening, and has come about so quickly that slow thinkers have not yet perceived it. The trouble started when women were taught to read and it was further augmented when the work was taken out of the homes and women were allowed to follow it. When all the work was done at home, and the women who did it, got only their board and keep, and had to keep civil tongues in their heads to get that, a man had a fairly good chance to keep his wife and daughters in proper subjection. But now with the girls earning their own money, paying their board at home, or living in a suite down town, father's authority is all but gone — and the attitude of some masculine minds is that something should be done about it!

And the first thing that should be done is to try and get men to believe that though they have lost a good, docile, capable servant, they have gained an understanding, intelligent friend and companion.

And on the other hand, we must try to convince women that they must not expect both tips and wages; that if they claim equality, they must play fair; that they cannot make economic dependence, which no longer exists, an excuse for letting men pay their bills; that they must look for no favors or special privileges, but with dignity, courtesy and straightforwardness go in and possess the land, or at least their share of it. . . .

In the new order [of companionship between men and women], which is happily coming, there will be a more enduring fellowship, a deeper understanding, a mutual respect and confidence that will wear better than the feverish romance of the good old days when blushes, and fleeting glances and stolen interviews behind hedges made up a courtship, and marriage too often brought disillusionment.

But these days of transition are full of heartburnings and discontents. Sex prejudice and the male superiority complex, built up since time began, will not go out in one generation. And we, who have emerged from the shadows of the past, and are set free from many of its illusions, but are not yet received as members in full standing of the human family, chafe under some of its restrictions that are still laid upon us.[29]

ARE WOMEN PERSONS?

The restrictions which Nellie now found so frustrating were more difficult to attack than those of her suffrage-movement days. Then it had been a question of dislodging a few old laws; now it was people's attitudes and habits which had to be changed. The tactics of direct political action looked less appropriate with every passing day.

But sometimes — though rarely — cases did come up which called for the old methods of assault. One of these was the matter of women's admission to the Canadian Senate. No female Senator had ever slumbered in the Upper House, and it was far from clear if any ever would, under the terms of the British North America Act. Section 24 of the Act announced that only "properly qualified persons" might be called to the Senate. Did this include women? It was still an open question whether women were legally persons, let alone "properly qualified" ones.

Emily Murphy had run into this troublesome word "persons" on her first day as police magistrate for Edmonton, back in 1916. A disgruntled lawyer had challenged her authority on the grounds of her sex: as a woman she was not eligible for the privilege of magisterial authority, he said. Emily set the challenge firmly to one side, but in the course of her off-duty research, she discovered there was some merit in her opponent's case. In 1876, a British court had resolved the matter of women's legal status with blunt clarity: "Women are persons in matters of pains and penalties, but are not persons in matters of rights and privileges." Since British common law had jurisdiction in Canada, this decree had the force of a precedent. The chance of a female being considered "properly qualified" to sit in the Senate did not look good.

The question attained a new importance in the early twenties when it became known to Emily Murphy's friends and to some of the women's organizations with which she was associated that she would happily don senatorial robes if an appointment could be arranged.[30] And so the lobbying began in earnest.

"Mrs. Murphy, as well as others of us," Nellie recalled, "had interviewed honorable gentlemen at Ottawa from time to time on the matter of appointing women to the Senate, and we had received the same reply. The gentlemen would like nothing better than to have women in the Senate but the British North . . . [America]' Act made no provision for women and the members feared that women could not be appointed until this great foundation of our liberties was amended and that would take time and careful thought."[31]

Unwittingly, in their innocent quest to have women admitted to the Red Chamber, the petitioners had stumbled into the quagmire of constitutional reform, though fortunately for their peace of mind they didn't know how deep and broad it would prove to be. By 1927 Emily Murphy was already tired of waiting for the B.N.A. Act to be changed,[32] and anyway she had discovered a much more direct and appealing means of assault. Section 60 of the Act provided that any five citizens could ask the government for an interpretation of constitutional law, so she called in four other Alberta feminists to plan strategy. They were Henrietta Edwards, an expert on women's legal status in Canada; Louise McKinney, W.C.T.U. leader and former Alberta M.L.A.; Irene Parlby, still a minister in the provincial cabinet; and Nellie.

A year earlier, Emily and Nellie had had a brief falling out over the liquor question. Emily, speaking on the basis of her experience as a magistrate, had publicly declared the new, liberalized liquor act to be a success. For this Nellie had taken her severely to task. She still fostered the idea that prohibition could be revived; it pained her to see government sale of liquor given a good press. In her reply to Emily's comments, she held little back for the sake of affection.[33] Emily, to her credit, took this criticism in her stride. "That was an awful bite you took out of me. . . ," she admitted in a letter written to explain her position. "Please love me still with all my faults . . . . I may improve sometimes. I *love you anyway." And she signed herself "Your old pal, J[aney] C[anuck]."*[34] *Whatever wounds the parties had sustained in this altercation apparently healed over quickly, though the two were naturally not as close after Nellie moved to Calgary as they had been during her Edmonton years.*[35]

In any case, Nellie was one of the five women gathered on Emily Murphy's veranda that hazy day in August 1927, to discuss petitioning the federal government about the meaning of Section 24. There was an obvious and simple way for them to pose their question: did the word "persons" in that clause include female persons? But the "Alberta five" were apprehensive about letting the vexatious term "persons" into the debate.[36] *So, to keep it out, Emily Murphy came up with three rather woolly and roundabout questions for the government to consider. Her ploy failed, though, for the deputy minister of justice, to whom the petition was eventually referred, rightly pointed out that the only real question was the meaning of "persons." Emily didn't accept this tactical defeat with grace, but ultimately she had little choice except to submit.*[37]

Weeks passed and then months as the women waited for word. They knew the matter was to go before the Supreme Court for adjudication, with Newton Wesley Rowell arguing their case and lawyers hired by the government of Quebec putting the negative. Finally, on 25 April 1927, the long-awaited verdict came: "In the opinion of the Supreme Court of Canada, women are not persons."

"Four out of the five judges based their judgment on the common law disability of women to hold public office. The other one believed the word 'person' in the B.N.A. Act meant male person because the framers of the Act had only men in mind when the clause was written."[38]

And so the five petitioners got together again, this time to consider their defeat.

Nellie L. McClung, 1945

Mrs. Murphy was still undaunted. We would appeal from the Supreme Court's decision. We would send our petition to the Privy Council. We asked what we would use for money for we knew that lawyer's fees, particularly when they take a case to the Supreme Court, are staggering. When a lawyer is writing his fee for a service of this kind, his hand often slips. Mrs. Murphy said she would write to the prime minister, and perhaps he could devise a way. This was every woman's concern and she believed that Mr. King would be glad to have it settled. The letter was written and we had a prompt reply.

Newton Wesley Rowell was going before the Privy Council in October and he would be glad to take our petition. The petition should have been in Mrs. Murphy's name, but it seems that names are arranged alphabetically so our petition appears on the record in the name of "Edwards and others."

On the morning of 18 October 1929, newspapers all over the British Empire carried black headlines: "Privy Council Declares That Women Are Persons!" It came as a surprise to many women in Canada at least who had not known that they were not persons until they heard it stated that they were.[39]

Nellie L. McClung, 1929

Our discontents are passing. We may yet live to see the day when women will be no longer news! And it cannot come too soon. I want to be a peaceful, happy, normal human being, pursuing my unimpeded way through life, never having to stop to explain, defend, or apologize for my sex. . . . I am tired of belonging to the sex that is called the Sex. And it is because the finding of the Privy Council that we are "persons," once and for all, will do so much to merge us into the human family, that we are filled with gratitude and joy. The *Winnipeg Tribune* is before me, and I have just read the interviews given by several prominent women. The lead says "indulgent laughter, mock congratulations and ironic expressions of gratitude greeted the news from London that their lordships had decided that women were legally persons within the meaning of the B.N.A. Act and were consequently entitled to sit in the Senate."

It does sound humorous. But there had to be a ruling on it. Women have been regarded as creatures of relationships rather than human beings with direct responsibilities. That is why one senator said women could not sit in the Senate, and give unbiased judgments, that is, married women, because they would naturally have to do what their husbands wished them to do. He might have gone on, and said any woman who had a male relative would owe her first allegiance to him. The world has gone on since that law prevailed, but the dear old fellow hasn't noticed. . . .

We cannot understand the mentality of the men who dare to set the boundaries of women's work. We object to barriers, just as the range horses despise fences. For this reason we protested the action of the Alberta Hotelmen's Association when they decided that women must not enter their beer parlors. Not but what we knew it was much better to be out than in, but we believe in equality.

And now, with the Senate doors open there are only the two great institutions, that will not accept women on equal terms.[40]

WOMEN AND THE CHURCH

The "two great institutions" which Nellie had in mind were the beer parlor — and the church. Nellie had first become concerned about the status of women in Christianity during her suffrage-campaign days. At that time, females had been excluded from all the governing bodies (or "courts") of the Methodist communion. And it went without saying that no member of the "gentle sex" had ever been allowed to seek ordination.

Nellie objected to both these restrictions in the strongest terms. "Woman has the same relation to the church as the hole to the doughnut," she once sniped.[41] For her, this was not just a matter of common justice, but of basic Christian doctrine. Sexual equality was fundamental to Christ's teachings, she thought. She pointed out the importance of women in His ministry — the woman at the well, Mary and Martha, the women at the tomb. She wasn't even persuaded that all the disciples had necessarily been male. Until very recently, she noted, women had been excluded from official tallies of the population. Mightn't they just as easily have been left off the list of apostles? "Christ's scribes were all men, and in writing down the sacred story, they would naturally ignore the woman's part of it."[42] But this was not Jesus's way, Nellie argued. The Master had valued women as full human beings, "with souls to save and lives to live" which were every bit as significant as those of the men.[43]

Nellie L. McClung, 1916

Christ was a true democrat. He was a believer in women; and never in his life did he discriminate against them.[44]

Nellie L. McClung, 1934

The case against women has always rested on the fact that women bear children, and this is such a holy office that women should be content with it. Christ made an utterance on this matter which should have cleared the thinking of the world, when he replied to the woman of the multitude who interrupted his preaching with her tribute to his mother. Carried away by the wisdom and beauty of his words, she exclaimed, "Blessed above all women is the woman who bore Thee!" And Christ, knowing that there was an error in her logic, halted his preaching to reply to her. "Yea verily," He said, not wishing to deny the honor paid to His mother "but" (and this word is significant, implying a correction) "blessed is every one that heareth the will of God and doeth it."

That should mean, if words have any meaning, that no biological function however important, not even bearing a Messiah, is to be compared to the possession of an ear that hears the will of God, and a soul that follows it. In other words, that women are human beings as men are in direct relation to God.[45]

Nellie L. McClung, 1915

The Christian church has departed in some places from Christ's teaching — noticeably in its treatment of women. . . .

Women have held a place all their own in the church. "I am willing that the sisters should labor," cried an eminent doctor of the largest Protestant church in Canada, when the question of allowing women to sit in the highest courts of the church was discussed. "I am willing that the sisters should labor," he said, "and that they should labor more abundantly, but we cannot let them rule." And so it was decreed.[46]

Nellie L. McClung, 1915

A Heart to Heart Talk with the Women of the Church
    by the Governing Bodies

> Go, labor on, good sister Anne,
> Abundant may thy labors be;
> To magnify thy brother man
> Is all the Lord requires of thee!

> Go raise the mortgage, year by year,
> And joyously thy way pursue,
> And when you get the title clear,
> We ll move a vote of thanks to you!

> Go, labor on, the night draws nigh;
> Go, build us churches — as you can.
> The times are hard, but chicken-pie
> Will do the trick. Oh, rustle, Anne!

> Go, labor on, good sister Sue,
> To home and church your life devote;
> But never, never ask to vote,
> Or we'll be very cross with you!

May no rebellion cloud your mind,
But joyous let your race be run.
The conference is good and kind,
And knows God's will for everyone![47]

Nellie L. McClung, 1915

One of the arguments advanced by the men who oppose women's entry into the full fellowship of the church is that women would ultimately seek to preach, and the standard of preaching would be lowered. . . . We assure the timorous brethren that women are not clamoring to preach; but if a woman should feel that she is divinely called of God to deliver a message, I wonder how the church can be so sure that she isn't. Wouldn't it be perfectly safe to let her have her fling? There was a rule given long ago which might be used yet to solve such a problem: "And now I say unto you, Refrain from these men, and let them alone, for if this council, or this work, be of men, it will come to naught, but if it be of God you cannot overthrow it, lest haply ye be found even to fight against God."

That seems to be a pretty fair way of looking at the matter of preaching; but the churches have decreed otherwise, and in order to save trouble they have decided themselves and not left it to God. It must be great to feel that you are on the private wire from heaven and qualified to settle a matter which concerns the spiritual destiny of other people.[48]

Mark McClung, 1975

[Would Nellie have liked to be a minister herself?] Absolutely. There's no question about it. She would have been a minister if the Methodist Church at that time had permitted it. . . . She would have been a humdinger of a clergyman. She would have filled the churches.[49]

SHALL WOMEN PREACH?

If Nellie really did aspire to the ministry, her hopes were never to be realized. When in 1918, the Methodist Church finally resolved the issue of women's role, the ruling was that females might sit on all the church's governing boards and committees but that they could not preach. Even achieving that much had been a "severe struggle," Nellie reported, and the decision had left her far from satisfied.[50] "I will confess to a peeved feeling every time I think of this," she told a church gathering.[51]

What really stung her was that the church — the Christian church — had lagged behind the state in extending women's sphere. In 1921, she found an international forum for these views when she was appointed as the lone female delegate from Canada to the Fifth Ecumenical Methodist Conference in England. *"The Church of Christ should have championed the woman's cause,"* she informed the august assemblage. *"It should have led all the reform forces in bringing liberty of soul and freedom of action to women. . . . It is a sore thought that the church has let us fight our battle against social inequalities alone."*[52]

The other delegates appreciated what they took to be her *"unconventional and daring sayings,"* but their opinion was of little practical account. As Nellie well knew, the battle had to be fought, not in England, but at home. This time it would be a straightforward contest over the right to ordination. *"Women should have a place in the pulpit,"* she continued to insist, *"and the time is coming, rather it is here, when women will refuse to be clubbed over the heads, even with a passage of scripture."*[53] But, unfortunately, a new obstacle had arisen. There was much hopeful talk of a union amongst Methodists, Congregationalists, and Presbyterians, a development with which Nellie was heartily in accord. To bring up such a controversial issue as women preachers might muddy the waters unduly, she could see, and so she allowed herself to be silenced for a while. But once the United Church was formed in 1925, the issue did not remain buried for very long. Nellie recalled the events which followed with considerable bitterness.

Nellie L. McClung, 1934

Once upon a time, this question of the ordination of women to preach the gospel, came very near to settlement in the largest church in Canada. There was a tide in the affairs of women flowing strongly toward complete equality.

It was in 1928.

It is easy to remember 1928, though to most of us it seems a lifetime ago. Everyone had money, and the markets were rising. Great oil and mining activities, great flurries in stocks and bonds had come in bewildering excitement, and even the elevator boys and little cash girls were seeing visions of wealth. It was hard to settle down to a routine job, when fortunes could be made so easily. Young men were leaving college to work in brokers' offices; farmers were deserting their ploughshares for oil shares, and even ministers were resigning their pulpits to promote new companies and not the new Jerusalem.

The Home and Foreign Missions Departments of the churches were alarmed. In the United Church of Canada there were fifty-five places where churches had been built, but there was no minister, not even a student who could be sent to take charge of them. Fifty-five districts, all in the western provinces, where there were no Sunday schools, no work among young people, no one to baptize the young or bury the dead. Sorrowing letters had come to the Home Mission Department saying "Our church is locked, spiders are spinning webs across the altar and dust lies thick on the pulpit Bible — Can't you send us someone — we would be glad to have even a woman."

Now the great United Church in the years preceding 1928, when pressed by some restless souls (and I was privileged to be one of them) to know when they were going to let down the bars of the ministry, had always discreetly said "Wait until some woman asks for ordination and then we will deal with the case on its merits. Give us a case!" And in the eventful year of 1928, there came a case before the General Council of the Church, which met in Winnipeg. The time had come!

A young woman [Miss Lydia Gruchy] was asking for ordination. She had completed her theological course some years before, at Saint Andrews in Saskatoon, taking the gold medal in a class of nineteen. She had already served on two fields, with marked success. She could speak French as well as English, play the organ, lead the singing, drive a car, keep house, hold her tongue and get along with people. She had established Sunday schools on her fields, organized literary societies, reading classes and ladies' aid societies. She was an able speaker, a clever student and a good pastor. And she was asking to be ordained. The case had arrived. In black and white had come a request for the ordination of a woman! . . .

Now I hate to have to join the chorus of those who blame women for everything that happens. It always seems like making [a] small answer to a big question. But I have to admit that the ordination of Miss Gruchy was killed at the 1928 General Council by the indifference of some of the women. . . .

It was on the day the Woman's Missionary Society brought in their reports. The Woman's Missionary Society has always seemed to me to be the spear-head of the church, with their hospitals and boarding schools at home, and their workers in the foreign field. The official report was being read by the chief executive, a good report of earnest work well done. Suddenly she stopped reading and said "You have not asked us what we think of the ordination of women — and it is just as well. You will find us very conservative."

That was all — but it was enough!

Across the aisle from me sat one of our old ministers who has worked for the equality of women all his life. I turned and looked at him in consternation — I wondered if he had heard what I did. I knew he had when I saw him draw his forefinger across his throat! It was a significant gesture. He knew the day was lost — and I knew it too. . . .

There was a futile and barren resolution adopted, saying "There is no bar in reason or religion against the ordination of women" but the whole matter had gone cold. The ordination of women has probably been delayed ten years, and occupies the shadowy place in the courts of the church once filled in British politics by the Deceased Wife's Sister's Bill.[54]

It will come, of course. In the meantime it makes me sad at heart to think that the church has been the last stronghold of prejudice. Every other profession has opened its doors, and women have entered, some to succeed, some to fail, thus proving their humanity. . . .

. . . the need for guidance in matters of religion was never more acute. The conditions of life are changing around us, old landmarks and roadsigns have gone, and many people, old and young are groping their way in uncertainty. . . . I know the church in its conservatism . . . [is] losing great leaders who would . . . [grace] the ministry and do much to make the church a greater force than it has yet been. . . .

I have been much discouraged since we missed the high tide of 1928. I knew then the defeat was a heavy one. Now we can see the tide has turned against women. See what has happened in Germany and Italy! In the United States there is a growing sentiment against women in employment. . . . Economic conditions now are pushing women back. It is an old rule that what is not used, be it a hand, or a house or a privilege, shrivels and deteriorates. Women had political power given to them in many parts of the world in the last twenty-five years, but they have not made full use of it, and now not only the liberty of women is threatened, but our whole civilization has a bomb under it. Armament makers may decide to have a war any day.

If the women of the world, the enfranchised women, had worked [with] intelligence and foresight and passionate earnestness, the spell of greed and graft might have been broken. . . . Someone will want to rise up here and cry out that I am laying too much responsibility on women — and that this is not fair. I am not saying it is fair, I merely say it is true. A nation rises no higher than its women. They have it in their hands to lead the race. Every fluffy haired little thing, with lips as red as a sword cut, and nails to match, running around lightly clad in body and mind, is a potential guardian of the future, and on her depends, the happiness, stability and morality of a home. And what is being done for her? . . .

There are great youth movements sweeping the world. Boys and girls are dissatisfied with the conduct of life as they see it. They are ready to follow positive leaders, either up or down. In the universities of our own country and of the United States of America, communistic doctrine is gaining ground, but that condition cannot be remedied by persecution or denunciation or deportation. It is the heroism in Communism that appeals to the young and adventurous.

Trained Christian leaders, young men and women, called to and prepared for the work, might have been able to catch the imagination of these young people, who are being led away into the dark and ugly ways of Communism, for Christianity is the most adventurous, heroic and romantic idea the world has ever known. It has been interpreted badly sometimes and made to appear stiff and stuffy, but look at it without prejudice! One young man with an idea, setting out to change the world, and doing it because his idea was a dynamic one! He knew that the human heart could be changed.[55]

CHAPTER TEN

LANTERN LANE

> ... changes are inevitable. What is true today
> may not be true tomorrow. All our opinions
> should be marked, 'Subject to change without
> notice.'

The human heart could be changed! As the unsettling decade of the twenties wore on, that conviction became of increasing importance in Nellie's thought. She had always known it, of course — people might be led to a new vision of human life — but it had never before been her main hope. At first, she had relied upon women, but they had proven too frail: they "hadn't the nerve; hadn't the courage. They were too afraid of being considered 'queer' if they failed to fall in line with custom."[1] *She had believed in the potency of ordinary people, "the common, honest, hard working, clear thinking people." "Government from the ground up" had been the rallying cry of the prairie reform movement, "a great movement" which, Nellie recorded with regret, "began, grew, flourished, triumphed, hesitated, languished — and sank — without a bubble."*
" 'From the ground up' did not work!"[2]

She had put her faith in legislation too, but that belief had not lasted her for long. "I used to think we could regenerate the world by laws," she had said in 1919. "I confess now to having been mistaken. It is not new laws we need, it is a new spirit in our people. The best law can be made of no effect, by selfish, unscrupulous people. The laws we need now, are the laws graven on human hearts."[3]

Before the war, the church had kept a tight hold on virtually all Canadians; Christian doctrine and values had shared the inevitability of physical law. But the war and the social dislocations which followed loosened many of the old sureties, and Nellie admitted as much: "we no longer believe in unsinkable ships, unbreakable treaties or inviolable contracts, gilt-edged securities. All these we have put away with Mrs.

Potts Irons and the stereoptican views. And the fruit of the tree of knowledge has been bitter on our tongues."[4]

The greatest loser in this process had been the church. Even Nellie had unwittingly adopted a more secular attitude. She no longer held God responsible for everything that happened and had begun to feel uncomfortable about indulging in blind faith. Remembering the poem she had written during the war, asking for grace to "run blindfolded in the race," she declared that in her "next re-incarnation," her prayers would "be for light."[5] What's more, the vision of a Kingdom of Heaven on earth, which had once shone so brightly in her mind, no longer attracted her. She had put aside the ideal of perfection: life had shown itself to be a matter of compensations, with the good making up for the bad. "There is no security in life," she had decided, "there is only balance."[6]

If people like Nellie had strayed a little from the tight old channels of thought, others had wandered much further. "Religion in the modern world is like an elderly chaperone at the dance," Nellie lamented. "No one takes much notice of her. The best the young dancers hope is that she will not spoil their fun."[7] As the church had lost its power, people's moral values had begun to bend and ripple and distort. Christian brotherhood and loving sacrifice permutated into sociability and self-service. People no longer seemed to care about one another; they were subsiding into insularity and self-indulgence. They had given up hope. "The curse of present day conditions is that our moral fiber is weakening," Nellie scolded. "We will not be bothered. We take the easy way."[8]

As Nellie's thought gradually modulated to take account of these changes, the need for spiritual education became her predominant theme. Her hopes came to rest on young people — "the valiant young," she optimistically called them. "They are our Last Reserves!"[9]

"There is so little to be done for grown-up people," she grudgingly acknowledged. "We can comfort them in sorrow, entertain them when they are dull, confirm them in what they already believe, but it is hard to change their way of thinking."[10] If she had her life to live over, she said, she would spend it as a leader and teacher of youth.[11] But the sad fact was that Nellie had begun to run out of time. By 1932, at age fifty-nine, she already suffered from arthritis and a bad heart, conditions which would become progressively worse. The doctors ordered her to slow down.

By happy coincidence, just as Nellie had to start restricting her activities, Wes was transferred again, this time to the lotus land of Canada — Victoria, British Columbia. The move made it easier for

Nellie to prune her schedule: she would write a weekly newspaper column, she decided, but resolved to give up making speeches. But even before she was properly unpacked in her new Victoria home, she had to admit that she'd broken this promise. "[The Woman's Missionary Society] . . . got after me and I fell," she confessed in a letter to a Calgary friend. "I spoke at two guest teas this week and will speak at one tomorrow. And I have two lectures to give. I think it is seven times I have addressed meetings, but I feel real well and am glad to be able to help a little."[12]

Public speaking was an entertainment for her, a stimulant, a way of staying connected to the world. She continued to travel east for speaking engagements now and then, even going on tour in Ontario once or twice in the thirties. When the Liberals called on her for help in the 1935 federal election campaign, she responded eagerly, not at all like the ailing old lady she was supposed to be.[13] It was a raucous, turbulent contest, and Nellie did nothing to quiet it down. Speaking in Vancouver, she kicked over the traces to advocate the enfranchisement of Orientals, a policy to which the local candidate and a large proportion of the hissing audience were opposed. "I don't think the presence of well-mannered meditative Orientals would lower the tone of political meetings in Vancouver," she chided the jeering crowd.[14]

Nineteen thirty-five was also the year when the Co-operative Commonwealth Federation made its first appearance in federal politics. Nellie was certainly not opposed to public ownership of basic services, but neither was she drawn to the new party. "Individually the C.C.F. are excellent people," she conceded from the campaign platform, "though I resent their mousy air of superior virtue when they allude to the old parties. They seem to think . . . [that] anyone who remains in either of the old parties is in the pay and service of the Big Interests."[15] Far better for everyone concerned, she thought, if the socialists had thrown their lot in with the other progressive-minded people — that is, the Liberals. "Anyone who gets a good idea, immediately wants to build a political party on it!" she complained. "The result is that the forces of progress are divided and subdivided, until their influence is watered down to nothing. You can chip down a good log, which might have been made into something beautiful and useful, until you have nothing but a pile of saw-dust!"[16]

Obviously, Nellie had not succeeded in disengaging herself from the excitement and turmoil of political life. "It is no use," she once wrote. "The cares of the world cannot be taken off like an overcoat, and hung in a dark closet. They follow us, wherever we go and sit on a picture frame,

*when we go to sleep ready to ... [greet us] with the first beam of
light."*[17]

Throughout the thirties, the *"cares of the world"* were numerous
enough to keep a worrier occupied full time — worldwide depression,
prohibitive tariff barriers, armament buildups, young men reduced to
begging handouts at the kitchen door. Nellie was well informed about
current events, but she had no time to fret over them. She knew what was
to blame for the world's problems — human mismanagement and man's
spiritual crassness — and she knew what was needed to solve them —
imagination and a moral revival. Her solution to the depression, for
example, was as simple to explain as it was difficult to accomplish. *"We
need ... more people who have the vision of a new Canada,"* she taught.
*"People who know unemployment is not a problem but a sin, a sin of
selfishness. ... We need new people, which is to say new hearts!"*[18] She
might lament over the state of the world or admonish her countrymen
like a latter-day prophet, but she was not inclined to brood.

In fact, her everyday life throughout these troublous years was
even-tempered and calm. In 1935, she and Wes found Lantern Lane, a
small farm at Gordon Head, six miles outside Victoria.[19] There was
peace here for Nellie and real deep-down contentment the likes of which
she hadn't known since leaving Manitou. After twenty-four years,
Nellie McClung was a country woman again.

Nellie L. McClung, 1936

... here am I in the place I have always wanted to be — on a
farm, near a city, within sight of the sea (with my onions planted in a
"warm rich soil on a sunny hillside, with natural drainage") and with
a large percentage of the things I have always craved, including glass
knobs on every door in the house, and a peach tree fastened to the
south wall.[20]

Nellie L. McClung, 1936

But to return to my onions. There they lie — the seeds I mean
— under an inch of soil in rows fourteen inches apart, according to
directions on the envelope, and when the rain falls now it will have a
new meaning for me, for it will start the little hard seeds to
germinate. And soon the little green threads will pierce the sod, and
then no longer on government papers, or other places, will I need to
give my occupation as "housewife," that pallid name which no
woman likes to own. I will boldly inscribe in that column this good
strong word — "Onion-Grower!"[21]

Nellie L. McClung, 1930s

I am a woman with a past, but when the fire burns, and I have
the flower catalogue in my hands, I turn my back to the gray shades
of disappointed hopes, and in imagination my soul goes forward.[22]

Nellie L. McClung, 1936

Yesterday afternoon I went down the woodland path to the
beach, thinking heavily of . . . things. . . . But though my mind was
clogged with perplexities, my feet soon began to feel the comfort of
the soft, springing soil of the deep woods, and the trees above me
whispered happily in the sunshine. I sat on a fallen log, covered with
moss, a great giant of a log that had fallen maybe fifty years ago, and
listened to the muted voices of the woods, the syncopated notes of
an ax and its echo, the rustle of leaves, and the wash of the waves
frilling on the gravelly beach below. . . .

And as I sat there on the fallen tree, looking out to sea, with the
sunlight falling around me and the cool, green, free essence of the
wild coming to me in the tang of the forest, I began to feel that the
center of gravity in my life was shifting and very pleasantly too.

Here were riches — beauty, silence, peace so deep it was
entering into the very marrow of my soul. How very little, after all,
we need to make us happy — a woody path to the sea, the scent of
wild flowers, the flash of a bluebird's wing, a few friends, books by
the fire on a winter's night and a plate of apples, a good conscience,
space in which to work — going tired to bed — and then another
day, rolling down like a scroll![23]

Nellie L. McClung, 1930s

All is not lost. The world still holds sane, normal people, who
live their lives in peace and happiness; whose morals are not jazzed;
whose tastes are not vitiated. The Mayfairs [neighbors] live within
their income; they are buying their own home; they keep up their
insurance; they are raising a family.[24]

Edna Jaques, 1930s

I am at Lantern Lane, the lovely country home of Nellie
McClung. The McClungs are satisfying people. You don't have to
"visit" them, you just come in the back door and are "home." After
three years of being away, it was just like that, no formalities, no
stiffness, no getting acquainted.

She saw us drive into the yard and came out, looking a bit frailer than three years ago, but smiling and friendly, and we went together, arm in arm, into the kitchen, where a warm fire was burning, and a little rack of slabs dripped sawdust on the floor and filled the house with the odor of fresh cut wood, than which there is no grander smell on earth. . . .

An old black cat walked in and out between us, arching his back, purring, rubbing against our legs. This cat is quite aware of his own importance. His name is King Faruk of Egypt and he has a little leather collar on with two tiny bells (that he loves) and a lucky penny that came from Dunkirk. . . .

Behind the kitchen stove is a little blue rocking chair with a cretonne cushion where Mr. McClung loves to sit. In fact, he sometimes used it at the table for meals and rocks happily between bites and sips, cutting his bread with his knife held like a jack-knife and enjoying his food with the fresh unspoiled appetite of a man who works hard and eats his food with all the relish of a boy. . . .

In the study[25] there are a cobble stone fireplace, a radio, easy chairs, flowers and pictures and "herself" behind the desk writing the hours away, gleaning her material from letters and stories, sorting out her papers, answering the fan mail that comes from every hamlet in Canada. Women writing to her for advice . . . asking her to intercede for their children, how to handle their husbands. . . .

Nellie McClung's little articles are syndicated in newspapers all across Canada and countless thousands of women read them.[26]

HER OWN STORY

Nellie L. McClung, 1930s

There is something in the air of this place that makes people write. It's the ambient air, unbroken by rude traffic sounds; the gulls wheeling over a rocky ledge; children at play in the sands below my window; the waves advancing and retreating, and pulling the gravel back with them. It's all this, and more. It's the feeling of completion; the conviction that life has entered upon its last era. Farther west I cannot go. So here my caravan will rest; and from here will I return in memory to the stirring scenes of other days.[27]

Nellie L. McClung, 1930s

The idea of writing my own story has often come to me. . . . But when the urge came . . . it was driven out by the immediate present and its demands. It was not a compulsion and running a house, raising five children, getting the vote for women, and baking the cake for the "talents tea," in the church were. But since I came to live in Victoria, British Columbia, I have thought of it more seriously. I have had more time to think. The family are scattered and gone. The ladies' aid knows me no more; women have more rights than they are using.

One day, recently, it suddenly came out of the fog. I was walking by the sea, near Gonzales Point with a friend of mine, formerly a newspaper woman on the prairie, and the matter was definitely propounded by her. We had just come to rest by the sea, on the green bench provided for weary travelers, and rolling her cane on her knees with her two small hands she said, "You should write your own story. You have seen western Canada evolve; you've seen political parties come and go; women come out of the kitchen and go into business, politics and finance. You have seen waist lines rise and fall, and disappear altogether only to come back stronger than ever. You can remember when women wore clothes for upholstering, then for warmth and covering, and now merely for decoration or just for instance; and you may see its abandonment. Why, you can remember when women had fibered chamois interlining in their skirts, and pockets in their petticoats and called their husbands 'Mister', and were not sure that it was quite right to curl their hair with curl papers. You've seen much in your day, and you should write it. . . ."

Under her [inducement] I was all ready to start. This was in the sunny April weather, and I tried to plan the story, as I lay in a hammock looking out to sea across the gulf to San Juan Island. I was going to write in the proper manner this time, with a plan, and diagrams. Surely this was the place for writing, where no harsh sounds break into one's reverie. . . .

Then, when a week or so had passed, and I had not put pen to paper, I grew alarmed. I knew what was happening, I was too comfortable. The anesthesia of Victoria was working on me. I took down the hammock and roused myself. I looked about and took warning. I considered the case of the two old warriors, who once fought each other in a prairie town, in the gallant red-blooded way that belongs to the vibrant prairie, and its exhilarating climate. Rival editors, political opponents, never missing a chance to revile each other, and doing it with considerable wit. How we loved their biting sarcasm.

Now they live on the island, on the same side of the street. They share a party line telephone. They talk amicably across the fence about fertilizers and slugs and sprays. Even exchange confidences on how their arteries are hardening; and send each other gifts of roses, and early violets wet with dew, and new potatoes, and swiss chard. When I heard about the swiss chard I could have wept, remembering the brave old days, when if any offering from the vegetable kingdom had passed between them, it had surely been a sheaf of poison ivy, girded with barbed wire. So I knew I must get along with my story, before I grow too mellow; and all the color fades from the canvas of my life. The things I gave my life to were real and absorbing, and vital. They mattered greatly to me, and to the world. At least I thought they did. I loved and I hated in my time, and I did both with right good will, and I do not want to forgive all my enemies before I write the story.[28]

Nellie L. McClung, 1933

To tell a personal story spontaneously, but against a background packed with significant description, allusion, and reference is my object, and I believe this has not been done for western Canada. I want to write a book, in which many people will find their own experiences, and I can see that I am doing it.[29]

Nellie L. McClung, 1934

I am doing all right with my book, and am stopping at the place where I got married. And I will write another one. I am calling this one *Clearing in the West*. . . . I write all day now and certainly do get tired, and stiff when night comes.[30]

Letter to Nellie
from her sister Lizzie, 1933

Hannah came over last night and we had a real feast reading your story. . . . I think it is fine; I wonder how you got so much of the real everyday happenings. . . .[31]

Letter from a fan, about 1935

. . . tell Mrs. McClung when you see her I burnt the spuds and let the beefsteak stew, and spoiled two nut loaves and the house is in a mess ever since I started to read . . . [*Clearing in the West*]. Pauline said "I sure hope Nellie McClung NEVER writes another book; every time I go near mother she screams at me to 'shut up, I'm reading.' "[32]

RETIREMENT?

For a woman who had theoretically gone into retirement in 1932, the Nellie McClung of 1936-37 had all the attributes of a dedicated professional writer — long working hours, a fat file of fan letters, and three new titles to her credit. Clearing in the West had quickly been followed by two anthologies of her recent newspaper articles, Leaves from Lantern Lane (1936) and More Leaves from Lantern Lane (1937). For the first time in her life she had the leisure to think and polish and revise, so, not surprisingly, the books she produced in these years contain much of her most beautiful and controlled work.

But writing was still not her only occupation, for in 1936, her twenty-year loyalty to Mackenzie King was rewarded by appointment to the board of governors of the infant Canadian Broadcasting Corporation. She was the first and only woman on the nine-member board. It was not a lucrative position — the honorarium amounted to about $200 a year — but it was responsible: the board formulated policy for public broadcasting in Canada.

The first few times Nellie had spoken over the radio herself, she'd found the experience a little nerve-wracking. "Looking into the horn," she'd confided, "[I'd] feel better if I could see Mrs. Beaubier, of Champion, or Mrs. Edwards of Edmonton."[33] But if she was diffident about using the new technology, she was not at all backward about appreciating its potential for public education. "I would rather be on the governing board of the Canadian Radio Corporation than on the board of the greatest university in the world," she declared, "for radio is the greatest university. Everyone belongs to it — and no one can be excluded because they have not passed."[34]

Her first thought had been of the use the churches might make of the new medium. By broadcasting services and sermons, they might regain some of the influence they'd lost in the preceding two decades. They might even begin to bring about the spiritual regeneration which, Nellie hoped, could pull mankind back from the prospect of another war. The United Church, unhappily, didn't share her vision: "she couldn't get the church to budge on this," her son Mark recollects, "and she was just livid."[35] Less conservative clergymen, however, were quick to appreciate the new opportunities, and in Alberta, William Aberhart used radio to achieve a great evangelical and political victory. Nellie at least had the sickly comfort of knowing she had been right.

The issue of religious broadcasting didn't come before the C.B.C. governors, but another moral question did: should the network permit liquor advertising? The discussions were prolonged and rancorous, and one day Nellie completely lost her temper with an opponent on the board, a man who happened to be a Jew. "I was so annoyed with him," she confessed to Mark afterwards, "I said, ([and] you remember the dates when Hitler was well in power), 'Mr. So-and-So, you're the sort of Jew that almost makes me an anti-Semite.'" And then she confided, "You know, as soon as I had said it, I could have bitten out my tongue. To say such a thing, to another human being — just intolerable."

"When she told me about this," Mark remembered, "there were tears in her eyes. She was a pretty emotional woman, and she said, 'I reached out and I took his hands and I said, 'I'm sorry, I apologize.' And he took her hands and they had a reconciliation right there.'"[36]

Nellie's side eventually won the advertising fight, but not until the board had threatened to resign en masse in protest over the interference of C. D. Howe, who wanted the corporation to accept liquor commercials. For once in his career, the all-powerful Howe was forced to back down.[37]

Though she had largely given up on women as an agency of reform, Nellie had not lost her sympathy for them or her faith in their potential.[38] In what was probably her first public statement after being appointed to the C.B.C. board, she argued that "women are the best listeners in radio" and said that she felt a special "responsibility about women's programs."[39] They should be more than a recital of recipes, she maintained. She also championed the cause of women working within the corporation, noting that female voices were on air only about one percent of the time.[40] The press of the day alleged that women's voices were too shrill for good transmission;[41] besides, women broadcasters were likely to be incompetent. "We'd like to hear one of them handle a professional hockey game this winter," the Niagara Falls paper sneered.[42] Nellie apparently made little headway against this opposition.

In 1938 she took a brief holiday from the frustrations of C.B.C. affairs, only to immerse herself in the fog of international politics. Late that summer, Mackenzie King invited her to serve as a Canadian delegate to that year's session of the League of Nations in Geneva. Ex-delegate Charlotte Whitton sent her congratulations and a warning: "good luck," she wrote, "though you will be sickeningly disillusioned."[43] And that was about the way it turned out. Nellie had long been a supporter of the League: she advocated international cooperation and conciliation and relief, all the things the League stood for. So it was disillusioning to discover the fractious and inconsequential reality which hid behind the idealistic facade. The business of the League, even in the "Fifth Committee" on social questions, where Nellie sat, was too easily bogged down in purposeless disputation and empty speeches. Too many of the delegates were overly concerned about getting credit for what they'd contributed. "I knew there were people here who had worked long and earnestly," Nellie remarked, "but surely that was no reason for them to act like young mothers at a baby show!"[44]

Meanwhile, in the last week of September 1938, as the meetings droned on, Hitler screamed out his threats of aggression against Czechoslovakia.

Nellie's impressions of her stay in Europe were not all negative, however, for she had taken a side trip to another international conference, this one held at Interlaken and sponsored by the Oxford Group or Moral Re-Armament. Here delegates from forty-five countries were gathered, "rich and poor, bishops and communists, coal miners and university professors, all united in one purpose — to know the will of God and do it."[45]

"The difference between Interlaken and the League of Nations," Nellie noted in her traveling diary, "is the difference between hope and fulfillment."

> At Interlaken we saw the Christian message in action. We saw the effect of changed lives. . . . We saw how old enemies, steeped in traditional hatreds could throw them all away, in a new alliance for God and their fellowmen. Interlaken is, in miniature, what the League of Nations should be, representatives of all nations meeting to help each other, being more anxious to give than to get, more concerned with opportunities for service than with the exercise of their rights. . . .
>
> Moral re-armament to me means being on duty every day to spread the good news that God does give guidance to us, if we will listen to him.[46]

"We are dwelling in the midst of alarms," she wrote on another occasion. "War in Spain, China, Japan; strikes, lockouts — poverty in the midst of plenty."

> Everyone knows that these things should not be. But we seem to be powerless to prevent them, yet we know God must have a remedy for them, and it is our business to find it.
>
> Individuals are praying, the churches are working, but it is the Oxford Group which has launched a world-wide

movement, in co-operation with every other human agency, to bring in that new day when God will control the affairs of men everywhere, and wars will cease and peace and plenty reign.[47]

The delegates at Interlaken had prayed for "a year of grace," Nellie reported, a year "in which to work for peace and now we are committed to this work."[48]

When the war came anyway, in spite of moral re-armament and the year of grace and the "settlement" at Munich and everything else which had been done to prevent it, Nellie accepted it with resignation.

> War is an ugly thing. No one tries to glorify it now. But there are some things uglier. Slavery for instance. I would like to be an out and out pacifist. I envy the Quakers who go about doing good, in and out of belligerent countries, welcome everywhere, with their quiet faces, compassionate eyes, hands of healing and words of hope.
>
> But the Quakers, I am afraid, even in their numbers were multiplied a hundred fold, could not bring peace to troubled Europe. Not now. It's too late. So the downy-faced boys, who kept pets and collected stamps and went hiking on Saturdays, have to be turned into fighting men. Fire has to be fought with fire, force with force. It is a hard remedy involving unspeakable horror and waste. No one likes it, but what else can we do?[49]

Strangely enough, the war actually gave Nellie new reason for hope, because it was at least plausible that the crisis might revive the spirit of heroism and self-sacrifice which could redeem mankind. After all, that was what she perceived to have happened during the Great War. "We can endure the world today only if we are working for its salvation," she preached.

Nellie's own efforts to save the world were now restricted to writing her weekly newspaper column. Her health was deteriorating seriously. Early in the forties, she suffered a sudden collapse which might easily have ended her life. But as her "brain cleared" after the worst of the illness passed, she was left with "a great longing to live." "The age of plenty is here, if only the heart of man can be prepared, and he can be made to see that what hurts one nation hurts all. What a time to be alive! And what a poor time to die. So I lived."[50]

Now it really was necessary for her to give up most of her activities, so she withdrew from the C.B.C. board, canceled her weekly column, and turned her attention to finishing the autobiography she'd left half done in 1935. The second and most eventful part of her story remained untold. It took two years to finish the project, for her progress was often interrupted by pain and fatigue. Then, in 1944, she was temporarily set back by another severe blow: her eldest son, Jack, by this time a highly successful and respected Edmonton jurist, committed suicide.

For Nellie, the cause of her son's death was obvious — the ordeal of World War I.

> When a boy who has never had a gun in his hands, never desired anything but the good of his fellow men, is sent out to kill other boys like himself, even at the call of his country, something snaps in him, something which may not mend.
>
> A wound in a young heart is like a wound in a young tree. It does not grow out. It grows in.[51]

Jack's death was the greatest calamity in Nellie's life, and she did not rebound easily. But she did rebound. First, she finished her book, The Stream Runs Fast, and saw it published in 1945. And then she simply carried on, hopefully, faithfully, busily, and, in time, even happily again.

Margaret Ecker Francis, 1947

... there is fire yet, in the gray-haired novelist, who will be seventy-four on 20 October. Even if it's heresy, she still thinks an intelligent woman should have her place in the world along with men of the same caliber. She's still so revolutionary she doesn't believe women belong wholly in kitchen and nursery. She still sees evil in alcohol. If those are war cries, she's still a firebrand. . . .

She was smart in a blue wool dress the day I met her, with a touch of red at the throat; her . . . eyes snapping with interest. She didn't look her years. She didn't talk her years.

"For one thing," she said, "I love writing. I plan to do another book yet. In fact I was planning one this morning, a new novel. It will grow on me, just like it does when I have a new plot sizzling in my mind. As I go along, I'll draw what I need from the world around me. Snatches of conversation will give me clues. Without meaning to, people will say things that will turn the whole plot. That's how I've always written."

That, maybe, is your recipe for how to be a successful novelist. Definitely, it's Nellie McClung's salute to the future.

Mrs. McClung has been a sick woman for the past few years.

As we stood and looked out of the wide window of her study, across green fields to an arm of the Pacific in the distance, she said,

"I sit a good deal in a sunny corner now, sheltered by a hedge, watching the world go by."

Through an open window came the heady perfume of flowers from her garden, distilled by a sudden shower. It was a graceful picture, a sort of pastoral Whistler's mother.

But the hostess shattered it in a minute. Briskly she turned from the window and went to her desk.

"Have you seen this?" She produced an article from a recent periodical.

"Did you hear Matthew Halton's broadcast on Sunday? Have you read this?" She dug a newly published book from among her papers. As she talked it was obvious that Lantern Lane is no quiet cloister, aloof from the world, but rather a radio set tuned to sound waves of affairs and opinions.

"Because I've got a bad heart my doctor has told me not to write." She made a wry face. "I assume he meant books, so I keep busy on letters, editorials and messages. And I read a lot. It's the first time in my life I've had enough time to read. . . ."

The conversation naturally kept coming back to books and writers. As one of the deans of Canadian writing, Mrs. McClung watches the work of young writers. Sometimes she likes what she sees; sometimes she doesn't. She's aware that it's a far cry from her homespun tales, folksy as gossip over the back fence, to the writing of today. Seldom did sex rear its head to leer at McClung characters.

"As far as I'm concerned the salacious and ugly have no place in literature," she said tartly; the corners of her eyes crinkled with the old McClung crusading spirit.

"I'm not a prude," she went on, "but I can't agree with some of our new Canadian writers that profanity is entertainment." She paused, evidently listing a few offenders in her mind. . . .

A tall, slightly-stooped man, with unruly hair and a twinkle in his eye, hesitated for a moment at the door.

"Ah, here's himself," exclaimed Mrs. McClung. "Now you've met him, you know the worst." The two grinned affectionately at each other. Wes McClung crossed to his wife's chair and put his hand protectingly on her arm for a moment. In a quiet voice he murmured something about not tiring herself and the two smiled at each other again, their smiles full of youthfulness and of some private joke. Together, somehow, they seemed much younger than they did separately.

"Yes, I suppose I've had my bit in this career," admitted the jolly man in the tweed jacket. "I'm both model and critic when my wife needs either," he said. He took down a book and went quietly to sit near his wife. One could still see the handsome young prairie druggist whom a young school teacher decided she was going to marry, and did. . . .

As they sat together, the last rays of the setting sun caught their faces in its glow. It was almost too much. It was the happy ending straight out of a McClung novel, two elderly people, after an eventful fifty-one years of married life, sitting quietly together in the setting sun.

But why shouldn't it be just that? It probably has been no trick at all for the pioneer girl who scribbled her way to fame, [and] managed to make more money than most Canadian writers ever have, to sign her own life with, "they lived happily ever after."[52]

Mark McClung, 1975

[My mother] . . . remained very cheerful all the time, through-out [her illness]. She was a woman of great fortitude, but I knew she was suffering, because she could only talk to me for a certain period. She would say, "I'm sorry, I'm tired. Come back tomorrow morning." . . . Nevertheless, she continued to write a good deal, with the assistance of my sister-in-law, Margaret McClung, who was a very good secretary and stenographer. She continued a lot of correspondence. There were also a lot of visitors to our home. One of the greatest deprivations she felt occurred when she was no longer able to go to church. She loved to go to church, naturally. And then the time came when she couldn't.[53]

Nellie L. McClung, no date

. . . the way I would like to go . . . [is] without pain, or weariness, or the loss of one's faculties. I dread a decrepit old age, beyond words. It does seem so cruel for old people to have to fade away bit by bit.[54]

Edna Jaques, 1977

It was the nicest experience I had in my life having her for a friend. She was the kindest person I ever knew.[62]

Nellie L. McClung, about 1916

What monument does any of us want . . . when we are dead and gone and out of the push and through with it all, other than that a few friends who knew us well, when they come together, may speak lovingly of us when their thoughts run upon old times. What better monument does any of us want than that?[63]

POSTSCRIPT

Nellie L. McClung, 1917

We know there is a future state, there is a land where the complications of this present world will be squared away. Some call it a day of judgment; I like best to think of it as a day of explanations. . . . Also I know we shall not have to lie weary centuries waiting for it. When the black curtain of death falls on life's troubled scenes, there will appear on it these words in letters of gold, "End of Part I. Part II will follow immediately."[64]

Nellie L. McClung, 1951

I have a few questions I will ask if happily I arrive at the heavenly country. . . . Especially do I want to know how it is that a just God has allowed the sins of the fathers to be visited on the children. Even the virtues of the mothers, inherited by the same law, do not balance the account.[65]

Nellie L. McClung, 1917

I want to hear God's side.[66]

NOTES

Epigraph: NLM, *The Stream Runs Fast*, Toronto: Thomas Allen, 1945, p. x.

Chapter One
PRAIRIE CHILD

Epigraph: NLM: "The Old Reader," *Leaves From Lantern Lane*, Toronto: Thomas Allen, 1936, p. 182.

1. Natalie Symmes, "Nellie McClung of the West: Writer, Lecturer, Cake Baker, Politician, Methodist, Mother," *Canada Monthly*, February 1916, p. 217.

2. "Cost of High Living Not High Cost of Living That We Are Paying These Days, According to Mrs. Nellie McClung of Edmonton," newspaper article, 28 May 1918, McClung Papers.

3. Personal interview.

4. NLM, *Clearing in the West*, Toronto: Thomas Allen, 1935, p. 226.

5. Ibid., p. 257.

6. Ibid., pp. 72-73, 116.

7. NLM, "The Spirit of the Times," *Agricultural Alberta*, July 1920, McClung Papers.

8. NLM, Undated notebook, McClung Papers.

9. NLM, quoted by Margaret Ecker Francis, "Nellie McClung," *Canadian Home Journal*, October 1947, p. 96.

10. NLM, Letter to Mr. F. C. Beech, Glenboro, Manitoba, 25 September 1946, McClung Papers.

11. NLM, "An Author's Own Story," *Women's Saturday Night*, 25 January 1913, McClung Papers.

12. NLM, *Clearing in the West*, pp. 106, 110, 112-14, 336.

13. Ibid., pp. 92, 96, 98-101.

14. Ibid., pp. 116-19.

15. Ibid., pp. 170-71.

16. NLM, "Lady Tweedsmuir Helps the Poets," *Leaves From Lantern Lane*, pp. 159-63.

17. NLM, Autobiographical sketch, circa 1920, McClung Papers.

18. Ibid.

19. NLM, *Clearing in the West*, p. 94.

20. NLM, "What Books Have Meant to Me," *Ontario Library Review*, no date, p. 38, McClung Papers.

21. NLM, *The Stream Runs Fast*, p. 71.

22. NLM, "Nellie's Christmas," newspaper article, December 1938, McClung Papers.

23. NLM, *Clearing in the West*, pp. 137-38.

24. Ibid., pp. 223-25.

Chapter Two
MARRIAGE OR A CAREER?

Epigraph: NLM, "What We Have Learned in Twenty-Five Years," typescript of a speech, McClung Papers.

1. NLM, *Clearing in the West*, p. 36.

2. NLM, quoted by Marjorie MacMurchy, "An Appreciation of Mrs. Nellie L. McClung," circa 1914, McClung Papers.

3. NLM, *Clearing in the West*, , p. 173.

4. Ibid., p. 227.

5. Ibid., p. 228.

6. Ibid., p. 234.

7. NLM, Undated notebook, McClung Papers. The quotation may date from any time in her adult life, for she never changed her mind on this point.

8. NLM, Notes for a speech, circa 1932, McClung Papers.

9. NLM, "An Author's Own Story," *Women's Saturday Night*, 25 January 1913, McClung Papers.

10. Letter to the author from Mrs. Clarence Truman, Midale, Saskatchewan, 17 September 1977.

11. The house in which she lived, furnished as she described it in *Clearing in the West*, is now maintained as a Nellie McClung museum by Bill Wallcraft on his farm near La Rivière, Manitoba.

12. NLM, "Can a Woman Raise a Family and Have a Career?" *Maclean's*, 15 February 1928, pp. 10, 70. See also *Clearing in the West*, pp. 268-69, 274-75, 286-88.

13. Nellie published two versions of this story. In the other, which appeared in "A Retrospect," *The Country Guide*, 2 December 1929, p. 3, she said that she and Mrs. Brown had asked only about the franchise and that Greenway had not seen the women's question. Instead it was discarded by the chairman of the meeting. "Mr. Greenway knew nothing about this," she wrote. "I know he would have answered our question, honestly, but he did not get a chance." Perhaps her loyalty to the Liberal party kept her from the truth in 1929. Perhaps she thought one version or the other made a better story. Or perhaps it was a simple lapse of memory.

14. NLM, *Clearing in the West*, p. 304, 306-8, 310.

15. NLM, Undated notebook, McClung Papers.

16. NLM, *Clearing in the West*, pp. 281-82. Though none of them held the same place in Nellie's affections as Dickens, she also admired the work of Robert Louis Stevenson, Rudyard Kipling, Bret Harte, and Olive Schreiner. She was influenced by many writers, for she read widely throughout her adult life.

17. Ibid., pp. 313-14.

18. Ibid., p. 313.

19. Ibid., p. 82.

20. Cited by Charles Rowell Wood, *The Historical Development of the Temperance Movement in Methodism in Canada*, p. 2.

21. Ibid., p. 43.

22. NLM, *Clearing in the West*, p. 292.

23. Ibid., pp. 351-54.

24. "Nellie L." was her name for herself, and the one which her closest friends often used in correspondence with her. Her official signature for the purposes of publication was "Nellie L. McClung," and she had no patience with editors who omitted the "L".

25. NLM, Notebook, McClung Papers.

26. NLM, *Clearing in the West*, pp. 374-76.

27. Letter to NLM from Nellie Sturdy, on the McClungs' golden wedding anniversary, 1946, McClung Papers.

Chapter Three
A LADY OF MANITOU

Epigraph: NLM, quoted in "Women's Place in the Universe," newspaper report of an address before the Ontario Equal Franchise Association, 1915, McClung Papers.

1. NLM, Letter to Mr. F. C. Beech, Glenboro, Manitoba, 25 September 1946, McClung Papers.

2. NLM, *The Stream Runs Fast*, pp. 16-17.

3. Ibid., p. 19.

4. Ibid., pp. 25-26.

5. NLM, *In Times Like These*, Toronto: McLeod and Allen, 1915, p. 25.

6. NLM, "Can a Woman Raise a Family and Have a Career?" *Maclean's*, 15 February 1928, pp. 71, 75.

7. NLM, *The Stream Runs Fast*, pp. 28-29.

8. NLM, Notebook, McClung Papers.

9. Note in NLM's handwriting, on a copy of Cora Hind's review of *Sowing Seeds in Danny*, McClung Papers.

10. Nellie was reading from *The Second Chance*, a novel she was writing at this time. See chapter four.

11. E. Cora Hind, "A Lady of Manitou," *Canadian Home Journal*, circa 1909, McClung Papers.

12. NLM, quoted in "Nellie McClung and Husband to Mark Golden Wedding Day," *Winnipeg Tribune*, 24 August 1946, McClung Papers.

13. Mark McClung, interviewed by Florence Bird, "The Incredible Nellie McClung," broadcast on CBC radio's *Between Ourselves*, 6 June 1975. It was not that Nellie didn't try to keep the household records in order. Scattered throughout her notebooks are list after list of expenditures for meat and milk and boots and services.

14. Miriam Green Ellis, "Nellie L. McClung," *Pathfinders*, Canadian Women's Press Club pamphlet, p. 14.

15. Mrs. A. H. Rodgers, past-president, Alberta Women's Institute, filmed interview, National Film Board of Canada.

16. NLM, "An Author's Own Story," *Women's Saturday Night*, 25 January 1913, McClung Papers.

17. NLM, *In Times Like These*, pp. 43, 44-45.

18. NLM, quoted in Margaret Ecker Francis, "Nellie McClung," *Canadian Home Journal*, October 1947, pp. 96-97.

19. NLM, *The Stream Runs Fast*, p. 27.

20. Coaching children to compete in recitation contests was one of Nellie's favorite projects in the W.C.T.U.

21. NLM, "To the Sound of Sleigh-bells," newspaper column, 7 January 1938, McClung Papers. See also *The Stream Runs Fast*, pp. 66-68.

22. NLM, Speech to a W.C.T.U. convention, Carmen, Manitoba, circa 1910, McClung Papers.

23. "W.C.T.U. Convention," *Grain Grower's Guide*, 17 May 1911, pp. 25-26.

24. There is evidence in one of Nellie's journals of how seriously she took this responsibility in her own family. Under the date of 26 June [1910], she wrote, "H.B.'s [Horace's] birthday passed off quietly but very hot. H.B. sat on F's knee at prayer time. Now he will sit beside father until he is five. Everybody loved him, but we gave him no present — the kingdom of God is not established by eating or drinking but righteousness, joy and peace."

25. NLM, "Mrs. McClung's Address," newspaper report of a speech given in Ontario, 20 December 1910, McClung Papers.

26. NLM, *The Stream Runs Fast*, pp. 58-62.

27. Charles Oke, "McCreary Man Recalls Kindness of Nellie McClung," *Western Producer*, 17 January 1974.

28. Personal interview, 1977. Mr. Wallcraft knew Nellie when he was a boy.

29. NLM, "Minding One's Own Business," McClung Papers.

30. NLM, newspaper article, *Calgary Albertan*, 1931, McClung Papers.

31. Mark McClung, newspaper article, 1973.

Chapter Four
AN AUTHOR, AT LAST

Epigraph: NLM, *The Stream Runs Fast*, p. 212.

1. NLM, Undated notebook, McClung Papers.

2. Letter to NLM from A. R. David, 12 September 1908, McClung Papers.

3. Ascheneth Sharp, now of Winnipeg, interview, 1977.

4. NLM, Undated notebook, McClung Papers.

5. NLM, *The Stream Runs Fast*, p. ix.

6. NLM, "Getting Acquainted," *Western Home Monthly*, 1925, McClung Papers.

7. NLM, *The Stream Runs Fast*, pp. 75-76.

8. McClung Papers. Caswell wrote from the Methodist Book and Publishing House, Toronto.

9. God eventually came to Pearlie's rescue: the window broke open during a thunderstorm.

10. NLM, *Sowing Seeds in Danny*, Toronto: William Briggs, 1908, pp. 69-71, 117-18, 124, 152-57, 160-61, 168, 176-81.

11. Letter to NLM from Rev. J. A. McClung, 15 November 1908, McClung papers.

12. NLM, *The Stream Runs Fast*, p. 69.

13. McClung Papers.

14. Letter to NLM from a friend, McClung Papers.

15. Interviewed by Florence Bird, "The Incredible Nellie McClung," broadcast on CBC radio's *Between Ourselves*, 6 June 1975. Nellie

later became something of a literary "nationalist." She thought it was important for Canadian writers to draw on their own history and for publishers to put out distinctively Canadian work. Her own fiction all developd western Canadian themes.

16. *Bookseller and Stationer,* circa 1908, McClung Papers.

17. Letter to NLM from F. S. Eweons, Methodist Book and Publishing Company, 3 November 1908, McClung Papers.

18. NLM, *The Stream Runs Fast,* p. 77.

19. "An Author Reciter," *Canadian Courier,* 2 April 1910, McClung Papers. Nellie spoke throughout Manitoba and, in 1910, toured in Ontario.

20. Letter to NLM from Mrs. G. C. Smith, Elkhorn, Manitoba, 2 September 1910, McClung Papers.

21. Brandon, Manitoba *Sun,* McClung Papers.

22. Letter to NLM from E. W. Walker, William Briggs Publishing Company, 11 May 1910, McClung Papers.

23. McClung Papers.

24. *Canadian Courier,* August 1909, McClung Papers.

25. *Toronto Globe,* 29 October 1910, McClung Papers.

26. *Canadian Thresherman,* circa 1912, McClung Papers.

Chapter Five
BRAVE WOMEN AND FAIR MEN

Epigraph: NLM in "Mrs. Nellie McClung's Appeal For the Boys," *Thomas Journal,* 10 June 1914, McClung Papers.

1. NLM, quoted in magazine article, *Canadian Thresherman,* McClung Papers.

2. Margaret McClung, Interview, 1977.

3. NLM, Autobiographical sketch, circa 1921, McClung Papers.

4. Emily F. Murphy (Janey Canuck), "What Janey Thinks of Nellie," *Maclean's,* 1 September 1921, p. 35.

5. NLM, Autobiographical sketch, circa 1921, McClung Papers. The convention in question was a get-together for soldiers' wives which Nellie, as president of the Edmonton Women's Institute, took a lead in organizing.

6. Press release for a speech in Calgary on behalf of the local branch of the Canadian Authors Association, probably prepared by Nellie herself, McClung Papers.

7. NLM, *The Stream Runs Fast*, p. 98.

8. Ibid., p. 99.

9. Alan Artibise, *Winnipeg: An Illustrated History*, Toronto: James Lorimer and National Museum of Man, 1977, pp. 199, 203.

10. Alan F. J. Artibise, *Winnipeg: a social history of urban growth, 1874-1914*, Montreal: McGill-Queen's University Press, 1975, p. 23 ff.

11. Clifford Sifton, Minister of the Interior, speech to the Toronto Board of Trade, 1922.

12. Artibise, *Winnipeg: a social history of urban growth*, p. 41.

13. NLM, Journal entry, 22 June [1910?], McClung Papers.

14. NLM, *Clearing in the West*, p. 52.

15. NLM, *The Stream Runs Fast*, pp. 53-57.

16. NLM, *The Second Chance*, Toronto: William Briggs, 1910, p. 71.

17. NLM, *The Stream Runs Fast*, pp. 99-100.

18. NLM, Journal entries, McClung Papers.

19. NLM, *The Stream Runs Fast*, pp. 101-7.

20. NLM, Journal entry, circa 1906, McClung Papers.

21. NLM, *The Stream Runs Fast*, p. 108.

22. Ibid., pp. 109-110.

23. NLM, in "Climax Reached in Brandon Reception," *Manitoba Free Press*, July 1914, McClung Papers.

24. NLM, Handwritten campaign speech, 1914 election, McClung Papers.

25. Natalie Symmes, "Nellie McClung of the West: Writer, Lecturer, Cake Baker, Politician, Methodist, Mother," *Canada Monthly*, February 1916, pp. 218-19.

26. NLM, "Mrs. McClung's Address," report of a speech given in Ontario, 20 December 1910, McClung Papers.

27. Nellie wrote a spirited verse about the death of one such woman which was a favorite recitation at Women's Institute meetings for

decades. See "Jane Brown," *Be Good to Yourself*, Toronto: Thomas Allen, 1930, pp. 12-18.

28. NLM, *In Times Like These*, p. 148.

29. NLM, Speech to an underwriters' convention, 24 August 1919, McClung Papers. For the whole hilarious story of her encounter with an insurance man, see *The Stream Runs Fast*, pp. 111-13.

30. "Odds and Ends of the Suffrage Campaign," Lillian Beynon Thomas Papers, Manitoba Archives.

31. NLM, "Women and Fashion," typescript, McClung Papers.

32. NLM, Letter to a woman in Birmingham, Washington, published as "Khaki Boys Hungry for Beauty While Flowers and Leaves Bring Thoughts of Home," *The Birmingham News*, 1917, McClung Papers.

33. NLM, "Nellie L. McClung Works Hard For Mothers of the West," newspaper report of an address to the Manitoba Liberal convention, 1914, McClung Papers.

34. Nellie L. McClung, "The Social Responsibilities of Women," typescript of a speech, McClung Papers.

35. NLM, *In Times Like These*, p. 100.

36. NLM, "A Retrospect," *The Country Guide*, 2 December 1929, p. 3.

37. *Manitoba Free Press*, 28 January 1914, p. 1.

38. *Carman Standard*, 11 June 1914, McClung Papers.

39. Personal interview, 1976.

40. The late H. B. Beynon, a member of the P.E.L. in 1914, explained in a 1976 interview that the "suffrage playlet" was included in the program in case the "parliament" were a flop.

41. *Winnipeg Tribune*, 29 January 1914, except for the "premier's speech," which is taken from handwritten notes, McClung Papers. The parliament was repeated in Winnipeg and then performed in Brandon. See *The Stream Runs Fast*, p. 117.

42. NLM, Typescript, McClung Papers.

43. NLM, quoted by Madge Macbeth in "Canadian Women in the Arts," *Maclean's*, September 1914, pp. 107-8.

Chapter Six
A WOMAN ON THE WARPATH

Epigraph: NLM, newspaper article, 1914, McClung Papers.

1. Newspaper report, *Portage la Prairie Liberal*, 11 June 1914, McClung Papers.

2. NLM, Typescript, McClung Papers.

3. Typescript, circa 1920, McClung Papers.

4. NLM, "Mennonites Leaving Canada," typescript, McClung Papers.

5. NLM, "Premier's reply to the delegation," typescript, McClung Papers.

6. W. L. Morton, *Manitoba: a History*, Toronto: University of Toronto Press, 1957, pp. 334-35.

7. NLM, "The Elusive Vote," *The Black Creek Stopping-House*, Toronto: William Briggs, 1912, pp. 187-208.

8. NLM, *The Stream Runs Fast*, p. 134.

9. Ibid., p. 134.

10. NLM, "A Woman on the Warpath," *Maclean's*, January 1920, p. 10.

11. Lillian Laurie (Lillian Thomas), "What Nellie L. McClung Made," newspaper report, circa 1915, McClung Papers.

12. McClung Papers.

13. "Mrs. McClung Has a Busy Day," Carman, Manitoba newspaper, 29 June 1914, McClung Papers.

14. "Roblin Encounters Contrary Winds," *Toronto Globe*, 6 July 1914, McClung Papers. It is important to remember that the press of 1914 was unabashedly partisan. Most of the quotations in this chapter come from Liberal papers.

15. McClung Papers.

16. McClung Papers.

17. McClung Papers.

18. "Mrs. Nellie McClung Conducting Whirlwind Campaign Through Province," *Brandon News*, 23 June 1914, McClung Papers.

19. Handwritten manuscript, McClung Papers.

20. "Mrs. Nellie McClung's Appeal for the Boys," *Neepawa Address*, 10 June 1914, McClung Papers.

21. "Mrs. McClung's Address," *The Swan River Star*, June 1914, McClung Papers.

22. Quoted in May L. Armitage, "Mrs. Nellie McClung," *Maclean's*, July 1915, p. 38.

23. NLM, "A Woman on the Warpath," *Maclean's*, January 1920, p. 9.

24. NLM, *The Stream Runs Fast*, pp. 125-30.

25. NLM, "Can a Woman Raise a Family and Have a Career?" *Maclean's*, 15 February 1928, p. 71.

26. NLM, *In Times Like These*, p. 6.

27. Quoted in "Orange Jingoes and Presbyterian Bulldogs," newspaper article, apparently from a Liberal paper, McClung Papers.

28. W. L. Morton, *Manitoba: a History*, p. 337.

29. *Winnipeg Tribune*, 11 July 1914, McClung Papers.

30. "Woman's Triumph: Miss McClung in Centre of Fight," *Ottawa Free Press*, 1 July 1914, McClung Papers.

31. "Mrs. McClung's Meeting is the Talk of the Town," *Manitoba Free Press*, [July?] 1914, McClung Papers.

32. "Mrs. McClung's Wonderful Reception by Crowded Walker Audience," *Manitoba Free Press*, [July?] 1914, McClung Papers.

33. Interviewed by Florence Bird, "The Incredible Nellie McClung," broadcast on CBC radio's *Between Ourselves*, 6 June 1975.

34. McClung Papers.

35. McClung Papers.

36. "The Anomaly," McClung Papers.

37. Alison Craig, journalist and suffragist, McClung Papers.

38. NLM, *The Stream Runs Fast*, p. 64.

. Chapter Seven
THE WAR THAT NEVER ENDS

Epigraph: NLM, Manuscript, McClung Papers.

1. NLM, *The Stream Runs Fast*, p. 137; interview with Ascheneth Sharp of Winnipeg, 1977.

2. "A Suffrage Tea," *The Canadian Thresherman and Farmer*, October 1913, McClung Papers.

3. NLM, *The Next of Kin*, Toronto: Thomas Allen, 1917, p. 32.

4. NLM, *The Stream Runs Fast*, p. 136.

5. NLM, "Beach Days," *The Next of Kin*, pp. 26-30, 31-32.

6. Ibid., p. 34.

7. NLM, *In Times Like These*, p. 208.

8. NLM, *The Stream Runs Fast*, pp. 139, 142-43.

9. The McClungs' first Edmonton home was at 11229 100 Avenue; later they moved to a spacious three-story house on 123 Street.

10. E. Cora Hind, "The Woman's Quiet Hour," *Western Home Monthly*, circa 1915, McClung Papers.

11. NLM, *The Stream Runs Fast*, p. 153.

12. May L. Armitage, "Mrs. Nellie McClung," *Maclean's*, July 1915, p. 38.

13. Newspaper report, 1915, McClung Papers.

14. See "May Be Lively Suffragette Meeting," *Edmonton Journal*, 3 February 1915. Other reports appeared on 4 and 8 February. One newspaper report claims that it was a visit from Nellie (then a resident of Winnipeg) which had prompted the formation of the Edmonton Equal Franchise League in 1914. In 1915, the year of the League's greatest successes, Nellie was first vice-president; the ladies elected a man as their president.

15. The Women's Canadian Club received her application for membership on 8 February 1915. Women's Canadian Club Papers, Provincial Archives of Alberta. "Press Women Feted by New Member," *Edmonton Journal*, 11 February 1915, p. 10.

16. Newspaper report, Edmonton Journal, 20 February 1915.

17. NLM, Typescript, McClung Papers.

18. "Doctors Agree Edmonton Car Steps Too High," newspaper report, 18 October 1915, Edmonton branch, Canadian Women's Press Club Papers, Provincial Archives of Alberta.

19. NLM, "The Neutral Fuse," *All We Like Sheep*, Toronto: Thomas Allen, 1926, p. 120.

20. EFM (Emily Ferguson Murphy), " 'The Next of Kin' — Edmonton Writer's Book Reviewed," newspaper report, 12 January 1918, McClung Papers.

21. Ibid.

22. "The Ungrateful Pigeons," "The Runaway Grandmother," *The Black Creek Stopping-House*, Toronto: William Briggs, 1912.

23. Manuscript, McClung Papers.

24. NLM, *In Times Like These*, p. 7.

25. See *In Times Like These*, pp. 19-23.

26. Ibid., pp. 32-33.

27. Ibid., pp. 161-62.

28. Ibid., p. 22.

29. Ibid., p. 161.

30. Review of *In Times Like These*, *Saturday Night*, 1 January 1916, McClung Papers.

31. " 'In Times Like These' Very Clever Book by Alberta Author," *Calgary Albertan*, 20 December 1915, McClung Papers.

32. Baltimore, Maryland newspaper, 1916, McClung Papers.

33. Pp. 13, 14, 26, 29, 143, 162-65.

34. "Politics Are an Uncut Book for Women, Nellie McClung Declares," *Calgary News Telegram*, 17 May 1917, p. 2, McClung Papers.

35. McClung Papers.

36. Speech in Vancouver, 1918, McClung papers.

37. "Women's Suffrage Before Legislature Next Year," *Edmonton Bulletin*, 26 February 1915.

38. Ibid.

39. Natalie Symmes, "Nellie McClung of the West: Writer, Lecturer, Cake Baker, Politician, Methodist, Mother," *Canada Monthly*, February 1916, p. 232.

40. *Edmonton Journal*, 20 July 1915, p. 7.

41. NLM, Address to the Strathcona Local of the United Farmers of Alberta, typescript, McClung Papers.

42. Natalie Symmes, "Nellie McClung of the West: Writer, Lecturer, Cake Baker, Politician, Methodist, Mother," *Canada Monthly*, February 1916, p. 232. The margin of victory was actually somewhat less than the two-to-one ratio which Symmes reports.

43. Telegram from F. O. Fowler, 28 July [1915], McClung Papers.

44. Telegram from Thomas H. Johnson, 28 July [1915], McClung Papers.

45. "Manitoba Shows Her Attitude to the World," *Manitoba Free Press*, 7 August 1915.

46. "Women's Suffrage for Alberta Will Be Passed At Next Session of the Legislature," *Edmonton Bulletin*, 20 September 1915, message from NLM.

47. Handwritten manuscript, McClung Papers.

48. McClung Papers.

49. NLM, "What Will They Do With It?" *Maclean's*, July 1916, pp. 36-38. According to Nellie, Alberta appointed its first public health nurses in 1917 and was the first province to have municipal hospitals and free health care for school children. See *The Stream Runs Fast*, p. 183.

50. "Women in Politics," newspaper report, 23 March 1916, McClung Papers.

51. NLM, *The Next of Kin*, pp. 100-101.

52. Ibid., pp. 44-45.

53. NLM, early draft of *The Next of Kin*, McClung Papers.

54. NLM, Journal entry, 4 December 1915, in *The Stream Runs Fast*, p. 155.

55. NLM, early draft of *The Next of Kin*, McClung Papers.

56. NLM, *The Next of Kin*, pp. 61, 62. Ontario women received the provincial franchise in 1917. It was extended in Nova Scotia, New Brunswick, and Prince Edward Island by 1922. Quebec held off until 1940.

57. Ibid., pp. 256-57.

58. NLM, *In Times Like These*, p. 32.

59. NLM, quoted in "Cost of High Living Not High Cost of Living That We Are Paying These Days, According to Mrs. Nellie McClung of Edmonton," newspaper report, 28 May 1918, McClung Papers.

60. NLM, "Compliments," *Toronto Globe and Mail*, 9 November 1937, McClung Papers.

61. "Mrs. Nellie McClung as Author, Orator, and Mother," *Toronto Daily News*, October 1915, McClung Papers.

62. Newspaper report, *Edmonton Journal*, October 1915, McClung Papers.

63. "Church Jammed to Doors; Many Turned Away," Toronto newspaper report, 1915, McClung Papers.

64. Headline, Ontario newspaper, October 1915, McClung Papers; headline, Ottawa newspaper, 1915, McClung Papers.

65. Quoted by Alison Craig, *Manitoba Free Press*, 20 November [1915?], McClung Papers.

66. "Bright, Breezy, Brimming With Optimism, Mrs. McClung Authoress Gives Interview," Toronto newspaper report, McClung Papers.

67. Ontario newspaper report, 1915, McClung Papers.

68. Quoted in an unsigned letter from Broadview, Saskatchewan, 3 December 1915, McClung Papers.

69. NLM, *The Stream Runs Fast*, p. 146.

70. Ibid., p. 147.

71. Ibid., p. 148.

72. Ibid., p. 147.

73. Ibid., p. 148.

74. Ibid., p. 145.

75. "Suffrage Victory in 5 Years Seen by National Leader," *Minneapolis Journal*, 8 May 1916.

76. Letter to NLM from Emilie J. Hubul, Racine, Wisconsin, 24 November 1916, McClung Papers.

77. Letter to NLM from Mary Ashburn McKay, 15 April 1917, McClung Papers.

78. "Ask Canadian Women About Vexing Things; Leaders of War Activities 'Interview' Mrs. McClung," Duluth newspaper report, 1917, McClung Papers; and "Khaki Boys Hungry for Beauty While Flowers and Leaves Bring Thoughts of Home," *Birmingham News*, McClung Papers.

79. NLM, *The Stream Runs Fast*, p. 170.

80. Newspaper report, Women's Canadian Club of Edmonton Papers, Provincial Archives of Alberta.

81. Minutes, Canadian Women's Press Club, Edmonton branch, September 1917, March 1918, Provincial Archives of Alberta.

82. "Vacant Lots Club to be Addressed by Two Enthusiasts: Lieut. Governor Brett and Mrs. Nellie McClung to Speak Next Monday," Edmonton newspaper report, 14 April 1916, p. 13.

83. May L. Armitage Smith and Elizabeth Baily Price, ed., *Club Women's Record*, Edmonton: Canadian Women's Press Club, 1916, p. 29-31.

84. "Overall Latest Thing Out in Women's Costume," *Edmonton Journal*, 12 January 1917.

85. Smith and Price, *Club Women's Record*, p. 37.

86. Newspaper report, *Edmonton Journal*, 2 February 1917, McClung Papers.

87. NLM, circa 1917, quoted in Rasmussen et al, *A Harvest Yet to Reap*, Toronto: Women's Press, 1976, p. 116.

88. "Spiritual Forces to Win War," *Pittsburg Dispatch*, 22 November 1917, McClung Papers.

89. Carolyn Cornell, "War . . . Increases Neighborliness, Curtails Selfishness — Inures All to Sacrifice," newspaper report, McClung Papers.

90. NLM, *The Next of Kin*, p. 213.

91. Ibid.

92. NLM, "Shall We Exclude German and Austrian Women from the International Council of Women," typescript, McClung Papers. Her answer to the question posed in the title of this article was "no."

93. NLM, *The Next of Kin*, p. 211.

94. "Mrs. McClung Agrees with Next-of-Kin Resolutions," newspaper report, 1917, McClung Papers.

95. "Franchise for Women," *Grain Growers' Guide,* 20 December 1916, p. 6.

96. NLM, *In Times Like These,* p. 76.

97. Ibid., p. 81.

98. Francis Marion Beynon, "The Foreign Woman's Franchise," *Grain Growers' Guide,* 27 December 1916.

99. NLM, "Mrs. McClung's Reply," *Grain Growers' Guide,* 24 January 1917.

100. "Work of Reconstruction May be Women's Greatest Opportunity," newspaper report in minute book, Women's Canadian Club of Edmonton Papers, Provincial Archives of Alberta.

101. NLM, "The Mobilization of Canadian Women," *Everywoman's World,* March 1918, McClung Papers.

102. NLM, *The Next of Kin,* p. 169.

103. Letter to Sir Robert Borden from Nellie L. McClung and Emily Ferguson Murphy, 11 February 1918, Borden Papers, Public Archives of Canada.

104. Telegram from N. W. Rowell, vice-chairman of the war committee of cabinet, 19 February 1918, McClung Papers.

105. NLM, Handwritten notes for a sermon, McClung Papers.

106. Typescript, McClung Papers.

107. NLM, Typescript, McClung Papers.

108. Minutes, Alberta Women's Institutes, 1919, Provincial Archives of Alberta.

109. "Ottawa Conference of Canadian Women," *Edmonton Journal,* 4 March 1918.

110. NLM, "Do We Want Women at the Peace Conference? Please — Yes." Typescript, McClung Papers.

Chapter Eight
THE MEMBER FOR EDMONTON

Epigraph: NLM, *In Times Like These,* p. 66.

1. Louise McKinney, "Editorial," *Canadian Home Journal*, August 1919.

2. Ibid.

3. NLM, "Editorial," *Canadian Home Journal*, January 1920, p. 5.

4. "Woman's place in the new order is to bring imagination to work on life's problems," she wrote in another article. "Without vision, which is another word for imagination — the people perish. It is vision that is needed now, rather than logic, and we have a right to expect it from women with their tender hearts and quick sympathies. We look to them to save the situation. The hand that rocks the cradle will surely never rock the boat!" "Woman's Place in the Band Wagon," McClung Papers.

5. NLM, Typescript, McClung Papers.

6. NLM, "Editorial," *Canadian Home Journal*, January 1920, p. 5.

7. Ibid.

8. NLM, "The Winnipeg General Strike," typescript, McClung Papers.

9. Ibid.

10. Ibid.

11. Ibid.

12. Ibid.

13. NLM, "Peace on Earth," typescript, 1920, McClung Papers.

14. NLM, "The Winnipeg General Strike," typescript, McClung Papers.

15. NLM, "Editorial," *Canadian Home Journal*, January 1920, p. 5.

16. NLM, Address to the Homemakers' Clubs, no date, McClung Papers.

17. "Politics are an Uncut Book for Women Nellie McClung Declares," *Calgary News Telegram*, 17 May 1917, p. 2. Nellie put one caveat on her optimistic expectations: "I am speaking, of course," she said, "of the real woman, not the parasite, who never did a day's work, or ate a meal that was not paid for by

someone else; but they are disappearing every day, and splendid, noble-souled women appearing in their places." "Loyalty," *Grain Growers' Guide*, 5 December 1917.

18. "An Idealistic Attitude," newspaper report, McClung Papers; "Mrs. McClung and Politics," *Calgary Daily Herald*, 17 May 1917, p. 8.

19. NLM, Autobiographical sketch, circa 1921, McClung Papers.

20. R. MacGregor Dawson, *William Lyon Mackenzie King, 1874-1923*, Toronto: University of Toronto Press, 1958.

21. NLM, "The Winnipeg General Strike," typescript, McClung Papers.

22. "After Much Balloting Liberals Selected Five Candidates For the City," *Edmonton Journal*, 29 June 1921.

23. Review of *Purple Springs*, *Zion's Herald*, 4 October 1922, McClung Papers.

24. Review of *Purple Springs*, *Cleveland Plain Dealer*, 11 March 1922, McClung Papers.

25. NLM, *Purple Springs*, Toronto: Ryerson, 1921, p. 299.

26. Ibid., p. 136.

27. "Here and There," *Edmonton Journal*, 11 July 1921.

28. Letter to NLM from J. Vernon MacKenzie, Editor of *Maclean's*, 21 July 1921, McClung Papers.

29. Agnes C. Laut, "Our Election Enigma — Woman," *Maclean's*, 15 November 1921, p. 21.

30. NLM, "Can a Woman Raise a Family and Have a Career?" *Maclean's*, 15 February 1928, p. 71.

31. Mark McClung, "Portrait of my Mother," speech delivered in Guelph, Ontario, 1975.

32. NLM, *The Stream Runs Fast*, pp. 175-76. Nellie admitted to being a puzzle addict. "I shun the puzzle page of a paper; and crossword puzzles turn me pale," she wrote. "I know what they could do to me, but their time is not yet. When the shades of evening gather about me, I know how I will pass the laggard hours. My grandchildren and great grand children will get no socks from me, done by my own frail, trembling old fingers. Not a sock. On the contrary, I will expect them to tell me what half an em is, and

what is the Portuguese word for bread!" "Getting Acquainted," *Western Home Monthly*, February 1925, McClung Papers.

33. Ibid., pp. 172-73. Amongst the issues on which Nellie voted against her party were the imposition of a two-cent-a-gallon surtax on gasoline (1922), a bill permitting government members to introduce private members bills without jeopardizing the tenure of the government (1922), and an extension of the powers of the Wheat Board (1923) — all of which she supported — and the prohibition question of 1923-26.

34. Clipping in the Alberta "newspaper hansard," 26 February 1926.

35. NLM, *The Stream Runs Fast*, p. 175. On 2 April 1924, Nellie and Irene Parlby collaborated on two resolutions asking the federal government to amend its laws. At that time, a Canadian woman lost her citizenship if she married an "alien" and the grounds for divorce were different for women than for men. (Women had to prove misconduct and two years of cruelty or desertion, while men only had to prove one act of adultery.) The two female M.L.A.s wanted both these laws revised.

36. *Edmonton Bulletin*, 25 February 1922.

37. Newspaper reports, *Edmonton Bulletin*, 10 March and 14 March 1922; *Edmonton Journal*, 14 March 1922, Alberta "newspaper hansard"; "Child Marriage is Legalized by Amendment," *Calgary Albertan*, circa 1925, McClung Papers.

38. Newspaper report, *Edmonton Journal*, 16 March 1923, Alberta "newspaper hansard"; see also reports on 21 March and 30 March 1923.

39. In addition to the issues enumerated in the text, Nellie took an interest in obtaining old-age pensions, sterilization of "mental defectives," make-work projects for the unemployed, allowances for single parents, and detention homes for delinquent girls. She also called for investigation of conditions at the provincial jails and asylums.

40. Newspaper report, *Edmonton Bulletin*, 17 February 1922, Alberta "newspaper hansard"; newspaper report, 17 March 1922, *Edmonton Journal*, Alberta "newspaper hansard."

41. Newspaper report, *Edmonton Journal*, 11 April 1923, Alberta "newspaper hansard."

42. "Opposition Objects to Form of Administration Provided in Hon. Mrs. Parlby's Bill," newspaper report, 2 March 1923, Alberta "newspaper hansard."

43. NLM, Speech to the Legislature, circa 1924, McClung Papers.

44. Newspaper reports, *Edmonton Bulletin*, 10 March and 14 March 1922; *Edmonton Journal*, 11 March and 14 March 1922. Alberta "newspaper hansard"; "Child Marriage is Legalized by Amendment," *Calgary Albertan*, circa 1925, McClung Papers.

45. "Member for Calgary Discussed Proposed Amendments to the Alberta Liquor Act — Believes If Beer Were Available, People Would Not Touch Moonshine Whiskey," *Edmonton Journal*, 21 March 1922, Alberta "newspaper hansard."

46. Ibid.

47. "Says Governmental Indifference is Working Greatest Harm In Enforcement of Temperance Act. Mrs. Nellie McClung Leads Social Service Delegation at Legislature Buildings, Which Was Received By Entire Cabinet — Representation Was Present From Everywhere in Province," newspaper report, 15 March 1921, McClung Papers.

48. NLM, "How Prohibition Is Working in Canada," typescript, McClung Papers.

49. NLM, "What Is Happening to Prohibition?" published magazine article, probably in *Canadian Home Journal*, McClung Papers.

50. NLM, "From Hired Man to Premier," *The Survey*, 1 September 1921.

51. Newspaper report, *Edmonton Journal*, 29 January 1923, Alberta "newspaper hansard"; address given by Nellie McClung to a Women's Institute Convention, 31 May 1923, later issued as a leaflet by the Alberta Prohibition Campaign Committee, McClung Papers.

52. NLM, Address to the Legislature, McClung Papers.

53. "Mrs. McClung is Keeping Keen Eye on Beer Petitions," *Edmonton Journal*, 19 February 1923, Alberta "newspaper hansard."

54. Headline, Edmonton newspaper, in Alberta "newspaper hansard," 13 March 1923.

55. NLM, Speech to the Legislature, 12 March 1923, McClung Papers.

56. "Mrs. Nellie McClung Finds Many Holes in Petition," Edmonton newspaper, in Alberta "newspaper hansard," 13 March 1923.

57. "Mrs. Nellie M'Clung Finds Many Holes In Petition," *Edmonton Journal*, 13 March 1923, Alberta "newspaper hansard."

58. Newspaper report, *Edmonton Journal*, 21 April 1923, Alberta "newspaper hansard."

59. NLM, Address to a Women's Institute Convention, 31 May 1923, McClung Papers.

60. NLM, Handwritten manuscript, McClung Papers.

61. NLM, Speech to the Legislature, McClung Papers.

62. NLM, Speech to the Legislature, 31 January 1924, McClung Papers.

63. "Two Lady Members Cross Swords in Legislature in Duel of Short Duration," newspaper report, 1 February 1924, Alberta "newspaper hansard."

64. Ibid.

65. NLM, Speech to the Legislature, McClung Papers.

66. "Liquor Control Act Debate Taken Up by Mrs. Nellie M'Clung," newspaper report, 15 February 1924, Alberta "newspaper hansard."

67. NLM, Speech to the Legislature, McClung Papers.

68. "Liquor Control Act Debate Taken up by Mrs. Nellie McClung," newspaper report, 15 February 1924, Alberta "newspaper hansard."

69. Newspaper report, *Edmonton Journal*, 14 March 1925, Alberta "newspaper hansard."

70. Mark McClung, interviewed by Florence Bird, "The Incredible Nellie McClung," broadcast on CBC radio's *Between Ourselves*, 6 June 1975.

71. NLM, Journal kept while attending the Fifth Ecumenical Methodist Conference in England, 1921, McClung Papers.

72. NLM, "How It Feels To Be a Defeated Candidate," typescript, McClung Papers.

73. NLM, "The Development of Personality," speech to the Island Underwriters, 10 December 1933, McClung Papers.

Chapter Nine
OUR PRESENT DISCONTENTS

Epigraph: NLM, Handwritten manuscript, circa 1941, McClung Papers.

1. NLM, Autobiographical sketch, circa 1921, McClung Papers.

2. NLM, *The Streams Runs Fast*, p. 243.

3. Letter to NLM from W. L. Mackenzie King, 5 June 1930, McClung Papers.

4. Letter, NLM to Louise Dean of Calgary, 20 October 1934, Papers of the Good Cheer Club, Glenbow-Alberta Institute.

5. *All We Like Sheep* contains stories and essays which Nellie had written for magazines. Two of them are of special note for their humor: "All We Like Sheep" which recounts her short and unhappy career as a sheep rancher (!), and "Banking in London," which tells of the trouble she had opening an account in an English bank. The latter, especially, is worth tracking down.

6. NLM, Autobiographical sketch, circa 1921, McClung Papers.

7. NLM, Autobiographical sketch, circa 1920, McClung Papers.

8. Sometimes, the stories Nellie heard demanded action. Once, for example, the tale of a husband's irresponsibility and cruelty prompted her to report the case to the Calgary chief of police. He sent one of his men out to lecture the erring husband, who took such a fright that he immediately reformed! "That was the beginning of a series of cases. . . ," Nellie reports, "where family problems told to me were unsnarled by the wise intervention of [Police] Chief Ritchie." *The Stream Runs Fast*, pp. 248-50.

9. NLM, "Wasted Time — Where mine has gone to!" McClung Papers.

10. NLM, Autobiographical sketch, circa 1921, McClung Papers.

11. Ibid.

12. NLM, Manuscript for "The Writer's Creed," McClung Papers.

13. NLM, Typescript, 12 January 1922, McClung Papers.

14. NLM, *The Stream Runs Fast*, p. 237.

15. Mark McClung, "Portrait of My Mother," speech given at Guelph, Ontario, 1975.

16. G. H. Melrose, "Nellie and Aimee," *Saturday Night*, mid-1920s, McClung Papers.

17. Mark McClung, "Portrait of My Mother."

18. NLM, *The Stream Runs Fast*, p. 258.

19. NLM, "The Domestic Help Problem," undated manuscript, McClung Papers.

20. NLM, quoted in "Gloomy Predictions of Anti-Suffragettes Contradicted By 1940 List of Candidates," Calgary newspaper, McClung Papers.

21. NLM, "What Do Women Want?" June 1938, McClung Papers.

22. NLM, "What Have We Gained in Sixty Years?" *Canadian Home Journal*, 1927, McClung Papers.

23. NLM, "Adam's Fall," *Be Good To Yourself*, Toronto: Thomas Allen, 1930, p. 174.

24. NLM, "Ladies and Leisure," *Farm and Ranch Review*, March 1931, McClung Papers.

25. NLM, "What Is Wrong With Women's Organizations?" typescript, written between 1923 and 1931, McClung Papers.

26. NLM, Letter to Irene Parlby, 1 May 1930, Parlby Papers.

27. The first and for many years the only female Member of Parliament in Canada was Agnes Macphail of Ontario.

28. NLM, Letter to the Calgary Business and Professional Women's Club, 27 June 1935, Glenbow-Alberta Institute.

29. NLM, "Our Present Discontents," *Canadian Home Journal*, March 1929, p. 30, McClung Papers.

30. Women's admission to the Senate was endorsed by the National Council of Women, the Women's Institutes, the W.C.T.U., and university women's clubs. Letter to NLM from Emily F. Murphy, 5 August 1927, McClung Papers.

31. NLM, *The Stream Runs Fast*, p. 186. A government-backed measure had gone before the Senate in June 1923, asking the King to endorse an amendment of the B.N.A. Act so that women might be appointed to the Senate. However, on the day this

motion was to be debated, its sponsor, a Senator McCoig, failed
to show up and it was never discussed.

   "We have now come to realize," Emily wrote, "that the
matter is one which cannot with any degree of fairness be
submitted for decision to a body of male persons, many of whom
have expressed themselves towards it in a manner that is
distinctly hostile." Letter to NLM from Emily F. Murphy, 5
August 1927, McClung Papers.

32. It was not until late in 1927 that she discerned the truth about
constitutional amendments. She had learned that ". . . no one has
the power to amend the B.N.A. Act but the Premiers of all the
Provinces and . . . *they* never will. Evidently this is how they hope
to get out of it [having women in the Senate]." Letter to NLM
from Emily F. Murphy, 2 December 1927, McClung Papers.

33. NLM, Handwritten notes, McClung Papers. In fairness to Nellie,
it should be noted that she found the article difficult to write.
There were several false starts as she worked out her anger and
frustration.

34. Letter to NLM from Emily F. Murphy, 9 August 1926, McClung
Papers.

35. In 1929, when the Privy Council verdict was announced, Nellie
gave all credit for the victory to Emily, a gesture which the latter
found moving. "No woman ever had a finer truer friend than I
have in you," she wrote, "and this message means more to me
than I can say." Letter to NLM from Emily F. Murphy, 18
October 1929, McClung Papers.

36. Letter, Emily F. Murphy to Mr. W. Stuart Edwards, Deputy
Minister of Justice, 9 November 1927, McClung Papers.

37. Letter to NLM from Emily F. Murphy, 2 December 1927,
McClung Papers.

38. NLM, *The Stream Runs Fast*, p. 187.

39. Ibid., pp. 187-88. The first woman senator was a Liberal party
worker from Ontario named Cairine Wilson. Although Emily
Murphy was hurt not to have received the nod herself, both she
and Nellie were swift to see the humor in one paper's satisfaction
with Senator Wilson's appointment: ". . . it is eminently fitting,"
the paper said, "that she should be the first appointee, rather
than one of the very industrious women politicians, spinsters

and others, who have talked incessantly of their rights as women without discharging any of their responsibilities as such."

"Lord! I think we ought to ask now for an interpretation of the word 'responsibilites,' " Emily exclaimed. Letter to NLM from Emily F. Murphy, 4 March 1930. Nellie was sometimes suggested as a possible Senate appointee though nothing ever came of it.

40. NLM, "A Retrospect," *The Country Guide*, 2 December 1929, p. 3, McClung Papers.

41. NLM, Undated notebook, McClung Papers.

42. NLM, *In Times Like These*, p. 106.

43. Ibid., p. 104.

44. NLM, "Women Have Never Set High Enough Value On Their Own Place In Life," *Edmonton Journal*, 1916, McClung Papers.

45. NLM, "Shall Women Preach?" typescript, McClung Papers.

46. NLM, *In Times Like These*, pp. 105, 112.

47. Ibid., pp. 102-3.

48. Ibid., pp. 115-16.

49. Interviewed by Florence Bird, "The Incredible Nellie McClung," broadcast on CBC radio's *Between Ourselves*, 6 June 1975.

50. "Novelist from Canada," *Methodist Record*, London, England, September 1921, McClung Papers.

51. NLM, Address to the Alberta Conference [Methodist Church], 22 March 1918, McClung Papers.

52. Transcript of an address by NLM, *The Proceedings of the Fifth Ecumenical Methodist Conference*, Toronto: Methodist Book and Publishing Company.

53. NLM, 1928, McClung Papers.

54. For once in her career, Nellie was unduly pessimistic. The United Church decided to ordain women in 1934, and Lydia Gruchy became its first female minister. Nellie found so little pleasure in this belated victory that she ignored the whole subject when it came time to write her autobiography.

55. NLM, "Shall Women Preach?" typescript, McClung Papers.

Chapter Ten
LANTERN LANE

Epigraph: NLM, *The Next of Kin*, p. 93.

1. NLM, "The Last Night," *More Leaves From Lantern Lane*, Toronto: Thomas Allen, 1937, p. 18.

2. NLM, "Women and Fashion," McClung Papers.

3. NLM, Address to an underwriters' convention, Calgary, 21 August 1919, McClung Papers.

4. NLM, "What We Have Learned in Twenty-Five Years," address to a Homemakers' Convention, Saskatoon, circa 1940, McClung Papers.

5. NLM, *The Next of Kin*, p. 257; *The Stream Runs Fast*, p. 144.

6. NLM, "Life's Balance," *Leaves From Lantern Lane*, p. 150.

7. NLM, "The Place of Religion in the Modern World, and Why," circa 1940, McClung Papers.

8. NLM, "The Flame of Youth ..." *The Farmers Advocate*, 9 December 1926.

9. NLM, "The Last Night," *More Leaves from Lantern Lane*, p. 19.

10. NLM, "What Life Has Taught Me," *Onward*, 30 December 1951, p. 827.

11. NLM, *The Stream Runs Fast*, p. 314.

12. Letter, NLM to Louise Dean of Calgary, 20 October 1932, Papers of the Good Cheer Club, Glenbow-Alberta Institute.

13. She repeated this performance in 1940, missing only one meeting in the campaign. Elizabeth Bailey Price, "It's Not a Man's World," 11 October 1941, McClung Papers. All this activity was not without its cost. In 1938, when she was debating whether or not to accept an invitation to address the Nova Scotia Women's Institutes, she chided herself for "middle-aged vanity." "Why am I tearing myself to pieces pretending I am as good as ever?" she asked herself.

14. "Mrs. M'Clung Defies Party," *Vancouver Daily Province*, 9 October 1935, McClung Papers.

15. NLM, Draft of a campaign speech, 1935, McClung Papers.

16. NLM, "Is Co-operation Coming?" *More Leaves . . .* p. 52.

17. NLM, Undated notebook, McClung Papers.

18. NLM, Newspaper article, May 1940, McClung Papers.

19. The farm had been planned as a joint venture for Nellie and Wes and their son and daughter-in-law, Horace and Margaret. But the arrangement didn't last for long. As Margaret tells the story, Horace had to spend too much of his time playing chauffeur to Nellie's numerous visitors from the prairies. The younger couple moved to a home of their own, but Margaret continued to work as Nellie's secretary, typing correspondence and the weekly column ("little doo-dabs," they called them) which Nellie was turning out.

20. NLM, "The Tyranny of Trifles," *Leaves From Lantern Lane*, p. 23.

21. NLM, "The Onion-Grower," *Leaves From Lantern Lane*, p. 18.

22. NLM, "Fruit Farming in the Okanagan Valley, B.C.," undated manuscript, McClung Papers.

23. NLM, "You Can't Make It Pay," *Leaves From Lantern Lane*, pp. 12-13.

24. NLM, Undated manuscript, McClung Papers.

25. The study was Nellie's private preserve, and Ruth Scott (Nellie's niece) remembered that Wes had put a teasing notice on the door. "Generally speaking," it read, "women are generally speaking."

26. "A Visit to Lantern Lane," magazine article, McClung Papers.

27. NLM, Undated manuscript, McClung Papers.

28. NLM, Undated manuscript, McClung Papers. In 1934 she conveyed pleasant messages to Rodmond Roblin via a mutal acquaintance and the next spring received the assurance that Roblin "has [not], nor ever had, any ill feeling or resentment against you, only admiration for the energetic manner you work to accomplish whatever you undertook to do." Along with this came congratulations on her successes and an invitation to visit him in Winnipeg. Letter to NLM from D. A. Ross, 20 May 1935, McClung Papers.

29. NLM, Letter to her publisher, Thomas Allen, 21 December 1933, McClung Papers.

30. NLM, Letter to her sister Hannah, 28 November 1934, in the possession of Weston Sweet.

31. Letter to NLM from Elizabeth Rae, 29 October 1933, McClung Papers.

32. McClung Papers.

33. NLM, Notes for a radio speech, 8 January 1924, McClung Papers.

34. "One Man's Meat, Another's Poison on Radio Program; Tolerance Needed Says Mrs. McClung Discussing C.B.C.: Crooner With Vaseline Voice May Be Loved by Neighbors," *Calgary Herald*, 22 May 1937, McClung Papers.

35. Mark McClung, "Portrait of My Mother," speech given at Guelph, Ontario, 1975.

36. Ibid.

37. Ibid.

38. After 1929, Nellie seldom raised women's issues. However, as late as 1941, there were still subjects on which she reacted "like an old fire-horse when he hears the fire alarm" — the army's plan to pay women recruits less than the men, for example, or the suggestion that women should give up their jobs after the war and have more babies. Manuscript of newspaper article, for release 13 December 1941, McClung Papers.

39. Newspaper report, *Regina Star*, 9 November 1936, McClung Papers.

40. "Women Should Get on Air," *Chatelaine*, circa 1937, McClung Papers.

41. See, for example, "Kindly Preserve Radio Public From More Feminine Announcers," *Trail Times*, 24 November 1937, McClung Papers.

42. Newspaper report, *Niagara Falls Review*, 10 November 1937, McClung Papers.

43. Letter, Charlotte Whitton to NLM, 26 August 1938, McClung Papers.

44. NLM, *The Stream Runs Fast*, p. 292.

45. Ibid., p. 297.

46. NLM, Handwritten diary, McClung Papers.

47. NLM, "The Oxford Group," *More Leaves From Lantern Lane*, pp. 199-200.

48. NLM, Handwritten diary, McClung Papers.

49. NLM, "A Rough Path, but Plain!," typescript, for release 27 January 1940, McClung Papers.

50. NLM, *The Stream Runs Fast*, pp. xi, xii.

51. Ibid., p. 195.

52. "Nellie McClung," *Canadian Home Journal*, October 1947, pp. 95-96, 102.

53. "Portrait of My Mother," speech given at Guelph, Ontario, 1975.

54. NLM, Undated letter of condolence, to a Miss Johnson, Alberta Archives.

55. NLM, Letter to Lillian Thomas, 14 September 1950, Thomas Papers.

56. Newspaper report, 1947, McClung Papers.

57. NLM, Undated manuscript, McClung Papers.

58. "Portrait of My Mother," speech given at Guelph, Ontario, 1975.

59. *Pathfinders*, p. 15.

60. Interviewed by Florence Bird, "The Incredible Nellie McClung," broadcast on CBC radio's *Between Ourselves*, 6 June 1975.

61. "Nellie McClung of Gordon Head," *Victoria Daily Colonist*, 21 October 1973, p. 15.

62. Interview, 1977.

63. NLM, Speech to a U.F.A. convention, about 1916, McClung Papers.

64. NLM, *The Next of Kin*, pp. 219-20.

65. NLM, "What Life Has Taught Me," *Onward*, 30 December 1951, p. 826.

66. NLM, *The Next of Kin*, p. 219.

BIBLIOGRAPHY

PRIMARY SOURCES

Nellie McClung's papers are held by the Provincial Archives of British Columbia in Victoria. The Glenbow-Alberta Institute in Calgary has the papers of the Good Cheer Club, which Nellie helped to lead, and a few files of clippings and miscellaneous correspondence. The Provincial Archives of Alberta in Edmonton has the papers of the Edmonton branch of the Canadian Women's Press Club, the Alberta Women's Institutes, and Louise McKinney, as well as isolated letters and clippings. There are two letters which Nellie wrote during her term as M.L.A. in the premiers' papers; she is also mentioned by Margaret H. Brine, Pansy L. Pue, Rev. Astor R. Schrag, Robert Andison, Sem Wissler Field, and John E. Brownlee in phonotaped interviews. Emily Murphy's papers are in the City of Edmonton Archives. The Provincial Archives of Manitoba has the records of the Winnipeg branch of the Canadian Women's Press Club, the Quill Club (a literary society with which Nellie was associated), and the Political Equality League, as well as the personal papers of Lillian Beynon Thomas. The Public Archives of Canada holds letters from Nellie to Agnes Macphail, Robert Borden, W. L. Mackenzie King, and Senator Cairine Wilson.

BY NELLIE L. McCLUNG: BOOKS

Sowing Seeds in Danny. Toronto: William Briggs, 1908. The first of the Pearlie Watson stories.

The Second Chance. Toronto: William Briggs, 1910. The Watson saga continued.

The Black Creek Stopping House. Toronto: William Briggs, 1912. A collection of short stories and a novella.

In Times Like These. Toronto: McLeod and Allen, 1915; rpt. Toronto: University of Toronto Press, 1975. Essays on temperance and women's suffrage.

The Next of Kin. Toronto: Thomas Allen, 1917. An exhortation to war service.

Three Times and Out: a Canadian Boy's Experience in Germany. Boston: Houghton Mifflin, 1918. The true story of Private Simmons told more or less in his own words.

Purple Springs. Toronto: Thomas Allen, 1921. Pearlie Watson's story concluded.

When Christmas Crossed "The Peace". Toronto: Thomas Allen, 1923. A moralistic but spirited novella.

Painted Fires. Toronto: Thomas Allen, 1925; published in Finland as *A Finnish Girl in America* in 1927. A novel about an immigrant girl.

All We Like Sheep. Toronto: Thomas Allen, 1930. Sketches, stories, and poems.

Be Good to Yourself. Toronto: Thomas Allen, 1930. Sketches, stories, and poems.

Flowers For the Living. Toronto: Thomas Allen, 1931. A book of short stories.

Clearing in the West: My Own Story. Toronto: Thomas Allen, 1935, 1976. Volume one of her autobiography.

Leaves From Lantern Lane. Toronto: Thomas Allen, 1936. An anthology of her newspaper columns.

More Leaves From Lantern Lane. Toronto: Thomas Allen, 1937. Another collection of newspaper columns.

Before They Call. . . Toronto: Board of Home Missions, United Church of Canada, 1937. A pamphlet on missionary work in Canada.

The Stream Runs Fast: My Own Story. Toronto: Thomas Allen, 1945. Volume two of her autobiography.

BY NELLIE L. McCLUNG: MAJOR MAGAZINE ARTICLES

"Speaking of Women," *Maclean's*, May 1916, pp. 25-26, 96-97. Nellie's submission in a magazine "debate" with Stephen Leacock on women's suffrage.

"What Will They Do With It?" *Maclean's*, July 1916, pp. 36-38. Predictions about women's use of the provincial franchise.

"A Woman On The Warpath—Myself and a Certain Manitoba Election and Other Experiences," *Maclean's*, January 1920, pp. 9-10, 87-88. Funny (sometimes poignant) stories about Nellie's experiences on the campaign trail.

"Banking in London," reprinted in *All We Like Sheep*. Toronto: Thomas Allen, 1926, pp. 176-83. An hilarious account of one of Nellie's misadventures in England in 1921.

"All We Like Sheep," *Maclean's*, 1 March 1920, pp. 14-16, 63-64; 15 March 1920, pp. 20-21, 62; reprinted in *All We Like Sheep*. Toronto: Thomas Allen, 1926, p. 1-37. Nellie's short and inglorious career as a sheep rancher.

"How It Feels To Be a Defeated Candidate," reprinted in *Be Good To Yourself*. Toronto: Thomas Allen, 1930, pp. 45-55. Nellie's election defeat, 1926.

"I'll Never Tell My Age Again," *Maclean's*, 15 March 1926, pp. 15, 55-56. A light-hearted essay on aging and women.

"Can a Woman Raise a Family and Have a Career?" *Maclean's*, 15 February 1928, pp. 10, 70-71, 75. Nellie's own experiences.

"Our Present Discontents," *Canadian Home Journal*, March 1929, pp. 9, 30. The position of women ten years after their full enfranchisement.

"A Retrospect," *Country Guide*, 2 December 1929, pp. 3, 58. Looking back from the vantage point of the Persons Case.

"Shall Women Preach?" *Chatelaine*, September 1934, pp. 14-15. A review of the ordination controversy in the United Church.

"Are We Uneasy? We Should Be," *Canadian Home Journal*, 31 January 1945, inside front cover, p. 31. A plea for temperance workers.

"What Life Has Taught Me," *Onward*, 30 December 1951, pp. 826-27. A biographical and philosophical comment, published posthumously.

SECONDARY SOURCES

ABOUT NELLIE L. McCLUNG: PRINTED SOURCES

Most of the standard reference works on Canadian writers include short biographies of Nellie McClung. A bibliography of sources, compiled by Ann Braden, is available from the library at Carleton University in Ottawa.

Armitage, May L. "Mrs. Nellie McClung," *Maclean's*, July 1915, pp. 37-38. Nellie as an energetic reformer.

Benham, Mary Lile. *Nellie McClung*. Toronto: Fitzhenry and Whiteside, 1975, 61 pages. An illustrated biography for younger readers.

Ellis, Miriam Green. "Nellie McClung," *Pathfinders*. Canadian's Women's Press Club, about 1957, pp. 14-15.

Francis, Margaret Ecker. "Nellie McClung," *Canadian Home Journal*, October 1947, pp. 94-96, 100. An interview with Nellie, aged seventy-four.

Harman, Eleanor. "Five Persons From Alberta," *The Clear Spirit*, ed. Mary Quayle Innis. Toronto: University of Toronto Press, 1966, pp. 158-178. Focus is on the Persons Case.

Jackel, Susan. "Prairie Wife: Female Characterization in Canadian Prairie Fiction." Unpublished M.A. thesis, University of Toronto, 1966, pp. 20-29.

Jaques, Edna. "Years Between," *Country Guide*, December 1942, pp. 42-43. A friend visits Lantern Lane.

—. *Uphill All the Way*. Saskatoon: Western Producer Prairie Books, 1978. One short chapter deals with Nellie McClung.

Jupp, Ursula. "Nellie McClung of Gordon Head," *Daily Colonist*, 21 October 1973, p. 13. A neighbor remembers.

Lambert, Norman. "A Joan of the West," *Canadian Magazine*, January 1916, pp. 265-69.

McClung, Mark. "Recollections of my Mother," *Perception*, 1975, p. 1. Report of a brief interview.

—. "Portrait of my Mother," transcript of a speech, available from Dr. Margaret Andersen, Department of Languages, University of Guelph, Guelph, Ontario. Intimate recollections.

McCourt, Edward. *The Canadian West in Fiction*. Toronto: Ryerson, pp. 71-76. A comment on Nellie as a writer.

MacKenzie, Jean. "Nellie Was a Lady," *United Church Observer*, October 1973, pp. 18-19.

McLean, Una. "The Famous Five," *Alberta Historical Review*, spring 1962, pp. 1-4. The Persons Case.

McMullen, M.J.G. *Nellie McClung: "Recalled to Life."* Priv. printed, Winnipeg, 1965. An illustrated pamphlet.

Matheson, Gwen. "Nellie McClung," *Canadian Dimension*, June 1975, pp. 42-48.

— and V. E. Lang. "Nellie McClung, Not a Nice Woman," *Women in the Canadian Mosaic*. Toronto: Peter Martin, 1976, pp. 1-20.

—. "No 'Nice Nelly' Was Nellie," *Chatelaine*, November 1974, pp. 54-55, 102-5.

Murphy, Emily. "What Janey Thinks of Nellie," *Maclean's*, 1 September 1921, pp. 15, 34-35. An appreciation of Nellie's political work by a friend.

Salverson, Laura Goodman. *Confessions of an Immigrant's Daughter*. Toronto: Ryerson, circa 1939. A friend tells how Nellie encouraged her to write.

Strong-Boag, Veronica. "Introduction," *In Times Like These*. Toronto: University of Toronto Press, 1973. A biographical and critical essay.

Symmes, Natalie. "Nellie McClung of the West: Writer, Lecturer, Cake Baker, Politician, Methodist, Mother," *Canada Monthly*, February 1916, pp. 217-19, 232.

Verkruysse, Patricia Louise. "Small Legacy of Truth: the Novels of Nellie McClung." Unpublished M.A. thesis, University of New Brunswick, 1975.

Zieman, Margaret K. "Nellie Was A Lady Terror," *Maclean's*, 1 October 1953, pp. 20-21, 62-66.

ABOUT NELLIE L. McCLUNG: OTHER MEDIA

Grant, Diane. *What Glorious Times They Had — Nellie McClung*. (A play originally created and performed by Redlight Theater). Toronto: Simon and Pierre, 1974.

Grandmother Was Not a Person, a series of five radio dramas, each fifteen minutes long, which follows the career of Nellie McClung from the 1890s to 1930. Written by Candace Savage and produced by Alberta School Broadcasts and Media Productions, Edmonton, 1979.

Great Grand Mother. A twenty-eight minute color film on pioneer women and suffrage feminism, by Anne Wheeler and Lorna Rasmussen. National Film Board of Canada.

"The Incredible Nellie McClung," *Between Ourselves.* A documentary broadcast by CBC Radio on 6 June 1975.

GENERAL REFERENCES

Allen, Richard. *The Social Passion: Religion and Social Reform in Canada, 1914-1928.* Toronto: University of Toronto Press, 1971.

—, ed. *The Social Gospel in Canada.* National Museums of Man, Mercury Series, History Division Paper No. 9, 1975.

Artibise, Alan. *Winnipeg: an illustrated history.* Toronto: James Lorimer and the National Museum of Man, 1977.

—. *Winnipeg: a social history of urban growth.* Montreal: McGill-Queen's University Press, 1975.

Bacchi-Ferraro, Carol-Lee. "The Ideas of the Canadian Suffragists, 1890-1920." Unpublished M.A. thesis, McGill University, 1970.

Beynon, Francis. *Aleta Day.* London: C. W. Daniel, 1919. A novel about the reform movement and the war.

Brown, Robert Craig and Ramsay Cook. *Canada, 1896-1921, A Nation Transformed.* Toronto: McClelland and Stewart, 1974.

Cleverdon, Catherine. "The Prairie Provinces," *The Women Suffrage Movement in Canada.* Second edition. Toronto: University of Toronto Press, 1974, pp. 46-83.

Cook, Ramsay. "Francis Marion Beynon and the Crisis of Christian Reformism," *The West and the Nation.* Toronto: McClelland and Stewart, 1977, pp. 187-208.

Creighton, Donald. *Canada's First Century.* Toronto: Macmillan, 1970.

Dawson, R. Macgregor. *William Lyon Mackenzie King, 1874-1923.* Toronto: University of Toronto Press, 1958.

Ferguson, Emily. *Janey Canuck in the West.* Toronto: J. M. Dent, 1917.

Gray, James H. *Booze: The Impact of Whisky on the Canadian West.* Toronto: Macmillan, 1972.

—. *The Roar of the Twenties.* Toronto: Macmillan, 1975.

—. *The Winter Years, The Depression on the Prairies.* Toronto: Macmillan, 1966.

Houghton, Walter E. *The Victorian Frame of Mind 1830-1870.* New Haven: Yale University Press, 1957.

MacGregor, James G. *A History of Alberta.* Edmonton: Hurtig, 1972.

Mitchell, David. *Monstrous Regiment: The Story of the Women of the First World War.* New York: Macmillan, 1965.

Morton, W. L. *Manitoba: A History.* Toronto: University of Toronto Press, 1957.

Nicholson, Barbara Jane. "Feminism in the Prairie Provinces to 1916." Unpublished M.A. thesis, University of Calgary, 1974.

O'Neill, William L. *Everyone Was Brave: The Rise and Fall of Feminism in America.* Chicago: Quadrangle Books, 1969.

Palmer, R. R. and Joel Colton. *A History of the Modern World.* Third edition. New York: Alfred A. Knopf, 1965.

Ramkhalawansingh, Ceta. "Women During the Great War," *Women at Work, Ontario, 1850-1930.* Toronto: Women's Press, 1974, p. 261-307.

Rasmussen, Linda, Lorna Rasmussen, Candace Savage, and Anne Wheeler. *A Harvest Yet to Reap: A History of Prairie Women.* Toronto: Women's Press, 1976.

Sanders, Byrne Hope. *Emily Murphy Crusader.* Toronto: Macmillan, 1945.

Strong-Boag, Veronica Jane. *The Parliament of Women: The National Council of Women of Canada 1893-1929.* National Museum of Man, Mercury Series, History Division Paper No. 18, 1976.

Thomas, L. G. "Alberta Politics and the War of 1914-1918," *The Liberal Party in Alberta: A History of Politics in the Province of Alberta, 1905-1921.* Toronto: University of Toronto Press, 1959, pp. 154-87.

Thompson, John Herd. "The Harvests of War: The Prairie West 1914-18." Unpublished Ph.D. dissertation, Queen's University, 1975.

Trofimenkoff, S. M., ed. *The Twenties in Canada.* National Museum of Man, Mercury Series, History Division Paper No. 1, 1972.

— and Alison Prentice, ed. *The Neglected Majority: Essays in Canadian Women's History.* Toronto: McClelland and Stewart, 1977.

Voisey, Paul. "The 'Votes for Women's Movement'," *Alberta History,* summer 1975, pp. 1-23.

Wilson, L. J. "Educational Role of the United Farm Women of Alberta," *Alberta History,* spring 1977, pp. 28-36.

Wood, Charles Rowell. "The Historical Development of the Temperance Movement in Methodism in Canada." Unpublished B.D. thesis, Emmanuel College, Victoria University of the University of Toronto, 1958.

INDEX

About the author

Candace Savage was born in 1949 and presently resides in Saskatoon, Saskatchewan. A recipient of numerous academic awards, including the Governor-General's Medal for 1971 at the University of Alberta, the author has pursued a career in writing and editing since her graduation. To date she has several publications to her credit. Her first work was entitled *Foremothers: Personalities and Issues From The History of Women in Saskatchewan*. In 1976 she co-authored *A Harvest Yet To Reap: A History of Prairie Women*. During the years 1976 to 1979 inclusive, she co-authored *Herstory: A Canadian Women's Calendar*.

Ms. Savage enjoys a variety of outdoor activities including hiking, canoeing, and swimming. She and her husband Arthur have one child.

Other Canadian Lives you'll enjoy reading

Canadian Lives is a paperback reprint series which presents the best in Canadian biography chosen from the lists of Canada's many publishing houses. Here is a selection of titles in the series. Watch for more Canadian Lives every season from Goodread Biographies. Ask for them at your local bookstore.

An Arctic Man by Ernie Lyall Ernie
Lyall's story of sixty-five years living with the Inuit people in the Arctic.
"What makes Lyall's book so exceptional is its Inuit orientation." — *Books in Canada* / 239 pages / 12 photos / $4.95

Boys, Bombs and Brussels Sprouts by J. Douglas Harvey
An irreverent, sometimes naughty, often moving account of the young Canadians who flew with Bomber Command in the Second World War. A bestseller in cloth — and in paperback! / 210 pages / $4.95

Brian Mulroney: The Boy from Baie-Comeau by Rae Murphy et al
A revealing personal portrait of Canada's 18th prime minister — his background, his values, his quest for power.
"Fascinating, informative." — *Kitchener-Waterloo Record* / 214 pages / 38 photos / $4.95

By Reason of Doubt by Ellen Godfrey
The story of university professor Cyril Belshaw, the mysterious death of his wife, and his trial for murder.
"Fascinating reading for lovers of mystery." — *Calgary Herald* / 208 pages / 12 photos / $4.95

Canadian Nurse in China by Jean Ewen
The story of a remarkable young nurse who travelled in war-torn China with Dr. Norman Bethune.
"A remarkably candid book by a no-nonsense nurse." — Pierre Berton / 162 pages / 12 photos / $3.95

The Company Store by John Mellor
The dramatic life of a remarkable and fiery idealist, J.B. McLachlan, and the battle of the Cape Breton coal miners.
"A man of exceptional humanity, resolute will and unshakable conviction." — Montreal *Gazette* / 400 pages / 35 photos / $5.95

Deemed Suspect by Eric Koch
The moving story of young refugees from the Nazis, locked in a prison camp in Quebec City during the Second World War.

"A fascinating story told with…warmth and wit." — Andrew Allentuck, Arts National / 259 pages / 37 photos / $5.95

Dual Allegiance by Ben Dunkelman
A hard-drinking, hard-fighting soldier tells his true-life adventure story.

"A fascinating story. I couldn't put it down." — *Quill and Quire* / 326 pages / 50 photos / $5.95

E.P. Taylor by Richard Rohmer
The best-selling biography of one of the most successful Canadian tycoons of all time.

"A marvellously comprehensive picture." — Montreal *Star* / 352 pages / $5.95

The Fighting Fisherman: Yvon Durelle by Raymond Fisher
A moving, honest account of the life of a great boxer from the Maritimes — his triumphs and his tragedies.

"An authentic Canadian tragic hero — superb!" — Montreal *Star* / 282 pages / 17 photos / $5.95

Halfbreed by Maria Campbell
The powerfully told life story of an unforgettable young Métis woman.

"The daring account of a strong-willed woman who defeated poverty, racism, alcohol and drug addiction by the age of thirty-three." — *Saturday Night* / 184 pages / $4.95

Her Own Woman by Myrna Kostash et al
Profiles of ten contemporary Canadian women, famous and not-so-famous, including Barbara Frum, Margaret Atwood, and sports hero Abby Hoffman.

"Insightful, well-written, wonderful to read." — Doris Anderson / 212 pages / 9 photos / $4.95

Hey Malarek! by Victor Malarek
A wonderfully written account of a young street-tough kid, in and out of boys' homes, in trouble with the cops — truly a good read!

"Very human." — *Calgary Herald* / 241 pages / $4.95

Hockey Is a Battle by Punch Imlach with Scott Young
One of the game's great coaches offers a lively, revealing account of his first thirty years in the game. More than 100,000 copies sold, this is an all-time Canadian bestseller. / 203 pages / 27 photos / $4.95

Hugh MacLennan: A Writer's Life by Elspeth Cameron
The prize-winning biography of one of Canada's greatest novelists.

"Deeply understanding of its subject, this impressive biography does justice to the man and his work." — Margaret Laurence / 420 pages / 23 photos / $5.95

The Indomitable Lady Doctors by Carlotta Hacker
Stories of courage, heroism and dedication — the experiences of Canada's pioneering women doctors.

"Admirable, enjoyable." — *Edmonton Journal* / 223 pages / 20 photos / $5.95

Letters from a Lady Rancher by Monica Hopkins
The lively, delightfully written adventures of a young woman who married a homesteader and started a new life in the West.

"Highly readable…an irrepressible personality." — James Gray / 171 pages / $4.95

Louis 'David' Riel: Prophet of the New World by Thomas Flanagan
A sympathetic portrayal of a great Métis leader — a man too often dismissed by historians as mad.

"Absorbing." — Hamilton *Spectator*. "A most sensitive job, neither obscuring the reality of madness nor dismissing the basic truths of the visionary." — *Calgary Albertan* / 215 pages / $4.95

Ma Murray by Georgina Keddell
The outspoken newspaperwoman who became a legend in her own time. / 301 pages / 12 photos / $5.95

The Making of a Secret Agent by Frank Pickersgill;
edited by G.H. Ford
The story of a young Canadian who abandons pacifism to become a spy — and whose courage and idealism cost him his life.

"A marvellous book, a Canadian classic." — Ramsay Cook, *Canadian Reader* / 274 pages / 10 photos / $5.95

Morgentaler by Eleanor Wright Pelrine
The surprising life story of the controversial Montreal doctor.

"Fascinating reading." — *Toronto Star* / 222 pages / $4.95

My Uncle, Stephen Leacock by Elizabeth Kimball
A young girl's memories of wonderful summers at the lake and of the Leacock clan at play.

"Draws you in to the Leacock family like a magnet. You hate to leave." — *Kitchener-Waterloo Record* / 174 pages / 13 photos / $4.95

Nathan Cohen: The Making of a Critic by Wayne Edmonstone
A book which captures in print a man who made an indelible impression on Canadian arts and entertainment.

"How did we ever produce such a giant?" — *Toronto Star* / 286 pages / 9 photos / $5.95

Our Nell: A Scrapbook Biography of Nellie L. McClung
by Candace Savage
The story of Nellie McClung, politician, writer, and vigorous advocate of women's rights

"A warm, sincere, vital human being who cared deeply about women." — *Upstream* / 203 pages / 51 photos / $5.95

The Patricks: Hockey's Royal Family by Eric Whitehead
The story of a four-generation family that has been right at the centre of hockey history for seventy years.

"A finely crafted book by a good storyteller...with fascinating anecdotes aplenty." — *Quill and Quire* / 280 pages / 19 photos / $5.95

The Prince and His Lady by Mollie Gillen
The love story of Edward, Duke of Kent, and his French mistress, and their years in Quebec and Halifax

"Enjoyable, fascinating reading." — Halifax *Chronicle-Herald* / 282 pages / 27 photos / $5.95

Radical Tories by Charles Taylor
A personal journey of discovery, and portraits of Canadians with a unique perspective on our country.

"An immensely readable book." — Dalton Camp / 215 pages / $4.95

Shaking It Rough: A Prison Memoir by Andreas Schroeder
The story of life inside, by a young writer who could understand the prison world because he bore no grudges.

"Crisp and telling." — *Maclean's*. "Fresh and interesting." — *New York Times* / 214 pages / $4.95

Something Hidden: A Biography of Wilder Penfield
by Jefferson Lewis
The life of the world-famous Canadian surgeon and scientist who explored the hidden mysteries of the brain — and the mind.

"One of the most valuable and fascinating biographies I have read in many years." — Hugh MacLennan / 311 pages / 22 photos / $5.95

Ticket to Hell by A. Robert Prouse
A young Canadian's story of three years in a German prisoner-of-war camp — told with warmth, humour and honesty.

"A fascinating, yet terrible, memoir of what it was like behind barbed wire." — Kingston *Whig-Standard* / 161 pages / 50 photos / $4.95

Tommy Douglas by Doris French Shackleton
A warm, lively account of one of Canada' most loved — and most successful — political leaders.

"Vivid, compelling, and authentic." — *Calgary Albertan* / 329 pages / 20 photos / $5.95

Tomorrow Is School by Don Sawyer
The adventures of two young teachers in an isolated Newfoundland outport.

"Honest and love-filled." — Canadian Press / 12 photos / 205 pages / $4.95

Troublemaker! by James Gray
One of western Canada's favourite historians relives his days as an irreverent newspaperman witnessing the golden age of western Canada, 1939-1955.

"Vividly portrays a span of western Canadian history." — Saskatoon *Star-Phoenix* / 315 pages / 22 photos / $5.95

A Very Double Life by C.P. Stacey
The true story of Mackenzie King's startling private life — the ladies of the night, the séances, the close women friends — sympathetically told.

"One of the strangest men ever to govern a democratic state." — *The Globe and Mail* / 227 pages / 23 photos / $5.95

Walter Gordon: A Political Memoir by Walter Gordon
The memoirs of an establishment businessman turned politician who fought for his vision of an independent Canada in the Pearson years. / 395 pages / 9 photos / $5.95

The Wheel of Things: A Biography of L.M. Montgomery by Mollie Gillen
The remarkable and tragic life story of the woman who created Canada's best-loved heroine, Anne of Green Gables.

"A perceptive and sympathetic portrait of a complex personality." — Ottawa *Journal* / 200 pages / 32 photos / $4.95

When I Was Young by Raymond Massey
The vivid account of growing up in the richest, most establishment family of the day in Toronto by a man with an actor's gift of recall and a refreshingly irreverent attitude. / 269 pages / 42 photos / $5.95

Within the Barbed Wire by Takeo Nakano
The moving story of a young Japanese-Canadian man, torn from his family by the events of the Second World War.

"Sensitive and moving...this book holds the bloom of a beautiful parable." — *United Church Observer* / 126 pages / 8 photos / $3.95

CANADIAN LIVES...ON FILM
Documentary films of the lives of many of the Canadians featured in the Goodread Biographies series have been produced by the CBC and the National Film Board, and are available to borrow from NFB distribution offices. Among those available are a film on Dr. Wilder Penfield written by Jefferson Lewis and based on his book, a film on E.P. Taylor, a film on Lucy Maud Montgomery, and one on Hugh MacLennan.